Engineering News-Record

SQUARE FOOT
COSTBOOK 2015 EDITION

ENR Square Foot Costbook 2015

ISBN 978-1-58855-165-8

Table of Contents

Square Foot Costs 1

Unit-In-Place Costs 35

Metro Area Multipliers 173

Index...179

Section One
Square Foot Costs

Building Type

The buildings in this book are all actual projects, not hypothetical models. For this reason, it is hoped that this book will give a more realistic picture of the wide range of square foot costs that occur due to all circumstances — from design variations to scheduling delays.

Graphic Representation

The graphic representations selected for this book have been chosen as the best overall illustration of the building's architectural features.

Description

Every case study is described in a short summary. These summaries are given to provide insight into the circumstances and the requirements behind the design. A building's function or location often influences the choice of building materials and thus the cost. Site limitations and local building and zoning codes are factors that have to be taken into consideration. Budget constraints, material availability and personal expertise of an individual builder all affect a project's outcome. Wherever appropriate, these types of issues are explained in the descriptions that accompany each case study. Further, when costs within one or more of the CSI divisions for the project are abnormally high or low, an explanation is usually provided.

Case Studies

Parking Garage 3
Mall Redevelopment 4
Theater & Conference Center 5
Market (Shell Only).................................. 6
Beauty Store (Shell Only) 7
Retail Store (Shell Only) 8
Discount Shoe Store (Shell Only) 9
Judicial Center & Courthouse............. 10
Fire Station 11
Fire Station 12
Industrial Facility 13
Industrial Facility 14
Senior Living Community..................... 15
Medical Office Building 16
County Hospital Expansion 17
County Hospital Parking Deck............ 18

Podiatry Clinic 19
Ambulatory Surgical Center 20
University Hall 21
Community College Building 22
Classroom & Admin. Building............. 23
University Hall 24
Science & Technology Building.......... 25
Airport Restaurant................................ 26
City Services Building.......................... 27
Church.. 28
Church.. 29
Men's Homeless Residential 30
Woman's/Family Homeless Res.......... 31
Retirement Living Facility................... 32
Retirement Community 33
Woman's Transformational Home 34

Project Notes

The façade of this garage is designed in a curvaceous, free-form sculptural style that reflects the area's artistic and modern environment. Located one block from the ocean, the organic contours of the exterior surface resemble the wind-filled sails of a ship.

The sails are designed to let natural light and ventilation into all parking levels while screening the vehicles from public view. This is important in creating a welcoming and safe environment while providing a structure that "does not look like a parking garage." Decorative lights project onto the exterior sails; multi-colored gels provide the ability to "paint" them a variety of colors relating to holidays and the seasons.

The ground level includes variety along the retail space, enhancing the pedestrian experience. Awnings and gumbo limbo trees provide shade. Serving as the transition from the garage to street level, an outdoor "lobby" continues the dynamic architectural dialogue with the pedestrian.

A simple floor plan, identical on each level, facilitates motorists' ability to navigate. The cast-in-place design eliminates shear walls and columns between parking spaces, while an open floor plan with high ceilings creates a bright, airy atmosphere that helps with visitor spatial orientation. The parking garage has spaces for 743 cars including four electric-car vehicle spaces, slots for 35 motorcycles, and accommodations for 74 bicycles with both long and short-term storage.

The project is LEED-CS v2009 Gold. Green components include an underground retention vault and cistern to store and treat storm water runoff from the site. A portion of the water is reused for the irrigation system. Interior materials surpass LEED® requirements for off-gassings of VOC's and other toxic chemicals. Energy consumption is reduced with LED lighting and an energy management system that only provides artificial light when and where it is needed. A solar carport is located on the roof and electric vehicle plug-ins are provided on the first floor.

Code	Division Name	Sq. Cost	Projected
00	Procurement	7.00	2,010,004
03	Concrete	18.66	5,355,820
04	Masonry	0.57	163,747
05	Metals	2.43	696,647
06	Wood & Plastics	0.07	20,520
07	Thermal & Moisture	0.50	142,340
08	Openings	2.95	846,363
09	Finishes	0.83	236,834
10	Specialties	0.28	79,050
11	Equipment	0.12	34,408
12	Furnishings	0.27	77,128
14	Conveying Systems	1.22	349,125
21	Fire Suppression	0.73	209,362
22	Plumbing	1.17	337,161
23	HVAC	0.88	251,256
26	Electrical	3.29	943,564
48	Elec. Power Generation	0.53	151,421
Total Building Costs		**41.47**	**11,904,749**

For a more in-depth report on this building or additional case studies contact DC&D
@ 800-533-5680, or www.DCD.com

3

Project Notes

The existing mall was designed and constructed circa 1982 as a covered mall building. The structure is a one-story steel structure with clearstory and skylight typically running down the center core of the structure. Steel wide flange girders and steel wide flange columns support the typical roof, and space frame trusses support the skylight system.

To create an attractive, inviting environment for mall visitors to experience, the new landscaped pedestrian plaza, with valet and drop off, is located adjacent to the cinema and the existing mall. The plaza is connected to shopping and the food court in the center of the existing mall through a newly featured clearstory glass entrance. The plaza, visible from inside the mall promenade, includes a wood gazebo structure, a water fountain, three concrete pads for kiosks, and a covered area with a shade structure that features a performance stage.

The project required the demolition of a portion of the mall, remodeling, reconfiguration of two mall entries, three new stand-alone buildings, and a new 14-screen cinema.

The demolition was strategically chosen, extending along major existing column lines to minimize the extent of structural work required, while maximizing the remaining leasable space defined by the new building line.

Within the plaza three pad areas are defined for future buildings. As part of the redevelopment a new exterior façade for the truncated end of the existing covered mall was replaced, forming new tenant spaces on both sides of the existing mall promenade.

The new mall exterior façades include storefronts, trellis, awnings and exterior patios for new tenants. In addition to the new façades, new monumental canopy entry system and curtain walls complete the transition from the existing mall interior to the new plaza area.

In the interior mall wing that extends from the plaza back to the food court, the interior space was updated with new floor tile infill areas, the existing storefronts and adjacent surfaces were modified and refinished to tie into the new construction and matching to the existing mall interior design.

Code	Division Name	Sq. Cost	Projected
01	General Requirements	7.45	371,086
03	Concrete	2.25	112,240
04	Masonry	1.07	53,187
05	Metals	7.73	384,944
07	Thermal & Moisture	4.48	222,910
08	Openings	6.73	334,960
09	Finishes	9.32	463,920
21	Fire Suppression	1.09	54,279
22	Plumbing	1.48	73,583
26	Electrical	3.46	172,130
Total Building Costs		**45.05**	**2,243,241**

Project Notes

Fort Collins' Lincoln Center is now the city's premier theater and conference center after a complete renovation and a new addition by Aller Lingle Massey Architects.

Aller Lingle Massey Architects completed a Master Plan for the 35-year-old performing arts and conference center that included 13,500 square feet of new enclosed space to enlarge the pre- and post-function lobbies, patron restrooms and circulation corridors, and three new permanent bars. The new addition also created larger entry vestibules with new ticketing and office space along with creating greatly needed dressing rooms, chorus rooms, green room and conference space. A new art gallery was also included in the project.

The design called for renovation of 24,660 square feet of the facility's conference spaces and a complete renovation of the Magnolia Theater, including reconfiguration of the seating, acoustical, sound system and finish upgrades to the Main Performance Hall.

Inspired by the client's design, the building's architectural image was completely updated. A new glazed curtain wall wraps the lobbies and public spaces, while a rainscreen wall assembly clad in multi-colored Trespa panels encloses the gallery, restrooms and other spaces. The result dramatically enhances the architectural expression of the Lincoln Center. The Lincoln Center will now meet the City's needs for another 35 years.

Code	Division Name	Sq. Cost	Projected
00	Procurement	1.99	75,749
01	General Requirements	46.99	1,793,247
03	Concrete	6.97	265,908
04	Masonry	1.33	50,692
05	Metals	12.35	471,433
06	Wood & Plastics	5.33	203,274
07	Thermal & Moisture	18.89	720,848
08	Openings	11.13	424,695
09	Finishes	19.29	736,086
10	Specialties	1.05	40,046
14	Conveying Systems	1.42	54,240
21	Fire Suppression	3.25	124,195
22	Plumbing	5.84	222,876
23	HVAC	14.64	558,658
26	Electrical	20.47	781,098
28	Electronic Safety/Security	1.06	40,553
Total Building Costs		**172.00**	**6,563,59**

Project Notes (*Continues through Page 7, 8, and 9*)

So what does a developer/owner do when your big box retailer, vacates more than 87,000 square feet in your retail center located in the heart of a retail district? You establish the creative goal of not only "filling the space," but improving the retail diversity and quality of the center.

Thus, via diligent and immediate efforts and with an innovative development plan, K-Mart's departure not only resulted in replacement retailers, but resulted in the introduction of new retail players in the Pensacola market:

-- The Fresh Market
-- Ulta Beauty
-- Marshalls
-- Discount Shoe Warehouse (DSW)

Joining the recent additions of: Florida Blue, Five Guys, PetCo and Graphicom, this Shopping Center is 100% leased and poised to remain a vibrant retail center...

Code	Division Name	Sq. Cost	Projected
00	Procurement	4.70	98,660
01	General Requirements	4.02	84,392
03	Concrete	17.05	358,003
04	Masonry	4.98	104,632
05	Metals	5.77	121,142
06	Wood & Plastics	0.29	6,170
07	Thermal & Moisture	4.08	85,613
08	Openings	2.64	55,456
09	Finishes	7.08	148,583
10	Specialties	1.18	24,764
11	Equipment	0.77	16,274
21	Fire Suppression	2.24	47,133
22	Plumbing	2.23	46,804
23	HVAC	5.37	112,748
26	Electrical	5.04	105,941
Total Building Costs		**67.44**	**1,416,316**

Project Notes

Continued from previous page…

Rather than settle with the new tenants (and to assist in landing these new retailers) the owner opted to renovate the entire center from Jersey Mike's to Kirklands. A complex undertaking, placing four new retailers while maintaining service for the remaining 161,000-plus square feet of operation.

The replacement of a big box retailer with four individual retailers created tremendous utility and service opportunities. Compounded by a restricted "rear" service drive thus over 11,000 square feet of the existing building was removed to accommodate service and utilities for the new tenants.

Each new tenant brings prototypical service and utility criteria.

This Final Site Plan offers an opportunity to view the implementation of the service and utility challenges identified. Each of the four tenants offered unique challenges. Stores 2, 3 and 4 are provided with new recessed truck docks and store 3 includes a compactor area, boxed storage and exterior grease interceptor located in the area previously occupied by the K-Mart building…

Code	Division Name	Sq. Cost	Projected
00	Procurement	9.09	98,660
01	General Requirements	(-3.28)	(-35,638)
03	Concrete	13.39	145,323
04	Masonry	5.51	59,837
05	Metals	6.08	66,006
06	Wood & Plastics	0.94	10,225
07	Thermal & Moisture	4.11	44,575
08	Openings	4.76	51,662
09	Finishes	12.13	131,662
10	Specialties	1.30	14,151
21	Fire Suppression	2.28	24,764
22	Plumbing	3.14	34,068
23	HVAC	8.41	91,285
26	Electrical	7.03	76,231
Total Building Costs		**74.91**	**812,813**

Project Notes

Continued from previous page…

    With coordinated efforts each tenant was provided new metered utilities including fire main, domestic water, electrical, telephone and sanitary sewer.

    The original 24-foot rear service drive contained only the sanitary sewer. Within this 24-foot drive all new utilities were designed and installed including new subsurface storm water collection for the recessed truck docks as well as the building drainage, paralleling the existing sanitary and the new service utilities. The final "impervious area" is actually reduced from pre-construction totals.

    Rather than totally demolish the existing K-mart structure the owner opted to utilize the structural chassis, modifying as noted for the "rear service areas" and to reconstruct the storefronts and provide new individual entrance canopies…

Code	Division Name	Sq. Cost	Projected
00	Procurement	3.80	98,660
01	General Requirements	2.15	55,900
03	Concrete	3.01	78,205
04	Masonry	4.33	112,503
05	Metals	4.12	107,162
06	Wood & Plastics	0.36	9,447
07	Thermal & Moisture	2.91	75,708
08	Openings	2.43	63,142
09	Finishes	9.96	258,947
21	Fire Suppression	0.41	10,613
22	Plumbing	0.56	14,682
23	HVAC	0.89	23,208
26	Electrical	4.08	105,991
Total Building Costs		**39.02**	**1,014,167**

Project Notes

Continued from previous page…

Success is often defined as the achievement of something planned or attempted. Thus this redevelopment was and is a success. The "hole" created by previous tenant departure was creatively filled with the creation of 75,840 square feet of new retail space. The entire center has been re-imaged. There are no vacant spaces.

The team preformed!

Project Scope

Replace vacated 87,000 square feet of tenant space with four tenant spaces totaling 75,840 square feet. The 11,552 square feet of demolished space was converted to exterior "rear" service areas.

The costs included are for the landlords shell only, including façade renovation to remaining stores, new site lighting, and new parking lot seal coat and striping.

The four new tenants were each responsible for their respective interior build-outs.

Code	Division Name	Sq. Cost	Projected
00	Procurement	5.72	103,020
01	General Requirements	7.94	142,857
03	Concrete	5.71	102,822
04	Masonry	3.43	61,707
05	Metals	4.91	88,316
06	Wood & Plastics	1.10	19,760
07	Thermal & Moisture	2.61	47,052
08	Openings	2.54	45,742
09	Finishes	8.29	149,268
10	Specialties	0.94	16,981
21	Fire Suppression	1.90	34,203
22	Plumbing	2.18	39,163
23	HVAC	7.64	137,434
26	Electrical	20.01	360,122

Total Building Costs	**74.91**	**1,348,446**

For a more in-depth report on this building or additional case studies contact DC&D
@ 800-533-5680, or www.DCD.com

9

Project Notes

Augusta, Georgia was in need of a new judicial center and courthouse. Services were scattered across a number of facilities in different locations. In addition, the facilities were outdated with inadequate courtroom technology, HVAC systems, and security.

The county's Capital Improvements Program Manager's first assignment was to review the judicial center's capital program that had been completed.

The review led to several suggestions including a reduction in the building's size from 300,000 to 180,000 square feet. This saved the county at least $30 million.

The county utilized the construction manager at-risk method for procuring the construction phase services for the project. By using CM at-risk, they were able to issue bid packages for the site, foundations, and concrete framework for early award and exceeded initial expectations for completion.

An unusual characteristic of the project was its location on a transitional plane between different geographic zones, The Piedmont and Coastal Plain. A geotechnical firm recognized the soil could potentially liquefy in the event of seismic activity. The solution was to drive more than 600 auger piles to stabilize the foundation and eliminate the possibility of movement.

The center includes the county's first sallyport, allowing officials to transport prisoners directly from police vehicles to holding cells. Separate elevators for prisoners, visitors, and judges offer an additional layer of security.

The lobby is impressive with 35-foot-high ceilings, blended limestone-porcelain tiles, wood panels, sound absorption panels, and an expansive bank of windows.

"Like the city itself, the building is gracious but simple," said Heery Project Manager Lindsay Johnson.

Looking back over the project, Johnson believes part of the facility's success stems from involving all user groups in the design and construction process. "The county now has a facility that not only meets budget requirements, but will serve judicial needs for years to come".

Code	Division Name	Sq. Cost	Projected
00	Procurement	1.42	259,732
01	General Requirements	37.71	6,912,890
03	Concrete	55.73	10,216,986
04	Masonry	19.10	3,502,508
05	Metals	5.82	1,067,184
06	Wood & Plastics	23.98	4,396,095
07	Thermal & Moisture	13.74	2,518,428
08	Openings	14.92	2,735,928
09	Finishes	51.06	9,360,801
10	Specialties	2.28	417,520
11	Equipment	8.51	1,560,013
12	Furnishings	0.91	166,305
14	Conveying Systems	5.71	1,046,257
21	Fire Suppression	3.13	573,384
23	HVAC	35.79	6,562,556
26	Electrical	47.56	8,719,300
Total Building Costs		**327.35**	**60,015,886**

Project Notes

The new location for Richardson Fire Station No. 4 was chosen to improve emergency response times throughout the city; however, constructing this building adjacent to an existing middle school inevitably raises some concerns from the community. Safety for the school children, potential traffic issues, and architectural image were the primary concerns from the neighbors. BRW participated in community meetings with the fire department to address these concerns and presented the new design, which included a rerouted school traffic pattern. Public feedback after the meetings was very positive and the new design was fully embraced.

The architectural design of the fire station needed to fit comfortably with the varied styles of the adjacent residential neighborhood, middle school, and a newly constructed recreation center. Traditional roof forms, brick details, and rough-cut stone combined with stained wood, exposed steel, and modern detailing helps to bridge the stylistic gap between the existing buildings.

A long covered porch directs visitors to the entry lobby, while stone-clad pylons with steel pipe struts support a large roof overhang highlighting the apparatus bay. The living wing is filled with natural daylight and accented by bamboo millwork and diamond polished concrete floors. Direct access from the dining area leads to a courtyard with barbeque grill and covered pavilion for the fire fighters to relax and gather.

As physical fitness is a priority within the Richardson Fire Department, a large room leading to a large covered porch was designed for cross-training activities. A concrete mezzanine within the apparatus bay will be used for "confined spaces" training, allowing for easy access to specialized training directly onsite. The many unique, customized features were included to address specific needs of the fire department in an effort to build a high-quality station that will provide many decades of service.

Code	Division Name	Sq. Cost	Projected
00	Procurement	4.77	67,246
01	General Requirements	34.91	491,912
03	Concrete	35.74	503,646
04	Masonry	31.38	442,140
05	Metals	41.54	585,271
06	Wood & Plastics	15.28	215,311
07	Thermal & Moisture	26.88	378,733
08	Openings	25.29	356,306
09	Finishes	13.48	189,866
10	Specialties	2.72	38,341
11	Equipment	2.34	33,005
12	Furnishings	1.53	21,612
21	Fire Suppression	2.41	33,897
22	Plumbing	21.18	298,479
23	HVAC	28.09	395,794
26	Electrical	35.00	493,155

Total Building Costs	322.55	4,544,715

For a more in-depth report on this building or additional case studies contact DC&D
@ 800-533-5680, or www.DCD.com

11

Project Notes

This fire station houses nine paid and 65 volunteer firefighters, is located along a retail corridor, and backs up to a residential neighborhood. To maintain both the scale and style of the commercial and residential area, BRW Architects incorporated a traditional pitched roof and utilized local building materials. To ensure that this facility will stand for years to come against 150 mph hurricane force winds, the structure is an economical mix of structural steel, concrete masonry, and wood construction.

The narrow site was able to accommodate pull through bays and a large drive apron to allow fire apparatus to safely enter and exit the station. Visitor parking is available near the entrance while an automated gate secures employee parking.

Visitors to the station enter through a reminiscent historical hose drying tower. Light from the clerestory windows at the top of the tower floods the entrance while the limestone from the exterior is carried inside to give the entrance a warm, natural feel. From the secured lobby, the public can contact the on-duty lieutenant via pass through window to his office or utilize the training room and restroom facilities for community events.

The rest of the first floor consists of private living areas for the fire personnel. Every square inch is utilized to the fullest as custom lockers are built into the walls of the corridor to provide storage for the volunteer staff members. A dorm room is provided for the volunteers while the 3 shifts of full-time fire fighters have private rooms with individual lockers. Three bathrooms service the private area of the station while a fourth one is provided directly off the apparatus bay. The entire crew can relax in the dayroom or complete continuing

education hours in the study while the rest enjoy the amenities in the gourmet kitchen and dining area. To work off the calories gained in the kitchen, the second floor houses a complete fitness room. To isolate the noise of the fitness room, innovative soundproofing techniques and specialized flooring where implemented.

The apparatus bays have quick opening bi-fold doors and diamond ground concrete floors to reduce slip resistance. Trench drains, ceiling mounted cord reels, and truck fill hose bibs are all included for efficiency and easy maintenance.

Code	Division Name	Sq. Cost	Projected
00	**Procurement**	5.60	62,522
01	**General Requirements**	25.66	286,389
03	**Concrete**	20.34	227,006
04	**Masonry**	17.72	197,856
05	**Metals**	14.59	162,901
06	**Wood & Plastics**	21.79	243,230
07	**Thermal & Moisture**	12.14	135,465
08	**Openings**	40.28	449,660
09	**Finishes**	14.72	164,352
10	**Specialties**	3.32	37,065
11	**Equipment**	3.19	35,614
12	**Furnishings**	0.32	3,561
21	**Fire Suppression**	7.62	85,078
22	**Plumbing**	14.26	159,208
23	**HVAC**	10.63	118,713
26	**Electrical**	29.19	325,802
27	**Communications**	0.95	10,552
28	**Electronic Safety/Security**	1.83	20,445
Total Building Costs		**244.15**	**2,725,421**

For a more in-depth report on this building or additional case studies contact DC&D

@ 800-533-5680, or www.DCD.com

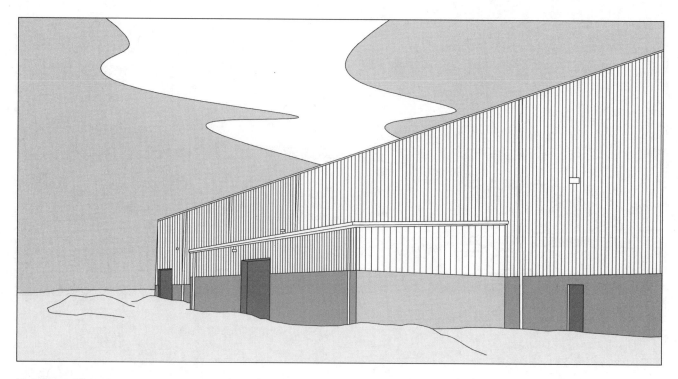

Project Notes

The owner of Lee Steel Corporation contacted Maltese Construction LLC to design and build a new industrial facility in Wyoming, Michigan. They did not have a site, but needed to start building soon in that area as their business was expanding. D. J. Maltese traveled to Wyoming, Michigan with the owners to find a site. Through their travels and communication with the City of Wyoming they came across a new Industrial Park. They were able to secure a site, close on it, design and build a facility while securing the owner tax credits for the development. The building was designed for future expansion.

Years later, the owner of Lee Steel contacted Maltese Construction to begin the process of expanding the original building as their business was growing. An agreement to design and build the addition to their current steel processing center was signed. The addition would include one new bay and pallet room.

The building addition is a pre-engineered building with pre-cast tilt-up walls at the front and back, and a polished masonry belt with steel siding above on the side. The total building height is about 42 feet. All materials look and match the existing building, so it does not look like an addition.

Soon the drawings were completed and building permits secured, steel ordered and site work started. Demolition work included removal of landscaping and two driveways from a private road to the existing building. New construction included underground drainage, foundations, steel, masonry, pre-cast concrete, service doors, overhead doors, HVAC, plumbing, electrical, concrete slab, site paving, machine pits, one new 35-ton crane and new landscaping.

Code	Division Name	Sq. Cost	Projected
00	Procurement	0.22	7,630
01	General Requirements	1.05	36,676
03	Concrete	15.03	523,294
04	Masonry	2.02	70,354
06	Wood & Plastics	0.06	2,046
07	Thermal & Moisture	0.05	1,673
08	Openings	3.77	131,264
09	Finishes	3.34	116,308
10	Specialties	2.77	96,412
11	Equipment	0.42	14,730
13	Special Construction	24.34	847,458
22	Plumbing	1.26	43,968
23	HVAC	3.49	121,621
26	Electrical	5.33	185,565
Total Building Costs		**63.15**	**2,198,998**

Project Notes

For expansion, SWF Industrial purchased a property that would allow them to construct a new facility. The site was selected for its close proximity to major roads and highways. After land development approvals were underway, Cornerstone Design-Architects was chosen to develop the project and work with the general contractor.

The design of the facility included two separate buildings attached by a connector. The office building serves as the location for office staff such as project managers, estimators, administrative personnel, etc. Additional spaces include a conference room, break room, and miscellaneous support spaces. The structure and mechanical ductwork were left exposed to allow a greater sense of interior height. Natural lighting is controlled by the installation of exterior sunshades and interior light shelves. This allows for natural light to be brought into the building, but controlled in an effort to reduce direct sunlight, glare, and heat gain. The exterior design of the office building was intended to showcase the owner's ability to fabricate and weld structural elements. The owner also wanted to create a modern feel to the building by creating curved parapet walls and including a large quantity of glass.

The design of the shop area consists of four separate bays including two structural bays, a stainless steel bay, and a production bay. A pre-engineered metal building was chosen for economy and the ability to free span long distances. Each bay serves a different purpose that may be required for the final product. Other spaces in the shop area include a lunch room, hazardous storage rooms, tool room, and field equipment storage. Each bay includes a full length crane rail, allowing personnel the ability to have full mobility in the shop area. A paint booth and a blast booth were also included.

Future expansion capacity was included in the design of both the site and building. This will allow the owner the flexibility in the future to expand the operations when needed.

Code	Division Name	Sq. Cost	Projected
01	General Requirements	4.20	320,180
03	Concrete	9.05	689,572
04	Masonry	0.89	68,011
05	Metals	1.74	132,351
06	Wood & Plastics	0.07	5,106
07	Thermal & Moisture	2.32	177,158
08	Openings	2.77	211,190
09	Finishes	2.12	161,798
10	Specialties	0.21	16,026
11	Equipment	0.23	17,679
12	Furnishings	0.22	16,836
13	Special Construction	12.66	964,732
22	Plumbing	5.68	433,203
26	Electrical	5.89	448,686
Total Building Costs		**48.05**	**3,662,530**

Project Notes

A craftsman inspired master plan created by CDH Partners includes four living communities: a 38,386-square-foot assisted living, a 65,000-square-foot independent living, 18,525-square-foot memory care home, and four 1,600-square-foot independent living cottages. The interior is organized as small homes and interconnected neighborhoods that are bright and open and comfortable enabling the residents to meet and build new relationships.

The design goal was to create a resident-centered sense of place and less of a clinical atmosphere. Therefore, each apartment was carefully designed to encourage residents to live as independently as possible, while providing 24-hour watchful oversight. Careful attention was also given to keeping the design intuitive so residents could move easily along with a greater sense of belonging, community, and security, which are needed to maintain a higher level of well-being and a sense of personal freedom.

The project is designed with sustainable features such as responsible landscape planning, high performance, low energy and water usage, and energy saving spray foam insulation.

The Oaks Senior Living, who is the family owned operator of the facility, has been serving the South's senior living community since 1998. This Braselton, Georgia location is the latest facility in a line of successful senior living communities for this company.

"We are committed to serving with faith, knowledge, compassion, and love," says company president Nelson Salabarria. "To achieve this mission, we strive to create an environment that promotes physical, social, and spiritual well-being. The design team at CDH Partners helped us achieve this goal. Our personal commitment to dignified

senior living combined with CDH's commitment to design excellence has produced a facility that contains well-planned spaces that are open and spacious. This is a state-of-the-art facility that is aesthetically pleasing and highly functional."

Code	Division Name	Sq. Cost	Projected
01	General Requirements	17.43	980,593
03	Concrete	6.69	376,338
04	Masonry	1.15	64,590
05	Metals	1.69	94,986
06	Wood & Plastics	17.31	973,669
07	Thermal & Moisture	5.90	332,104
08	Openings	1.31	73,926
09	Finishes	9.88	555,783
10	Specialties	2.48	139,669
11	Equipment	2.65	149,005
12	Furnishings	2.81	158,310
13	Special Construction	2.81	158,310
21	Fire Suppression	2.77	155,777
22	Plumbing	7.25	407,806
23	HVAC	6.80	382,540
26	Electrical	12.36	695,297
Total Building Costs		**101.31**	**5,698,702**

For a more in-depth report on this building or additional case studies contact DC&D
@ 800-533-5680, or www.DCD.com

15

Project Notes

This new 8,900-square-foot medical office building houses Primary and Specialty Care and Immediate Care services with additional out-patient services of radiology and phlebotomy for Southern New Hampshire Health System.

Dennis Mires PA, The Architects were sensitive through massing and appropriate detail that the facility fulfills the design program without overwhelming the scale of Windham Road near the Town Center in Pelham.

The visitor is greeted by a corner entry with a glass vestibule that leads to a common check-in area. A waiting area serves the smaller south wing that provides immediate care services. Another waiting area serves the north wing that provides the Primary and Specialty care services.

Each wing has a central nurses station and support services surrounded by treatment rooms. X-ray and phlebotomy services are available to all patients with core administrative services shared by each wing.

Code	Division Name	Sq. Cost	Projected
00	Procurement	28.25	237,246
01	General Requirements	22.46	188,608
03	Concrete	10.43	87,588
04	Masonry	0.09	737
05	Metals	7.16	60,160
06	Wood & Plastics	14.62	122,791
07	Thermal & Moisture	27.66	232,314
08	Openings	7.08	59,439
09	Finishes	21.44	180,106
10	Specialties	2.38	19,969
11	Equipment	0.17	1,460
12	Furnishings	0.16	1,304
21	Fire Suppression	6.50	54,584
22	Plumbing	4.78	40,130
23	HVAC	17.21	144,555
26	Electrical	15.08	126,673
Total Building Costs		**185.46**	**1,557,665**

Project Notes

The Oktibbeha County Hospital Regional Medical Center (OCH) located in Starkville, Mississippi is a county-owned and operated facility that was founded over 35 years ago. Its mission is clear: provision of high quality health care to the people of the hospital's seven-county service area responding to changing community needs. Dean and Dean/Associates Architects, P.A. was commissioned with the task of helping Oktibbeha County Hospital fulfill this mission as its growth created the need for a major renovation and expansion.

This 23.4 million dollar construction project consists of a new five-story, 87,116-square-foot addition, new parking garage and interior renovation to the existing Oktibbeha County Hospital. At the first floor level, the design features a new Main Entrance, Lobby, Gift Shop, Coffee Bar, Community Education facilities, and shell space for future expansion. The upper floors provide 52 new private Medical/Surgical Patient Rooms and a state-of-the-art Women's Center comprised of a Birthing Suite with eight Labor/Delivery/Recovery (LDR) rooms, two C-Section rooms/Recovery, three Triage Rooms/Observation Rooms, and new Nursery Suite to include a Well Baby Nursery and High Risk Nursery with Neo-Natal Intensive Care.

In addition, the project includes 30,263 square feet of renovations to existing patient bed floors. This renovation features enlargement and refurbishment of undersized and outdated patient rooms and baths into 30 new Medical/Surgical Patient Rooms/Baths which meet contemporary standards. Also a new six bed Intensive Care Unit, an ICU Waiting Area, and a Family Quiet Room were welcomed additions to this area. To further enhance this updated modern facility new entrance driveways and a 240-space parking structure were constructed.

Oktibbeha County Hospital has over 650 employees. In 2012 their new 96-bed facility was opened and today these employees continue to proudly serve the community and carry out the mission begun over 35 years ago.

Code	Division Name	Sq. Cost	Projected
00	Procurement	4.42	385,090
01	General Requirements	41.75	3,637,434
03	Concrete	31.51	2,745,111
04	Masonry	3.21	279,211
05	Metals	7.21	628,186
06	Wood & Plastics	5.19	452,037
07	Thermal & Moisture	18.80	1,637,478
08	Openings	15.82	1,378,303
09	Finishes	21.47	1,870,048
10	Specialties	1.37	119,342
11	Equipment	0.23	20,272
12	Furnishings	0.57	50,041
14	Conveying Systems	8.24	717,704
21	Fire Suppression	2.55	222,471
22	Plumbing	15.96	1,389,975
23	HVAC	62.16	5,415,281
26	Electrical	25.15	2,190,833

Total Building Costs	**265.61**	**23,138,817**

Project Notes

The Oktibbeha County Hospital Regional Medical Center (OCH) located in Starkville, Mississippi is a county-owned and operated facility that was founded over 35 years ago. Its mission is clear: provision of high quality health care to the people of the hospital's seven-county service area responding to changing community needs. Dean and Dean/Associates Architects, P.A. was commissioned with the task of helping Oktibbeha County Hospital fulfill this mission as its growth created the need for a major renovation and expansion.

This 23.4 million dollar construction project consists of a new five-story, 87,116-square-foot addition, new parking garage and interior renovation to the existing Oktibbeha County Hospital. At the first floor level, the design features a new Main Entrance, Lobby, Gift Shop, Coffee Bar, Community Education facilities, and shell space for future expansion. The upper floors provide 52 new private Medical/Surgical Patient Rooms and a state-of-the-art Women's Center comprised of a Birthing Suite with eight Labor/Delivery/Recovery (LDR) rooms, two C-Section rooms/Recovery, three Triage Rooms/Observation Rooms, and new Nursery Suite to include a Well Baby Nursery and High Risk Nursery with Neo-Natal Intensive Care.

In addition, the project includes 30,263 square feet of renovations to existing patient bed floors. This renovation features enlargement and refurbishment of undersized and outdated patient rooms and baths into 30 new Medical/Surgical Patient Rooms/Baths which meet contemporary standards. Also a new six bed Intensive Care Unit, an ICU Waiting Area, and a Family Quiet Room were welcomed additions to this area. To further enhance this updated modern facility new entrance driveways and a 240-space parking structure were constructed.

Oktibbeha County Hospital has over 650 employees. In 2012 their new 96-bed facility was opened and today these employees continue to proudly serve the community and carry out the mission begun over 35 years ago.

Code	Division Name	Sq. Cost	Projected
03	Concrete	28.57	2,854,083
04	Masonry	0.82	82,193
05	Metals	0.69	68,494
07	Thermal & Moisture	0.21	20,549
08	Openings	0.23	22,819
09	Finishes	0.32	31,955
14	Conveying Systems	2.66	265,452
21	Fire Suppression	0.16	15,891
23	HVAC	1.32	131,792
26	Electrical	1.51	151,104
Total Building Costs		**36.49**	**3,644,332**

Project Notes

Thirty years ago, CDH Partners was asked to design a medical facility for Marietta. This longtime client contacted CDH once again with the request to renovate a building they had just purchased and add a new building adjacent to the renovated facility.

The 7,200-square-foot single story clinic is residential in style and is constructed of wood frame with a mansard roof. It has a rustic brick exterior and sits on 1.43 acres.

The building has been systematically laid out with future expansion in mind. The new surgery center was placed at the entry level to the site to the west of the existing clinic.

The CDH team began by renovating the group's clinic, which was original to the facility and implemented sustainable design principles. The new ambulatory surgery center also contains a physical therapy space and exam modules.

The design team applied a system-wide approach to patient and family centered care. Only finish upgrades were required but this still allowed the CDH team to follow a comprehensive process through every phase of the project, resulting in a well-conceived product that is both holistic and well planned. One exam module was converted into a naturally lit physical therapy area, requiring some minor structural and MEP changes.

The different occupancies and fire separations required the buildings be ten feet apart connected by a lite corridor. In order to make the two sections into a cohesive whole, the original entry to the clinic was redesigned to have a similar canopy to the addition. Brick from the original clinic was matched for a pull away detail on the surgery center entrance.

Intricate details are binding elements that bring a final layer of comfort and thoughtfulness to a project. The waiting room was updated for patient comfort. Subdued lighting was added along with a wireless network access and coffee station.

Code	Division Name	Sq. Cost	Projected
01	General Requirements	45.89	201,898
03	Concrete	9.07	39,894
04	Masonry	2.39	10,512
05	Metals	13.97	61,457
06	Wood & Plastics	7.04	30,965
07	Thermal & Moisture	17.35	76,332
08	Openings	12.61	55,471
09	Finishes	26.84	118,090
10	Specialties	1.98	8,709
22	Plumbing	14.04	61,763
23	HVAC	23.41	103,016
26	Electrical	13.50	59,384
Total Building Costs		**188.07**	**827,492**

Project Notes

The first problem was to fit the addition with a complex program to the narrow site with tight setbacks. The stepping of the façade that was necessitated by the setbacks turned into a design opportunity.

Another challenge was to create a clear path of circulation within the facility to guide patients from the waiting areas to the treatment areas. The key to overcoming the challenges was to transform the dark and uninviting parking area below the existing second story into what became known as the "Gallery". This enclosure wraps around the original building forming a link to the new treatment areas, while serving as the waiting room with views over the creek below toward downtown Stroudsburg beyond.

The exterior façade of the addition is finished with stone veneer from Dutch Quality along with the EIFS installation of Energex-PB Drainage Wrap System selected to both insulate and match the stucco of the existing facility.

Natural light is an important amenity for the new addition. A clerestory above the pre-op and recovery areas allows natural light deep into the patient and nurse areas. It has become well documented as to the health benefits of exposure to natural lighting in the healing process. In terms of massing, the modernist clerestory creates a playful dialogue with the mansard roof of the existing Victorian structure. The three new operating rooms on the south side of the building afford relaxing views of the tree-lined berm outside.

While the existing building is of wood frame construction, the new addition is steel frame. Both the existing and the addition are provided with an automatic sprinkler system. Systems required to serve the addition include medical gas. The HVAC system includes roof mounted air handlers feeding VAV boxes. The air handlers serving the OR's include pre-filters and HEPA final filters. Additional electrical requirements for the facility include a Type I 80 KW emergency electrical service generator.

Code	Division Name	Sq. Cost	Projected
01	General Requirements	2.47	49,299
03	Concrete	12.44	247,871
04	Masonry	5.43	108,187
05	Metals	20.43	407,192
06	Wood & Plastics	8.51	169,671
07	Thermal & Moisture	20.13	401,232
08	Openings	13.48	268,617
09	Finishes	20.16	401,857
10	Specialties	10.33	205,872
21	Fire Suppression	2.64	52,564
22	Plumbing	22.76	453,672
23	HVAC	45.24	901,606
26	Electrical	40.27	802,617
27	Communications	0.66	13,143
Total Building Costs		**224.97**	**4,483,400**

Project Notes

Rider University, understanding the need for additional academic and faculty space, opened its new facility, North Hall. The building, with its nine classrooms, two seminar rooms, sixteen faculty and departmental offices, and multi-purpose conference room, is the first strictly academic facility to be built on campus since 1988. The building houses the History and Philosophy department offices, but its classrooms serve all programs throughout the University, including one of the large seminar rooms acting as the President's Board Room.

North Hall is certified LEED® Gold by the U.S. Green Building Council. Some of its sustainable features include sunshades, green roof, VOC-free paints and adhesives, rapidly renewable materials, low flow fixtures, daylighting, detention basin for storm water management, fly ash content in concrete, green power purchase, recycling storage, water efficient landscaping, bike racks, and regionally-sourced materials. North Hall was designed and constructed from beginning to end with sustainability as a driving force.

Rider University has committed itself to sustainability. "Achieving LEED Gold for North Hall just shows how far Rider has come with its green initiatives," said Melissa Greenberg, sustainability manager at Rider University.

Beginning with a master plan, in conjunction with a carbon neutrality study and action plan, Rider University, with Spiezle providing the guidance and expertise, has carved a path to be a leader in sustainability among higher education institutions. In fact, earlier this year, Rider University was named one of the most environmentally responsible colleges and universities in the United States and Canada by The Princeton Review, which selected Rider for inclusion in the third annual edition of The Princeton Review's Guide to 322 Colleges. North Hall is another step in the University's charter of providing the optimal learning environment in a sustainable approach.

Code	Division Name	Sq. Cost	Projected
01	General Requirements	19.99	452,854
03	Concrete	12.83	290,626
04	Masonry	27.59	625,097
05	Metals	19.88	450,496
06	Wood & Plastics	3.94	89,337
07	Thermal & Moisture	14.80	335,392
08	Openings	20.20	457,593
09	Finishes	18.40	416,916
10	Specialties	0.84	19,057
14	Conveying Systems	2.09	47,352
21	Fire Suppression	3.33	75,422
22	Plumbing	8.21	185,915
23	HVAC	25.65	581,109
25	Integrated Automation	5.90	133,708
26	Electrical	21.05	476,856
27	Communications	1.56	35,355
28	Electronic Safety/Security	2.46	55,799
Total Building Costs		**208.71**	**4,728,88**

Project Notes

This project reflects the results of a truly collaborative design process that experienced success on a myriad of fronts.

The public portion of the building includes a 293-seat lecture hall equally capable of hosting small concerts and theatrical performances; serving a unique role on the Northern Wake Campus. Adjacent to the lecture hall, a multi-purpose prefunction space encourages gathering during performance events. The plaza, an extension of the interior public spaces, collects campus pathways that weave through the building, blurring the distinction between exterior and interior.

The remaining building program consists of general classrooms, labs, and offices equipped with cutting edge, adaptive technology to allow for flexibility in teaching and learning. In addition, the facility houses specifically tailored classroom, practical lab, and office space to meet the growing demand of the Certified Nursing Assistant Program. Other spaces include music rehearsal rooms, computer and networking labs, and study lounge space.

The building achieved LEED® Gold certification through the U.S. Green Building Council making this the first campus in the country to be completely LEED certified. Sustainable design features include a green rooftop terrace to absorb carbon dioxide and generate oxygen, reflective roofing materials, solar shading devices, daylight harvesting, high-efficiency glazing, occupancy sensors for lighting, high-efficiency plumbing fixtures, a future tie-in to the municipal reclaimed gray water system, radiant heating and cooling mechanical systems, and a high-efficiency displacement ventilation system located under the stepped seating in the lecture hall resulting in over 50% reduction in energy use and over 45% reduction in water use.

Code	Division Name	Sq. Cost	Projected
00	Procurement	0.98	78,977
01	General Requirements	40.08	3,239,226
03	Concrete	14.02	1,132,988
04	Masonry	11.08	895,710
05	Metals	31.20	2,521,384
06	Wood & Plastics	0.94	75,770
07	Thermal & Moisture	31.81	2,571,175
08	Openings	19.45	1,572,229
09	Finishes	23.63	1,909,829
10	Specialties	5.67	457,935
11	Equipment	2.77	223,627
12	Furnishings	10.35	836,468
14	Conveying Systems	2.99	241,652
21	Fire Suppression	2.68	216,351
22	Plumbing	11.43	923,889
23	HVAC	31.94	2,581,594
26	Electrical	27.37	2,212,351
27	Communications	0.80	64,946
28	Electronic Safety/Security	3.80	307,004

Total Building Costs	**272.99**	**22,063,105**

Project Notes

The Classroom and Administration Building initiated the first phase of The Awty International School's newly developed master-plan prepared by Bailey Architects. Bailey Architects, a Houston-based architecture firm, has had an on-going client relationship with Awty, one of the country's premier private international schools, since 2001 beginning with the adaptive reuse of a two-story warehouse for a lower school, a 24.5-acre master plan, athletic complex, and 450-car parking garage. Plans are on the boards for a new preschool and construction started in June 2013 on a lower school expansion as the school anticipates growth from the current 1,504 student enrollment to 1,550 students.

Tasked with efficiently incorporating a diverse program on a very limited site, Bailey Architects designed the Classroom and Administration Building to house 33 classrooms, art studios, a dining hall, and the school's administrative headquarters in addition to relocating an existing soccer field to support Awty's athletic program. Conversion of the dining hall to 10 more classrooms is anticipated.

Multiple first-floor entrances direct students, visitors, and staff to enter the building separately, and zone academic, administrative, support, and dining operations. The new classroom building enhances Awty's ability to respond to a growing student body and curriculum, and to continue providing excellent academic programs. The building design achieved LEED Silver from the USGBC LEED for Schools program for its sustainable site approach, water conservation, energy efficiency, selection of materials and products with recycled content, and special consideration for improved indoor air quality.

Established in 1956, Awty is currently the largest international school in the United States and ranks the largest among ISAS (Independent Schools Association of the Southwest) member schools in Houston. The school offers parallel programs from Preschool to Grade 12 leading to either the International Baccalaureate or the French Baccalaureate.

Code	Division Name	Sq. Cost	Projected
00	Procurement	1.81	118,261
01	General Requirements	19.33	1,260,806
03	Concrete	9.31	607,191
04	Masonry	5.09	332,161
05	Metals	19.78	1,290,443
06	Wood & Plastics	6.05	394,659
07	Thermal & Moisture	7.93	517,038
08	Openings	15.79	1,030,151
09	Finishes	20.45	1,334,056
10	Specialties	7.64	498,555
11	Equipment	0.82	53,378
12	Furnishings	0.82	53,486
14	Conveying Systems	2.00	130,396
21	Fire Suppression	1.83	119,465
22	Plumbing	6.44	420,370
23	HVAC	25.65	1,673,250
26	Electrical	18.77	1,224,450
27	Communications	5.71	372,628
28	Electronic Safety/Security	2.98	194,438
Total Building Costs		**178.21**	**11,625,181**

For a more in-depth report on this building or additional case studies contact DC&D
@ 800-533-5680, or www.DCD.com

23

Project Notes

The restoration of and addition to historic Middleton Hall was commissioned by Mississippi State University. Mississippi State University is located in the northeastern section of the state and serves a student population of over 20,000. Middleton Hall houses the Army and Air Force ROTC Programs on the Mississippi State University campus. The historic classification of Middleton Hall puts it under the Mississippi Department of Archives and History regulations, which require a Mississippi Landmark permit. Five years prior to this addition and renovation phase, Shafer & Associates, PLLC restored the exterior within the context of Archives and History regulations.

The scope of the addition and renovation project included additional wings on the north and south sides of the building, restoration of the existing space, new interior walls, mechanical and electrical systems, and refurbished windows along with new interior fixtures and finishes. The building is on a very tight site leaving little space for additions. The major design criteria were to respect the existing building while renovating and expanding it to meet the additional space and functional requirements and to bring the building into code compliance. The north and south wing additions provide ADA compliant restrooms on the first and second floors, three additional offices and two additional vaults (in the basement). The renovation of the existing historic building includes three standard lecture-style classrooms (14, 21, and 18 seats) and a personnel room (13 seats).

The restoration/renovation/addition of Middleton Hall preserves the historic landmark building while updating it for current and future departmental/program needs. The benefit to Mississippi State University and the state are in the preservation and effective reuse of an existing structure, which is an important piece of state history.

Shafer & Associates, Pllc - Office of Architecture produces well-designed, budget-conscious solutions for a broad client-base. The practice concentrates on affordable education, civic, and housing projects and is well resourced, and staffed with talented and committed professionals.

Code	Division Name	Sq. Cost	Projected
00	Procurement	32.31	476,534
01	General Requirements	13.09	193,043
03	Concrete	7.35	108,409
04	Masonry	15.39	226,978
05	Metals	1.26	18,599
06	Wood & Plastics	16.40	241,937
07	Thermal & Moisture	4.89	72,133
08	Openings	12.61	186,035
09	Finishes	26.18	386,036
10	Specialties	1.86	27,375
11	Equipment	0.80	11,783
14	Conveying Systems	5.38	79,388
21	Fire Suppression	5.97	87,975
22	Plumbing	16.51	243,496
23	HVAC	34.83	513,706
26	Electrical	28.17	415,505
Total Building Costs		**223.01**	**3,288,931**

Project Notes

The new Science & Technology Building serves as a hub for academics; science; and social interaction. The LEED® Silver targeted project responds to several new FSU climate, energy, and sustainability initiatives.

The new building completes an L-shaped quad of existing science buildings. The west lab and classroom wing completes the U of the quad and resolves a significant grade change, replacing a 10-foot tall entry staircase with a gently sloping lawn and on-grade entry.

There is no formal lobby; rather, the first floor is a cafe with extended hours that serves the entire campus. Above the cafe, the upper levels contain seminar rooms, each with a series of "dormers" framing views of the quad. The Discovery Forum also connects the laboratory and faculty office wings with a highly transparent multi-level bridge containing wide seating areas and planned access to a future roof garden.

Rotated in plan, the office wing floats in the quad between the original Lyons building and a major north-south pedestrian axis. The two brick-clad wings are connected on the upper levels by a glass bridge that forms part of the Discovery Forum. Beneath the bridge, the quad flows freely through and around the office wing, forming an open, inviting natural amphitheater for both formal and informal uses. Shielded from intense mid-day sun, a formal plaza containing outdoor café seating extends to the north from the building's main façade.

The classrooms and laboratories are tall, airy spaces with generous windows. Open ceilings perform multiple duties, promoting building flexibility, ease of maintenance,

and engaging students in a real-world way about science, energy, and sustainability.

Working in a tough economy, the entire project team: design, construction, and owner, were inspired by the opportunities this project represented. The creativity exhibited by all parties resulted in strategies that fulfilled all of FSU's project goals, with an iconic new building now representing FSU's future.

Code	Division Name	Sq. Cost	Projected
00	Procurement	4.96	322,395
01	General Requirements	52.23	3,397,300
03	Concrete	45.44	2,955,708
04	Masonry	12.51	813,580
05	Metals	37.30	2,426,530
07	Thermal & Moisture	22.39	1,456,741
08	Openings	21.01	1,366,981
09	Finishes	27.18	1,768,307
10	Specialties	1.04	67,500
12	Furnishings	16.75	1,089,326
14	Conveying Systems	4.65	302,499
21	Fire Suppression	4.43	288,122
22	Plumbing	19.70	1,281,157
23	HVAC	92.15	5,994,355
26	Electrical	44.94	2,923,338
27	Communications	16.10	1,047,203
28	Electronic Safety/Security	15.95	1,037,380

Total Building Costs	**438.73**	**28,538,420**

For a more in-depth report on this building or additional case studies contact DC&D
@ 800-533-5680, or www.DCD.com

25

Project Notes

Goodwyn, Mills and Cawood were challenged to design a two-sided restaurant in an existing vacant space to accommodate passengers on the secure and non-secure side of the TSA security. To accomplish this task, a security wall was created that was half glass and half wall with a full bar on each side.

The kitchen is located on the secure side and serves food on both sides of the restaurant. The food conveyance system, which was designed around TSA requirements, is what makes this concept work. The architect used a Sally Port system that has been used in three other airports across the county. What is unique about this location is that this is the first time it has been used to convey food and drink products from secure server to non-secure server, while the three other locations serve food from a secure kitchen to a non-secure dining room. This unit moves in one direction and a server operates it manually. If anything moves too far around the Sally Port it falls in to a "dump" so nothing can pass through from the non-secure side to the secure side.

Code	Division Name	Sq. Cost	Projected
00	Procurement	82.10	190,478
01	General Requirements	8.02	18,614
06	Wood & Plastics	1.43	3,309
07	Thermal & Moisture	0.89	2,068
08	Openings	17.42	40,421
09	Finishes	42.29	98,113
10	Specialties	0.74	1,719
21	Fire Suppression	3.31	7,690
22	Plumbing	22.94	53,222
23	HVAC	34.28	79,523
26	Electrical	23.48	54,485
Total Building Costs		**236.92**	**549,643**

Project Notes

The Rockport City Services Building is designed as several pods interconnected by corridors. Each pod is home to one or more of the City's public works departments including water, wastewater, natural gas, building and development, permits and inspections, code enforcement and environmental services. This complex of interconnected pods is designed to provide a convenient, one-stop facility for the public and developers.

Elements of the exterior are designed to reflect a traditional seacoast community with repetitive metal roof lines and colors reminiscent of the sea.

The building complex is designed to withstand Category 3 hurricanes and is intended to be used as a base for recovery operations after major storms. Showers, toilets and training rooms were sized for a temporarily increased occupancy by emergency personnel. In the event of such an emergency, the complex can become self-sustaining and can house up to 100 emergency personnel.

A combination of ICF (insulated concrete forms) walls, impact-resistant insulated glass, and spray foam insulated roofs provides a very tight and energy-efficient structure. In addition to being thermally efficient, the ICF walls, impact resistant glazing, and standing seam metal roofing provide protection against hurricane force winds.

Particular care, was taken when positioning the facility, to preserve the natural beauty of the nine-acre site, with it's windswept oaks and natural vegetation. Taking advantage of existing topography and vegetation was a crucial part of the site design which, constructed under a separate contract, includes storage yards and buildings, a one-million gallon elevated water tower, and a sanitary sewer lift station.

Code	Division Name	Sq. Cost	Projected
00	Procurement	2.93	58,808
01	General Requirements	33.57	673,549
03	Concrete	25.80	517,595
05	Metals	0.72	14,501
06	Wood & Plastics	26.28	527,136
07	Thermal & Moisture	10.94	219,525
08	Openings	13.41	269,096
09	Finishes	11.17	224,184
10	Specialties	3.07	61,611
11	Equipment	0.77	15,494
21	Fire Suppression	5.05	101,235
22	Plumbing	5.51	110,516
23	HVAC	15.57	312,458
26	Electrical	32.11	644,274
28	Electronic Safety/Security	2.46	49,423
Total Building Costs		**189.38**	**3,799,406**

For a more in-depth report on this building or additional case studies contact DC&D
@ 800-533-5680, or www.DCD.com

27

Project Notes

Good Shepherd Catholic Church and the St. Joseph Diocese of Kansas City hired HMN with Castrop Design Group to design a new church for the parish relocation. Creating a master plan for the 32-acre site was the first step. It included space for the church, chapel, school, gym, day care, outdoor recreation and rectory.

After completing the master plan, the HMN design team began designing the first phase. The clients' goal was to create a building that was historically symbolic utilizing traditional ecclesiastic design elements. It features a 70-foot bell tower, 500-seat church, a fellowship narthex (foyer), offices, parish hall with a commercial kitchen, as well as School of Religion classrooms. Design features include a column free basement of long span composite concrete floor, which is a stiffer and less expensive approach. The worship space is expandable to 700 seats. A future 70-seat adoration apse was included in the design.

The project team encountered several challenges on the project. The first was obtaining utilities economically. HMN negotiated with the city for shared costs of public infrastructure. Another challenge was the integration of multiple construction systems. Concrete block, heavy timber, steel and formed concrete were used to achieve the design the client desired without being cost prohibitive.

Code	Division Name	Sq. Cost	Projected
00	Procurement	1.38	34,306
01	General Requirements	17.26	428,273
03	Concrete	17.33	430,011
04	Masonry	13.76	341,335
05	Metals	16.44	407,932
06	Wood & Plastics	13.26	329,055
07	Thermal & Moisture	9.58	237,767
08	Openings	8.18	202,922
09	Finishes	20.10	498,623
10	Specialties	0.64	15,773
14	Conveying Systems	1.32	32,653
21	Fire Suppression	1.49	36,873
22	Plumbing	4.80	119,157
23	HVAC	21.77	540,212
26	Electrical	17.19	426,514
Total Building Costs		**164.51**	**4,081,407**

Project Notes

Due to the economic collapse of the region, a church was able to purchase a partially completed two-story office building in an upscale location. Originally designed as a six building office condominium campus, the site had been abandoned three years earlier due to foreclosure.

As the church and architect first walked on the site, they were overcome by the impression that the unfinished masonry walls recalled the stone walls of a European cathedral during construction or after a WWII bombing raid.

There were two other major design cues. First, the winter home of Frank Lloyd Wright (Taliesin West) is located only a few miles away. Some of the colors and architectural graphics are inspired by Wright's regional influences. Second, the American "home" for the Episcopal faith is represented by the Episcopal "National Cathedral" in Washington, DC. National Cathedral inspired some of the gothic window shapes, the structurally necessary CMU buttresses and the massing of the steeple and gable façade to the south. Additionally, there is a touch of joviality found in how the tops of COTN's buttresses mimic the infamous "Darth Vader" gargoyle located on the National Cathedral.

More seriously, the intent was to also allow the design of the interior spaces and finishes to represent the "sacredness" of the building.

The nave has mostly hard surfaces and natural materials, allowing COTN to have one of the longest controlled acoustical reverberation times in the state of Arizona. This helps enhance the worship experience, especially when led by the organ or choir. However, the church also has a state of the art line array sound system for speech intelligibility, which can be adjusted on an iPad from any chair in the nave.

There are also two sets of high lumen video projectors and retractable screens for less traditional services.

Code	Division Name	Sq. Cost	Projected
00	Procurement	1.03	18,789
01	General Requirements	18.55	339,212
03	Concrete	2.85	52,129
04	Masonry	8.51	155,658
05	Metals	11.87	217,049
06	Wood & Plastics	5.35	97,861
07	Thermal & Moisture	5.41	99,025
08	Openings	11.47	209,723
09	Finishes	13.58	248,400
10	Specialties	2.02	36,936
21	Fire Suppression	1.70	31,062
22	Plumbing	2.86	52,239
23	HVAC	9.27	169,453
26	Electrical	9.79	179,097
27	Communications	2.14	39,223
Total Building Costs		**106.40**	**1,945,855**

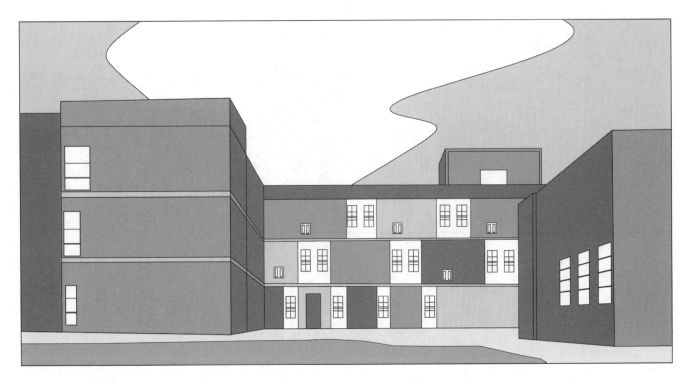

Project Notes

Determined to change the plight of its homeless population, the City of San Antonio provided a comprehensive "campus of transformation," which addresses and treats most of these causes.

Architects and stakeholders also held collaborative design charrettes and project progress meetings with service providers, interest groups, law enforcement, and surrounding neighborhood associations. The campus applies sustainable design practices through the reuse of previously abandoned warehouses and the revitalization of a derelict portion of downtown San Antonio. The most important sustainability result, however, is how it positively affects the City and each of its residents.

Haven for Hope is a 37-acre homeless transformational campus located near downtown San Antonio. The $60 million project includes 15 buildings of approximately 300,000 square feet of total space, with 998 beds and the capacity to sleep an additional 500+ individuals in the courtyard. It is the largest and most comprehensive homeless facility in the United States and houses more than 78 San Antonio-based non-profits and government agencies.

Located adjacent to San Antonio's Central Business District, Haven for Hope combines 140,000 square feet of abandoned warehouse space with 160,000 square feet of new construction. Instead of a jail-like structure with four walls surrounding the campus keeping the homeless in and the community out, Haven was designed to be an open, integrated and welcoming facility. Ample public courtyards between the buildings serve as important gathering spaces that allow members to redevelop social skills and create meaningful relationships. Spaces within the campus include

classrooms and conference rooms, a library and learning center, mail center, barbershop, exercise and recreational areas, a chapel, a childcare center with an after-school program, and even a pet shelter service center with a seeing-eye dog-training program.

Code	Division Name	Sq. Cost	Projected
01	General Requirements	36.17	2,456,245
03	Concrete	50.48	3,427,918
04	Masonry	13.15	892,994
05	Metals	6.09	413,535
06	Wood & Plastics	2.75	186,602
07	Thermal & Moisture	12.96	880,267
08	Openings	19.82	1,345,713
09	Finishes	20.86	1,416,621
10	Specialties	1.72	116,810
14	Conveying Systems	4.18	283,674
21	Fire Suppression	3.99	270,835
22	Plumbing	2.77	188,023
23	HVAC	38.13	2,589,059
26	Electrical	19.76	1,342,151
27	Communications	0.87	58,922

Total Building Costs	**233.69**	**15,869,370**

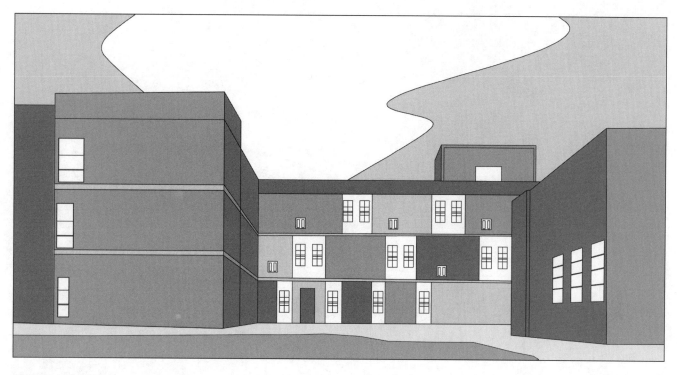

Project Notes

Determined to change the plight of its homeless population, the City of San Antonio provided a comprehensive "campus of transformation," which addresses and treats most of these causes.

Architects and stakeholders also held collaborative design charrettes and project progress meetings with service providers, interest groups, law enforcement, and surrounding neighborhood associations. The campus applies sustainable design practices through the reuse of previously abandoned warehouses and the revitalization of a derelict portion of downtown San Antonio. The most important sustainability result, however, is how it positively affects the City and each of its residents.

Haven for Hope is a 37-acre homeless transformational campus located near downtown San Antonio. The $60 million project includes 15 buildings of approximately 300,000 square feet of total space, with 998 beds and the capacity to sleep an additional 500+ individuals in the courtyard. It is the largest and most comprehensive homeless facility in the United States and houses more than 78 San Antonio-based non-profits and government agencies.

Located adjacent to San Antonio's Central Business District, Haven for Hope combines 140,000 square feet of abandoned warehouse space with 160,000 square feet of new construction. Instead of a jail-like structure with four walls surrounding the campus keeping the homeless in and the community out, Haven was designed to be an open, integrated and welcoming facility. Ample public courtyards between the buildings serve as important gathering spaces that allow members to redevelop social skills and create meaningful relationships. Spaces within the campus include

classrooms and conference rooms, a library and learning center, mail center, barbershop, exercise and recreational areas, a chapel, a childcare center with an after-school program, and even a pet shelter service center with a seeing-eye dog-training program.

Code	Division Name	Sq. Cost	Projected
03	Concrete	50.20	3,020,852
04	Masonry	14.23	856,616
05	Metals	6.38	383,876
06	Wood & Plastics	4.74	285,563
07	Thermal & Moisture	13.45	809,739
08	Openings	21.22	1,276,852
09	Finishes	22.10	1,329,958
10	Specialties	2.06	123,995
14	Conveying Systems	4.07	244,791
21	Fire Suppression	4.72	284,111
22	Plumbing	2.52	151,401
23	HVAC	44.51	2,678,881
26	Electrical	23.10	1,390,234
27	Communications	1.35	81,220
28	Electronic Safety/Security	10.46	629,651
Total Building Costs		**225.11**	**13,547,740**

Project Notes

Cornerstone Design Architects worked alongside Country Meadows to develop a new, 50-unit Independent Living Facility which adjoins the existing buildings on campus.

Taking into consideration the new building would unite with the existing facility, the focus for the articulation of the exterior façade was to provide a look that would tie into the existing buildings but provide an updated look. Exterior materials included EIFS, brick, and vinyl railings. The interior of the new facility offers a brand new commercial kitchen, dining space, resident apartments, outdoor courtyards, club room, lounge spaces, and resident storage.

Features of the apartments include unique, varying layouts, full operating kitchen with stainless steel appliances, private patios, courtyard access, and individual temperature controls. The apartments are available in studio, one, and two bedroom models, with a range of sizes available in each apartment type. The unique layouts provide a sense of individuality for the residents, in what could otherwise be an environment that fosters standardized layouts, treating every resident as if they have the same space needs.

Features of the common spaces include the dining room, where residents can order meals as though eating at their favorite restaurant, again promoting a sense of individuality for each resident. A feature of the dining room is the double-sided stone fireplace, occupying a prominent location in the center of the room and towering to the underside of the vaulted ceiling, with beams running across the vaulted space. The lounge spaces, club room, and various seating areas foster a sense of community and provide spaces for residents to interact and build relationships. The overall atmosphere, regarding finishes, is an elegant yet homelike feeling, with warm tones, multi-textural materials, and quality furnishings throughout. Eschewing the institutional feel of many outdated retirement facilities today, the new independent living facility at Country Meadows succeeds in providing a place that residents can be proud to call home.

Code	Division Name	Sq. Cost	Projected
01	General Requirements	10.45	556,365
03	Concrete	4.56	242,619
04	Masonry	5.10	271,702
05	Metals	3.86	205,739
06	Wood & Plastics	21.10	1,123,519
07	Thermal & Moisture	8.97	477,585
08	Openings	5.66	301,069
09	Finishes	11.82	629,172
11	Equipment	7.65	407,383
12	Furnishings	0.27	14,232
21	Fire Suppression	3.76	200,421
22	Plumbing	12.55	667,916
23	HVAC	11.60	617,348
26	Electrical	12.22	650,771
27	Communications	2.11	112,200
Total Building Costs		**121.68**	**6,478,042**

Project Notes

This renovation transforms a dated, cool-toned and institutional lobby, mail, and library space into an updated, warm and homelike environment. The formal dining space was also updated, and a brand new informal cafe and dining area were constructed to replace the existing outdated spaces. The overall square footage of renovation totaled approximately 14,255 square feet, and the construction occurred over several phases while maintaining existing operations.

Serving as a main entrance for residents and prospective residents alike, the lobby space is a key element for Landis Homes to make a lasting first impression. The lobby incorporates a raised ceiling with curving bulkheads, leading the eye into the space and giving it an aura of spaciousness, a central fireplace and seating area, improved lighting, and a reception desk easily visible from the main entrance but not dominant, keeping the focus on the fireplace and seating.

The newly created mail and library space are centrally located within the resident apartments and dining, as opposed to their former locations in the lobby and an enclosed room. These spaces are open and inviting, providing a central gathering space and fostering interaction and sense of community among residents as they check their mail or enjoy a book at the library. The library is filled with natural light due to the addition of windows. Additionally, window seats were provided along the corridor leading from the lobby to the mail and library area, allowing natural light to infiltrate the space and providing a place of rest for residents along a commonly traveled path.

The dining spaces, both formal and informal, received upgraded finishes, new equipment, and a greater sense of openness. The formal dining space, formerly a low, dimly lit space with limited natural light was provided with new skylights, illuminating the interior of the dining room with ample natural lighting and giving the space an open feeling above. The informal dining area and cafe were updated, and the serving line was reworked to give residents the flexibility of al-a-carte dining and made-to-order selections.

Code	Division Name	Sq. Cost	Projected
01	General Requirements	6.22	88,643
03	Concrete	1.35	19,242
04	Masonry	1.06	15,081
05	Metals	1.61	22,904
06	Wood & Plastics	1.56	22,286
07	Thermal & Moisture	1.52	21,736
08	Openings	5.84	83,295
09	Finishes	15.00	213,789
10	Specialties	0.47	6,633
11	Equipment	19.60	279,445
Total Building Costs		**54.23**	**773,054**

Project Notes

Sally's House was in need of a major expansion to accommodate the increased homeless population. However, with the existing facility situated on a small lot in downtown Houston, the lack of available land on which to build was a major challenge of the design. This "challenge" of a limited site was turned into an opportunity, in which design of the new two-story addition makes the most use of the limited lot by elevating the programmatic living spaces above the required on-site vehicle parking.

The building addition, which is a free-standing structure, is accessed through a double-height ground level security lobby, which houses an administration office, elevator and grand stairway to access the living quarters above. The second level utilizes a series of open lounge areas with seating and television monitors to create a sky-lit concourse that provides access to an office, a nurse's station, meeting rooms and the dormitory/sleeping area. Daylight floods the building's interior and uses colorful accents of structural and mechanical elements to provide visual interest.

Though situated in the downtown of a large metropolitan city, the design incorporates residential "transitional" forms and human scaled components to act as a foil to the larger surrounding buildings. The building's textures work in harmony to reflect a "sense of home" in the harsh downtown environment. Sustainable strategies were an important part of the project's design approach providing an opportunity for users to benefit from the investment, while allowing the owner's to be good stewards of the environment. The site's constraints enhance the overall sustainable design approach. The designers implemented best practice strategies towards energy conservation. Exterior windows are (low-E) double insulated glazing. The exterior sheathing is covered with R-19 insulation at the walls and R-30 at the roof. Due to comprehensive day-lighting strategies, the energy consumption is significantly reduced compared to the existing facility.

Code	Division Name	Sq. Cost	Projected
00	Procurement	2.66	20,776
01	General Requirements	40.45	315,978
03	Concrete	19.40	151,544
04	Masonry	10.48	81,883
05	Metals	22.68	177,208
06	Wood & Plastics	4.07	31,775
07	Thermal & Moisture	25.66	200,429
08	Openings	12.98	101,437
09	Finishes	21.59	168,654
10	Specialties	1.86	14,543
14	Conveying Systems	7.20	56,218
21	Fire Suppression	8.60	67,217
22	Plumbing	7.04	54,996
23	HVAC	7.35	57,440
26	Electrical	14.55	113,658
28	Electronic Safety/Security	1.96	15,277
Total Building Costs		**208.53**	**1,629,032**

Section Two

Unit-In-Place Costs

DIVISION 1 GENERAL CONDITIONS

DIVISION 2 SITEWORK

DIVISION 3 CONCRETE

DIVISION 4 MASONRY

DIVISION 5 METALS

DIVISION 6 WOOD & PLASTICS

DIVISION 7 THERMAL & MOISTURE PROTECTION

DIVISION 8 DOORS & WINDOWS

DIVISION 9 FINISHES

DIVISION 10 SPECIALTIES

DIVISION 11 EQUIPMENT

DIVISION 12 FURNISHINGS

DIVISION 13 SPECIAL CONSTRUCTION

DIVISION 14 CONVEYING

DIVISION 15 MECHANICAL

DIVISION 16 ELECTRICAL

	Unit	Total
01020.10 ALLOWANCES		
Overhead		
$20,000 project		
Minimum	PCT.	15.00
Average	PCT.	20.00
Maximum	PCT.	40.00
$100,000 project		
Minimum	PCT.	12.00
Average	PCT.	15.00
Maximum	PCT.	25.00
$500,000 project		
Minimum	PCT.	10.00
Average	PCT.	12.00
Maximum	PCT.	20.00
Profit		
$20,000 project		
Minimum	PCT.	10.00
Average	PCT.	15.00
Maximum	PCT.	25.00
$100,000 project		
Minimum	PCT.	10.00
Average	PCT.	12.00
Maximum	PCT.	20.00
$500,000 project		
Minimum	PCT.	5.00
Average	PCT.	10.00
Maximum	PCT.	15.00
Professional fees		
Architectural		
$100,000 project		
Minimum	PCT.	5.00
Average	PCT.	10.00
Maximum	PCT.	20.00
$500,000 project		
Minimum	PCT.	5.00
Average	PCT.	8.00
Maximum	PCT.	12.00
Structural engineering		
Minimum	PCT.	2.00
Average	PCT.	3.00
Maximum	PCT.	5.00
Mechanical engineering		
Minimum	PCT.	4.00
Average	PCT.	5.00
Maximum	PCT.	15.00
Taxes		
Sales tax		
Minimum	PCT.	4.00
Average	PCT.	5.00
Maximum	PCT.	10.00
Unemployment		
Minimum	PCT.	3.00
Average	PCT.	6.50
Maximum	PCT.	8.00
Social security (FICA)	PCT.	7.85
01050.10 FIELD STAFF		
Superintendent		
Minimum	YEAR	94,600
Average	YEAR	118,200
Maximum	YEAR	142,000
Foreman		
Minimum	YEAR	62,800
Average	YEAR	100,500
Maximum	YEAR	117,700

	Unit	Total

01050.10 FIELD STAFF (Cont.)

Bookkeeper/timekeeper
Minimum	YEAR	36,400
Average	YEAR	47,500
Maximum	YEAR	61,400

Watchman
Minimum	YEAR	27,100
Average	YEAR	36,200
Maximum	YEAR	45,700

01330.10 SURVEYING

Surveying
Small crew	DAY	890.00
Average crew	DAY	1,350
Large crew	DAY	1,800

Lot lines and boundaries
Minimum	ACRE	640.00
Average	ACRE	1,350
Maximum	ACRE	2,250

01380.10 JOB REQUIREMENTS

Job photographs, small jobs
Minimum	EA.	120.00
Average	EA.	180.00
Maximum	EA.	420.00

Large projects
Minimum	EA.	610.00
Average	EA.	910.00
Maximum	EA.	3,050

01410.10 TESTING

Testing concrete, per test
Minimum	EA.	21.00
Average	EA.	35.00
Maximum	EA.	70.00

01500.10 TEMPORARY FACILITIES

Barricades, temporary
Highway
Concrete	L.F.	16.96
Wood	L.F.	6.07
Steel	L.F.	5.87

Pedestrian barricades
Plywood	S.F.	5.30
Chain link fence	S.F.	4.72

Trailers, general office type, per month
Minimum	EA.	210.00
Average	EA.	340.00
Maximum	EA.	690.00

Crew change trailers, per month
Minimum	EA.	120.00
Average	EA.	140.00
Maximum	EA.	210.00

01505.10 MOBILIZATION

Equipment mobilization
Bulldozer
Minimum	EA.	200.00
Average	EA.	410.00
Maximum	EA.	680.00

Backhoe/front-end loader
Minimum	EA.	120.00
Average	EA.	200.00
Maximum	EA.	450.00

	Unit	Total

01505.10 MOBILIZATION (Cont.)

Equipment mobilization
  Backhoe/front-end loader

	Unit	Total
Minimum	EA.	490.00
Average	EA.	760.00
Maximum	EA.	1,300

01525.10 CONSTRUCTION AIDS

Scaffolding/staging, rent per month
  Measured by lineal feet of base

	Unit	Total
10' high	L.F.	12.50
20' high	L.F.	22.50
30' high	L.F.	31.50

  Measured by square foot of surface

	Unit	Total
Minimum	S.F.	.55
Average	S.F.	.95
Maximum	S.F.	1.69

Tarpaulins, fabric, per job

	Unit	Total
Minimum	S.F.	.25
Average	S.F.	.43
Maximum	S.F.	1.11

01570.10 SIGNS

Construction signs, temporary
  Signs, 2' x 4'

	Unit	Total
Minimum	EA.	35.00
Average	EA.	83.75
Maximum	EA.	300.00

  Signs, 4' x 8'

	Unit	Total
Minimum	EA.	73.50
Average	EA.	190.00
Maximum	EA.	820.00

  Signs, 8' x 8'

	Unit	Total
Minimum	EA.	94.25
Average	EA.	300.00
Maximum	EA.	2,950

01600.10 EQUIPMENT

Air compressor
  60 cfm

	Unit	Total
By day	EA.	92.50
By week	EA.	280.00
By month	EA.	840.00

  300 cfm

	Unit	Total
By day	EA.	190.00
By week	EA.	600.00
By month	EA.	1,850

Air tools, per compressor, per day

	Unit	Total
Minimum	EA.	38.25
Average	EA.	47.75
Maximum	EA.	66.75

Generators, 5 kw

	Unit	Total
By day	EA.	95.25
By week	EA.	280.00
By month	EA.	880.00

Heaters, salamander type, per week

	Unit	Total
Minimum	EA.	110.00
Average	EA.	160.00
Maximum	EA.	340.00

Pumps, submersible
  50 gpm

	Unit	Total
By day	EA.	76.25
By week	EA.	230.00
By month	EA.	680.00

	Unit	Total

01600.10 EQUIPMENT (Cont.)

Pickup truck

By day	EA.	140.00
By week	EA.	420.00
By month	EA.	1,300

Dump truck

6 cy truck

By day	EA.	380.00
By week	EA.	1,150
By month	EA.	3,450

10 cy truck

By day	EA.	470.00
By week	EA.	1,450
By month	EA.	4,300

16 cy truck

By day	EA.	760.00
By week	EA.	2,300
By month	EA.	6,850

Backhoe, track mounted

1/2 cy capacity

By day	EA.	780.00
By week	EA.	2,400
By month	EA.	7,050

Backhoe/loader, rubber tired

1/2 cy capacity

By day	EA.	470.00
By week	EA.	1,450
By month	EA.	4,300

3/4 cy capacity

By day	EA.	570.00
By week	EA.	1,700
By month	EA.	5,150

Bulldozer

75 hp

By day	EA.	670.00
By week	EA.	2,000
By month	EA.	6,000

Cranes, crawler type

15 ton capacity

By day	EA.	860.00
By week	EA.	2,550
By month	EA.	7,700

Truck mounted, hydraulic

15 ton capacity

By day	EA.	810.00
By week	EA.	2,450
By month	EA.	7,000

Loader, rubber tired

1 cy capacity

By day	EA.	570.00
By week	EA.	1,700
By month	EA.	5,150

	Unit	Total

02115.66 SEPTIC TANK REMOVAL

Remove septic tank

1000 gals	EA.	200.00
2000 gals	EA.	250.00

02210.10 SOIL BORING

Borings, uncased, stable earth

2-1/2" dia.	L.F.	30.75
4" dia.	L.F.	35.00

Cased, including samples

2-1/2" dia.	L.F.	40.75
4" dia.	L.F.	70.00

Drilling in rock

No sampling	L.F.	64.50
With casing and sampling	L.F.	81.75

Test pits

Light soil	EA.	410.00
Heavy soil	EA.	610.00

02220.10 COMPLETE BUILDING DEMOLITION

Building, complete with disposal

Wood frame	C.F.	.35

02220.15 SELECTIVE BUILDING DEMOLITION

Partition removal

Concrete block partitions

8" thick	S.F.	2.98

Brick masonry partitions

4" thick	S.F.	2.23
8" thick	S.F.	2.79

Stud partitions

Metal or wood, with drywall both sides	S.F.	2.23

Door and frame removal

Wood in framed wall

2'6"x6'8"	EA.	32.00
3'x6'8"	EA.	37.25

Ceiling removal

Acoustical tile ceiling

Adhesive fastened	S.F.	.45
Furred and glued	S.F.	.37
Suspended grid	S.F.	.28

Drywall ceiling

Furred and nailed	S.F.	.50
Nailed to framing	S.F.	.45

Window removal

Metal windows, trim included

2'x3'	EA.	44.75
3'x4'	EA.	55.75
4'x8'	EA.	110.00

Wood windows, trim included

2'x3'	EA.	24.75
3'x4'	EA.	29.75
6'x8'	EA.	44.75

Concrete block walls, not including toothing

4" thick	S.F.	2.48
6" thick	S.F.	2.63
8" thick	S.F.	2.79

Rubbish handling

Load in dumpster or truck

Minimum	C.F.	.99
Maximum	C.F.	1.49

Rubbish hauling

Hand loaded on trucks, 2 mile trip	C.Y.	37.75
Machine loaded on trucks, 2 mile trip	C.Y.	24.50

	Unit	Total

02225.13 CORE DRILLING

Concrete
6" thick
3" dia. .... EA.   42.00
8" thick
3" dia. .... EA.   58.75

02225.15 CURB & GUTTER DEMOLITION

Removal, plain concrete curb .... L.F.   6.13
   Plain concrete curb and 2' gutter .... L.F.   8.46

02225.20 FENCE DEMOLITION

Remove fencing
Chain link, 8' high
For disposal .... L.F.   2.23
For reuse .... L.F.   5.58
Wood
4' high .... S.F.   1.49
Masonry
8" thick
4' high .... S.F.   4.46
6' high .... S.F.   5.58

02225.25 GUARDRAIL DEMOLITION

Remove standard guardrail
Steel .... L.F.   8.17
Wood .... L.F.   6.29

02225.30 HYDRANT DEMOLITION

Remove and reset fire hydrant .... EA.   1,250

02225.40 PAVEMENT and SIDEWALK DEMOLITION

Concrete pavement, 6" thick
No reinforcement .... S.Y.   16.25
With wire mesh .... S.Y.   24.50
With rebars .... S.Y.   30.75
Sidewalk, 4" thick, with disposal .... S.Y.   8.17

02225.42 DRAINAGE PIPING DEMOLITION

Remove drainage pipe, not including excavation
12" dia. .... L.F.   10.25
18" dia. .... L.F.   13.00

02225.43 GAS PIPING DEMOLITION

Remove welded steel pipe, not including excavation
4" dia. .... L.F.   15.25
5" dia. .... L.F.   24.50

02225.45 SANITARY PIPING DEMOLITION

Remove sewer pipe, not including excavation
4" dia. .... L.F.   9.81

02225.48 WATER PIPING DEMOLITION

Remove water pipe, not including excavation
4" dia. .... L.F.   11.25

02225.50 SAW CUTTING PAVEMENT

Pavement, bituminous
2" thick .... L.F.   1.88
3" thick .... L.F.   2.36
Concrete pavement, with wire mesh
4" thick .... L.F.   3.62
5" thick .... L.F.   3.93
Plain concrete, unreinforced
4" thick .... L.F.   3.14
5" thick .... L.F.   3.62

	Unit	Total

02230.10 CLEAR WOODED AREAS

Clear wooded area

Light density	ACRE	6,150
Medium density	ACRE	8,150
Heavy density	ACRE	9,800

02230.50 TREE CUTTING & CLEARING

Cut trees and clear out stumps

9" to 12" dia.	EA.	490.00
To 24" dia.	EA.	610.00
24" dia. and up	EA.	820.00

Loading and trucking
For machine load, per load, round trip

1 mile	EA.	98.00
3 mile	EA.	110.00
5 mile	EA.	120.00
10 mile	EA.	160.00
20 mile	EA.	250.00

Hand loaded, round trip

1 mile	EA.	240.00
3 mile	EA.	270.00
5 mile	EA.	310.00
10 mile	EA.	380.00
20 mile	EA.	470.00

02315.10 BASE COURSE

Base course, crushed stone

3" thick	S.Y.	4.35
4" thick	S.Y.	5.61
6" thick	S.Y.	8.11

Base course, bank run gravel

4" deep	S.Y.	3.72
6" deep	S.Y.	5.38

Prepare and roll sub base

Minimum	S.Y.	.67
Average	S.Y.	.83
Maximum	S.Y.	1.11

02315.20 BORROW

Borrow fill, F.O.B. at pit
Sand, haul to site, round trip

10 mile	C.Y.	33.75
20 mile	C.Y.	42.75
30 mile	C.Y.	53.75

Place borrow fill and compact

Less than 1 in 4 slope	C.Y.	27.17
Greater than 1 in 4 slope	C.Y.	29.40

02315.30 BULK EXCAVATION

Excavation, by small dozer

Large areas	C.Y.	1.88
Small areas	C.Y.	3.14
Trim banks	C.Y.	4.71

Hydraulic excavator
1 cy capacity

Light material	C.Y.	4.09
Medium material	C.Y.	4.90
Wet material	C.Y.	6.13
Blasted rock	C.Y.	7.01

1-1/2 cy capacity

Light material	C.Y.	1.67
Medium material	C.Y.	2.22
Wet material	C.Y.	2.67

	Unit	Total

02315.30 BULK EXCAVATION (Cont.)

Wheel mounted front-end loader

7/8 cy capacity

Light material	C.Y.	3.34
Medium material	C.Y.	3.81
Wet material	C.Y.	4.45
Blasted rock	C.Y.	5.34

1-1/2 cy capacity

Light material	C.Y.	1.91
Medium material	C.Y.	2.05
Wet material	C.Y.	2.22
Blasted rock	C.Y.	2.43

2-1/2 cy capacity

Light material	C.Y.	1.57
Medium material	C.Y.	1.67
Wet material	C.Y.	1.78
Blasted rock	C.Y.	1.91

Track mounted front-end loader

1-1/2 cy capacity

Light material	C.Y.	2.22
Medium material	C.Y.	2.43
Wet material	C.Y.	2.67
Blasted rock	C.Y.	2.97

2-3/4 cy capacity

Light material	C.Y.	1.33
Medium material	C.Y.	1.48
Wet material	C.Y.	1.67
Blasted rock	C.Y.	1.91

02315.40 BUILDING EXCAVATION

Structural excavation, unclassified earth

3/8 cy backhoe	C.Y.	17.75
3/4 cy backhoe	C.Y.	13.25
1 cy backhoe	C.Y.	11.00
Foundation backfill and compaction by machine	C.Y.	26.75

02315.45 HAND EXCAVATION

Excavation

To 2' deep

Normal soil	C.Y.	49.50
Sand and gravel	C.Y.	44.75
Medium clay	C.Y.	55.75
Heavy clay	C.Y.	63.75
Loose rock	C.Y.	74.50

To 6' deep

Normal soil	C.Y.	63.75
Sand and gravel	C.Y.	55.75
Medium clay	C.Y.	74.50
Heavy clay	C.Y.	89.25
Loose rock	C.Y.	110.00

Backfilling foundation without compaction, 6" lifts	C.Y.	28.00

Compaction of backfill around structures or in trench

By hand with air tamper	C.Y.	32.00
By hand with vibrating plate tamper	C.Y.	29.75
1 ton roller	C.Y.	47.00

Miscellaneous hand labor

Trim slopes, sides of excavation	S.F.	.07
Trim bottom of excavation	S.F.	.09
Excavation around obstructions and services	C.Y.	150.00

	Unit	Total

02315.50 ROADWAY EXCAVATION

Roadway excavation
    1/4 mile haul .... C.Y.   2.67
    2 mile haul .... C.Y.   4.45
    5 mile haul .... C.Y.   6.67
  Spread base course .... C.Y.   3.34
    Roll and compact .... C.Y.   4.45

02315.60 TRENCHING

Trenching and continuous footing excavation
  By gradall
    1 cy capacity
      Light soil .... C.Y.   3.81
      Medium soil .... C.Y.   4.11
      Heavy/wet soil .... C.Y.   4.45
      Loose rock .... C.Y.   4.85
      Blasted rock .... C.Y.   5.13
  By hydraulic excavator
    1/2 cy capacity
      Light soil .... C.Y.   4.45
      Medium soil .... C.Y.   4.85
      Heavy/wet soil .... C.Y.   5.34
      Loose rock .... C.Y.   5.93
      Blasted rock .... C.Y.   6.67
    1 cy capacity
      Light soil .... C.Y.   3.14
      Medium soil .... C.Y.   3.34
      Heavy/wet soil .... C.Y.   3.56
      Loose rock .... C.Y.   3.81
      Blasted rock .... C.Y.   4.11
    1-1/2 cy capacity
      Light soil .... C.Y.   2.81
      Medium soil .... C.Y.   2.97
      Heavy/wet soil .... C.Y.   3.14
      Loose rock .... C.Y.   3.34
      Blasted rock .... C.Y.   3.56
    2 cy capacity
      Light soil .... C.Y.   2.67
      Medium soil .... C.Y.   2.81
      Heavy/wet soil .... C.Y.   2.97
      Loose rock .... C.Y.   3.14
      Blasted rock .... C.Y.   3.34
  Hand excavation
    Bulk, wheeled 100'
      Normal soil .... C.Y.   49.50
      Sand or gravel .... C.Y.   44.75
      Medium clay .... C.Y.   63.75
      Heavy clay .... C.Y.   89.25
      Loose rock .... C.Y. 110.00
    Trenches, up to 2' deep
      Normal soil .... C.Y.   55.75
      Sand or gravel .... C.Y.   49.50
      Medium clay .... C.Y.   74.50
      Heavy clay .... C.Y. 110.00
      Loose rock .... C.Y. 150.00
    Trenches, to 6' deep
      Normal soil .... C.Y.   63.75
      Sand or gravel .... C.Y.   55.75
      Medium clay .... C.Y.   89.25
      Heavy clay .... C.Y. 150.00
      Loose rock .... C.Y. 220.00
  Backfill trenches
    With compaction
      By hand .... C.Y.   37.25
      By 60 hp tracked dozer .... C.Y.   2.36

	Unit	Total

02315.70 UTILITY EXCAVATION

Trencher, sandy clay, 8" wide trench

18" deep	L.F.	2.09
24" deep	L.F.	2.36
36" deep	L.F.	2.69

Trench backfill, 95% compaction

Tamp by hand	C.Y.	28.00
Vibratory compaction	C.Y.	22.25
Trench backfilling, with borrow sand, place & compact	C.Y.	42.75

02315.75 GRAVEL AND STONE

F.O.B. PLANT

No. 21 crusher run stone	C.Y.	37.50
No. 26 crusher run stone	C.Y.	37.50
No. 57 stone	C.Y.	37.50
No. 67 gravel	C.Y.	37.50
No. 68 stone	C.Y.	37.50
No. 78 stone	C.Y.	37.50
No. 78 gravel, (pea gravel)	C.Y.	37.50
No. 357 or B-3 stone	C.Y.	37.50

Structural & foundation backfill

No. 21 crusher run stone	TON	27.50
No. 26 crusher run stone	TON	27.50
No. 57 stone	TON	27.50
No. 67 gravel	TON	27.50
No. 68 stone	TON	27.50
No. 78 stone	TON	27.50
No. 78 gravel, (pea gravel)	TON	27.50
No. 357 or B-3 stone	TON	27.50

02315.80 HAULING MATERIAL

Haul material by 10 cy dump truck, round trip distance

1 mile	C.Y.	5.24
2 mile	C.Y.	6.28
5 mile	C.Y.	8.57
10 mile	C.Y.	9.42
20 mile	C.Y.	10.50
30 mile	C.Y.	12.50
Site grading, cut & fill, sandy clay, 200' haul, 75 hp dozer	C.Y.	3.77
Spread topsoil by equipment on site	C.Y.	4.19

Site grading (cut and fill to 6") less than 1 acre

75 hp dozer	C.Y.	6.28
1.5 cy backhoe/loader	C.Y.	9.42

02340.05 SOIL STABILIZATION

Straw bale secured with rebar	L.F.	9.04
Filter barrier, 18" high filter fabric	L.F.	6.29
Sediment fence, 36" fabric with 6" mesh	L.F.	9.90
Soil stabilization with tar paper, burlap, straw and stakes	S.F.	.42

02360.20 SOIL TREATMENT

Soil treatment, termite control pretreatment

Under slabs	S.F.	.63
By walls	S.F.	.68

02370.40 RIPRAP

Riprap

Crushed stone blanket, max size 2-1/2"	TON	105.75
Stone, quarry run, 300 lb. stones	TON	109.50
400 lb. stones	TON	106.50
500 lb. stones	TON	104.50
750 lb. stones	TON	102.75
Dry concrete riprap in bags 3" thick, 80 lb. per bag	BAG	9.49

	Unit	Total
02455.60 STEEL PILES		
H-section piles		
8x8		
36 lb/ft		
30' long	L.F.	30.00
40' long	L.F.	27.51
Tapered friction piles, fluted casing, up to 50'		
With 4000 psi concrete no reinforcing		
12" dia.	L.F.	25.32
14" dia.	L.F.	28.26
02455.65 STEEL PIPE PILES		
Concrete filled, 3000# concrete, up to 40'		
8" dia.	L.F.	34.75
10" dia.	L.F.	42.00
12" dia.	L.F.	47.25
Pipe piles, non-filled		
8" dia.	L.F.	30.88
10" dia.	L.F.	37.11
12" dia.	L.F.	43.61
Splice		
8" dia.	EA.	189.25
10" dia.	EA.	199.25
12" dia.	EA.	230.00
Standard point		
8" dia.	EA.	229.25
10" dia.	EA.	269.25
12" dia.	EA.	300.00
Heavy duty point		
8" dia.	EA.	350.00
10" dia.	EA.	450.00
12" dia.	EA.	510.00
02455.80 WOOD AND TIMBER PILES		
Treated wood piles, 12" butt, 8" tip		
25' long	L.F.	30.50
30' long	L.F.	29.00
35' long	L.F.	27.25
40' long	L.F.	25.90
02465.50 PRESTRESSED PILING		
Prestressed concrete piling, less than 60' long		
10" sq.	L.F.	26.10
12" sq.	L.F.	34.11
Straight cylinder, less than 60' long		
12" dia.	L.F.	32.40
14" dia.	L.F.	41.56
02510.10 WELLS		
Domestic water, drilled and cased		
4" dia.	L.F.	101.00
6" dia.	L.F.	111.75
02510.40 DUCTILE IRON PIPE		
Ductile iron pipe, cement lined, slip-on joints		
4"	L.F.	23.81
6"	L.F.	27.71
8"	L.F.	34.41
Mechanical joint pipe		
4"	L.F.	28.68
6"	L.F.	33.25
8"	L.F.	41.25
Fittings, mechanical joint		
90 degree elbow		
4"	EA.	259.75
6"	EA.	324.25

	Unit	Total

02510.40 DUCTILE IRON PIPE (Cont.)

Fittings, mechanical joint
90 degree elbow

8"	EA.	464.75

45 degree elbow

4"	EA.	219.75
6"	EA.	294.25
8"	EA.	414.75

02510.60 PLASTIC PIPE

PVC, class 150 pipe

4" dia.	L.F.	11.19
6" dia.	L.F.	16.21
8" dia.	L.F.	22.26

Schedule 40 pipe

1-1/2" dia.	L.F.	3.91
2" dia.	L.F.	4.68
2-1/2" dia.	L.F.	5.85
3" dia.	L.F.	7.08
4" dia.	L.F.	9.23
6" dia.	L.F.	14.71

90 degree elbows

1"	EA.	8.46
1-1/2"	EA.	9.39
2"	EA.	11.17
2-1/2"	EA.	18.23
3"	EA.	20.92
4"	EA.	29.00
6"	EA.	71.75

45 degree elbows

1"	EA.	9.01
1-1/2"	EA.	10.18
2"	EA.	11.68
2-1/2"	EA.	18.23
3"	EA.	24.42
4"	EA.	34.50
6"	EA.	72.50

Tees

1"	EA.	10.28
1-1/2"	EA.	11.53
2"	EA.	13.67
2-1/2"	EA.	23.75
3"	EA.	29.00
4"	EA.	41.50
6"	EA.	107.00

Couplings

1"	EA.	8.26
1-1/2"	EA.	8.63
2"	EA.	9.95
2-1/2"	EA.	12.94
3"	EA.	16.21
4"	EA.	19.45
6"	EA.	41.00

Drainage pipe
PVC schedule 80

1" dia.	L.F.	4.67
1-1/2" dia.	L.F.	5.09
ABS, 2" dia.	L.F.	5.94
2-1/2" dia.	L.F.	7.46
3" dia.	L.F.	8.46
4" dia.	L.F.	10.89
6" dia.	L.F.	16.46
8" dia.	L.F.	22.45
10" dia.	L.F.	28.91
12" dia.	L.F.	42.92

	Unit	Total

02510.60 PLASTIC PIPE (Cont.)

Drainage pipe
ABS, 2" dia., 90 degree elbows

1"	EA.	10.83
1-1/2"	EA.	11.66
2"	EA.	13.21
2-1/2"	EA.	21.18
3"	EA.	22.42
4"	EA.	33.50
6"	EA.	63.75

45 degree elbows

1"	EA.	12.94
1-1/2"	EA.	14.44
2"	EA.	16.79
2-1/2"	EA.	25.18
3"	EA.	27.17
4"	EA.	44.00
6"	EA.	91.25

02530.20 VITRIFIED CLAY PIPE

Vitrified clay pipe, extra strength

6" dia.	L.F.	16.46
8" dia.	L.F.	18.00
10" dia.	L.F.	21.82

02530.30 MANHOLES

Precast sections, 48" dia.

Base section	EA.	530.00
1'0" riser	EA.	253.00
1'4" riser	EA.	290.00
2'8" riser	EA.	360.00
4'0" riser	EA.	510.00
2'8" cone top	EA.	450.00

Precast manholes, 48" dia.

4' deep	EA.	1,130
6' deep	EA.	1,580
7' deep	EA.	1,800
8' deep	EA.	2,070
10' deep	EA.	2,380

Cast-in-place, 48" dia., with frame and cover

5' deep	EA.	1,850
6' deep	EA.	2,190
8' deep	EA.	2,800
10' deep	EA.	3,300

Brick manholes, 48" dia. with cover, 8" thick

4' deep	EA.	1,180
6' deep	EA.	1,400
8' deep	EA.	1,680
10' deep	EA.	2,030

Frames and covers, 24" diameter

300 lb	EA.	414.75
400 lb	EA.	439.50

Steps for manholes

7" x 9"	EA.	21.43
8" x 9"	EA.	25.92

02530.40 SANITARY SEWERS

Clay

6" pipe	L.F.	16.09

PVC

4" pipe	L.F.	10.12
6" pipe	L.F.	14.45

	Unit	Total

02540.10 DRAINAGE FIELDS

Perforated PVC pipe, for drain field

	Unit	Total
4" pipe	L.F.	7.91
6" pipe	L.F.	10.46

02540.50 SEPTIC TANKS

Septic tank, precast concrete

	Unit	Total
1000 gals	EA.	1,310
2000 gals	EA.	3,260

Leaching pit, precast concrete, 72" diameter

	Unit	Total
3' deep	EA.	1,070
6' deep	EA.	1,700
8' deep	EA.	2,110

02630.70 UNDERDRAIN

Drain tile, clay

	Unit	Total
6" pipe	L.F.	9.97
8" pipe	L.F.	12.92

Porous concrete, standard strength

	Unit	Total
6" pipe	L.F.	9.52
8" pipe	L.F.	10.10

Corrugated metal pipe, perforated type

	Unit	Total
6" pipe	L.F.	11.77
8" pipe	L.F.	13.12

Perforated clay pipe

	Unit	Total
6" pipe	L.F.	12.45
8" pipe	L.F.	14.50

Drain tile, concrete

	Unit	Total
6" pipe	L.F.	8.68
8" pipe	L.F.	10.73

Perforated rigid PVC underdrain pipe

	Unit	Total
4" pipe	L.F.	6.00
6" pipe	L.F.	8.57
8" pipe	L.F.	11.06

Underslab drainage, crushed stone

	Unit	Total
3" thick	S.F.	1.07
4" thick	S.F.	1.28
6" thick	S.F.	1.54
Plastic filter fabric for drain lines	S.F.	.60

02740.20 ASPHALT SURFACES

Asphalt wearing surface, flexible pavement

	Unit	Total
1" thick	S.Y.	6.74
1-1/2" thick	S.Y.	9.42

Binder course

	Unit	Total
1-1/2" thick	S.Y.	8.86
2" thick	S.Y.	11.50

Bituminous sidewalk, no base

	Unit	Total
2" thick	S.Y.	12.25
3" thick	S.Y.	17.07

02750.10 CONCRETE PAVING

Concrete paving, reinforced, 5000 psi concrete

	Unit	Total
6" thick	S.Y.	46.50
7" thick	S.Y.	52.25
8" thick	S.Y.	58.00

02810.40 LAWN IRRIGATION

Residential system, complete

	Unit	Total
Minimum	ACRE	15,900
Maximum	ACRE	30,300

	Unit	Total

02820.10 CHAIN LINK FENCE

Chain link fence, 9 ga., galvanized, with posts 10' o.c.

4' high	L.F.	9.90
5' high	L.F.	13.04
6' high	L.F.	15.83

Corner or gate post, 3" post

4' high	EA.	93.25
5' high	EA.	103.00
6' high	EA.	115.25

Gate with gate posts, galvanized, 3' wide

4' high	EA.	196.50
5' high	EA.	260.00
6' high	EA.	280.00

Fabric, galvanized chain link, 2" mesh, 9 ga.

4' high	L.F.	5.14
5' high	L.F.	6.26
6' high	L.F.	8.48

Line post, no rail fitting, galvanized, 2-1/2" dia.

4' high	EA.	38.25
5' high	EA.	41.75
6' high	EA.	45.25

Vinyl coated, 9 ga., with posts 10' o.c.

4' high	L.F.	10.45
5' high	L.F.	12.70
6' high	L.F.	15.83

Gate, with posts, 3' wide

4' high	EA.	220.00
5' high	EA.	270.00
6' high	EA.	290.00

Fabric, vinyl, chain link, 2" mesh, 9 ga.

4' high	L.F.	5.14
5' high	L.F.	6.26
6' high	L.F.	8.48

Swing gates, galvanized, 4' high

Single gate

3' wide	EA.	310.00
4' wide	EA.	330.00

6' high

Single gate

3' wide	EA.	410.00
4' wide	EA.	430.00

02880.70 RECREATIONAL COURTS

Walls, galvanized steel

8' high	L.F.	23.43
10' high	L.F.	27.17
12' high	L.F.	31.50

Vinyl coated

8' high	L.F.	22.68
10' high	L.F.	26.92
12' high	L.F.	30.50

Gates, galvanized steel

Single, 3' transom

3'x7'	EA.	560.00
4'x7'	EA.	620.00
5'x7'	EA.	790.00
6'x7'	EA.	890.00

Vinyl coated

Single, 3' transom

3'x7'	EA.	880.00
4'x7'	EA.	980.00
5'x7'	EA.	1,020
6'x7'	EA.	1,100

	Unit	Total

02910.10 TOPSOIL

Spread topsoil, with equipment
Minimum	C.Y.	13.25
Maximum	C.Y.	16.75
By hand		
Minimum	C.Y.	44.75
Maximum	C.Y.	55.75
Area prep. seeding (grade, rake and clean)		
Square yard	S.Y.	.36
By acre	ACRE	1,800
Remove topsoil and stockpile on site		
4" deep	C.Y.	11.00
6" deep	C.Y.	10.25
Spreading topsoil from stock pile		
By loader	C.Y.	12.25
By hand	C.Y.	130.00
Top dress by hand	S.Y.	1.33
Place imported top soil		
By loader		
4" deep	S.Y.	1.33
6" deep	S.Y.	1.48
By hand		
4" deep	S.Y.	4.96
6" deep	S.Y.	5.58
Plant bed preparation, 18" deep		
With backhoe/loader	S.Y.	3.34
By hand	S.Y.	7.44

02920.10 FERTILIZING

Fertilizing (23#/1000 sf)		
By square yard	S.Y.	.18
By acre	ACRE	890.00
Liming (70#/1000 sf)		
By square yard	S.Y.	.23
By acre	ACRE	1,140

02920.30 SEEDING

Mechanical seeding, 175 lb/acre		
By square yard	S.Y.	.32
By acre	ACRE	1,360
450 lb/acre		
By square yard	S.Y.	.65
By acre	ACRE	2,630
Seeding by hand, 10 lb per 100 s.y.		
By square yard	S.Y.	.70
By acre	ACRE	2,890
Reseed disturbed areas	S.F.	.28

02930.10 PLANTS

Euonymus coloratus, 18" (Purple Wintercreeper)	EA.	10.05
Hedera Helix, 2-1/4" pot (English ivy)	EA.	8.53
Liriope muscari, 2" clumps	EA.	9.00
Santolina, 12"	EA.	9.66
Vinca major or minor, 3" pot	EA.	5.31
Cortaderia argentia, 2 gallon (Pampas Grass)	EA.	20.96
Ophiopogan japonicus, 1 quart (4" pot)	EA.	9.00
Ajuga reptans, 2-3/4" pot (carpet bugle)	EA.	5.31
Pachysandra terminalis, 2-3/4" pot (Japanese Spurge)	EA.	5.62

	Unit	Total

02930.30 SHRUBS

Item	Unit	Total
Juniperus conferia litoralis, 18"-24" (Shore Juniper)	EA.	55.75
Horizontalis plumosa, 18"-24" (Andorra Juniper)	EA.	58.25
Sabina tamar-iscfolia-tamarix juniper, 18"-24"	EA.	58.25
Chin San Jose, 18"-24" (San Jose Juniper)	EA.	58.25
Sargenti, 18"-24" (Sargent's Juniper)	EA.	55.75
Nandina domestica, 18"-24" (Heavenly Bamboo)	EA.	43.25
Raphiolepis Indica Springtime, 18"-24"	EA.	45.25
Osmanthus Heterophyllus Gulftide, 18"-24"	EA.	47.25
Ilex Cornuta Burfordi Nana, 18"-24"	EA.	51.25
Glabra, 18"-24" (Inkberry Holly)	EA.	49.25
Azalea, Indica types, 18"-24"	EA.	53.25
Kurume types, 18"-24"	EA.	57.50
Berberis Julianae, 18"-24" (Wintergreen Barberry)	EA.	41.00
Pieris Japonica Japanese, 18"-24"	EA.	41.00
Ilex Cornuta Rotunda, 18"-24"	EA.	45.25
Juniperus Horiz. Plumosa, 24"-30"	EA.	47.75
Rhodopendrow Hybrids, 24"-30"	EA.	90.00
Aucuba Japonica Varigata, 24"-30"	EA.	45.50
Ilex Crenata Willow Leaf, 24"-30"	EA.	47.75
Cleyera Japonica, 30"-36"	EA.	57.75
Pittosporum Tobira, 30"-36"	EA.	62.00
Prumus Laurocerasus, 30"-36"	EA.	92.00
Ilex Cornuta Burfordi, 30"-36" (Burford Holly)	EA.	62.00
Abelia Grandiflora, 24"-36" (Yew Podocarpus)	EA.	45.50
Podocarpos Macrophylla, 24"-36"	EA.	60.25
Pyracantha Coccinea Lalandi, 3'-4' (Firethorn)	EA.	49.75
Photinia Frazieri, 3'-4' (Red Photinia)	EA.	62.50
Forsythia Suspensa, 3'-4' (Weeping Forsythia)	EA.	49.75
Camellia Japonica, 3'-4' (Common Camellia)	EA.	66.25
Juniperus Chin Torulosa, 3'-4' (Hollywood Juniper)	EA.	68.75
Cupressocyparis Leylandi, 3'-4'	EA.	62.25
Ilex Opaca Fosteri, 5'-6' (Foster's Holly)	EA.	177.25
Opaca, 5'-6' (American Holly)	EA.	237.25
Nyrica Cerifera, 4'-5' (Southern Wax Myrtles)	EA.	75.25
Ligustrum Japonicum, 4'-5' (Japanese Privet)	EA.	66.00

02930.60 TREES

Item	Unit	Total
Cornus Florida, 5'-6' (White flowering Dogwood)	EA.	137.25
Prunus Serrulata Kwanzan, 6'-8' (Kwanzan Cherry)	EA.	154.75
Caroliniana, 6'-8' (Carolina Cherry Laurel)	EA.	174.75
Cercis Canadensis, 6'-8' (Eastern Redbud)	EA.	135.00
Koelreuteria Paniculata, 8'-10' (Goldenrain Tree)	EA.	215.75
Acer Platanoides, 1-3/4"-2" (11'-13')	EA.	284.50
Rubrum, 1-3/4"-2" (11'-13') (Red Maple)	EA.	234.50
Saccharum, 1-3/4"-2" (Sugar Maple)	EA.	354.50
Fraxinus Pennsylvanica, 1-3/4"-2"	EA.	204.50
Celtis Occidentalis, 1-3/4"-2"	EA.	274.50
Glenditsia Triacantos Inermis, 2"	EA.	254.50
Prunus Cerasifera 'Thundercloud', 6'-8'	EA.	154.75
Yeodensis, 6'-8' (Yoshino Cherry)	EA.	154.75
Lagerstroemia Indica, 8'-10' (Crapemyrtle)	EA.	235.75
Crataegus Phaenopyrum, 8'-10'	EA.	335.75
Quercus Borealis, 1-3/4"-2" (Northern Red Oak)	EA.	234.50
Quercus Acutissima, 1-3/4"-2" (8'-10')	EA.	234.50
Saliz Babylonica, 1-3/4"-2" (Weeping Willow)	EA.	152.00
Tilia Cordata Greenspire, 1-3/4"-2" (10'-12')	EA.	414.50
Malus, 2"-2-1/2" (8'-10') (Flowering Crabapple)	EA.	244.50
Platanus Occidentalis, (12'-14')	EA.	349.25
Pyrus Calleryana Bradford, 2"-2-1/2"	EA.	274.50
Quercus Palustris, 2"-2-1/2" (12'-14') (Pin Oak)	EA.	294.50
Phellos, 2-1/2"-3" (Willow Oak)	EA.	329.25
Nigra, 2"-2-1/2" (Water Oak)	EA.	284.50

	Unit	Total

02930.60 TREES (Cont.)

Magnolia Soulangeana, 4'-5' (Saucer Magnolia)	EA.	157.25
Grandiflora, 6'-8' (Southern Magnolia)	EA.	214.75
Cedrus Deodara, 10'-12' (Deodare Cedar)	EA.	344.50
Gingko Biloba, 10'-12' (2"-2-1/2")	EA.	334.50
Pinus Thunbergi, 5'-6' (Japanese Black Pine)	EA.	137.25
Strobus, 6'-8' (White Pine)	EA.	154.75
Taeda, 6'-8' (Loblolly Pine)	EA.	139.25
Quercus Virginiana, 2"-2-1/2" (Live Oak)	EA.	329.25

02935.10 SHRUB & TREE MAINTENANCE

Moving shrubs on site		
3' high	EA.	44.75
4' high	EA.	49.50
Moving trees on site		
6' high	EA.	54.50
8' high	EA.	61.25
10' high	EA.	81.75
Palm trees		
10' high	EA.	81.75
40' high	EA.	490.00

02935.30 WEED CONTROL

Weed control, bromicil, 15 lb./acre, wettable powder	ACRE	510.00
Vegetation control, by application of plant killer	S.Y.	.20
Weed killer, lawns and fields	S.Y.	.33

02945.20 LANDSCAPE ACCESSORIES

Steel edging, 3/16" x 4"	L.F.	1.21
Landscaping stepping stones, 15"x15", white	EA.	8.06
Wood chip mulch	C.Y.	70.50
2" thick	S.Y.	3.39
4" thick	S.Y.	5.99
6" thick	S.Y.	8.66
Gravel mulch, 3/4" stone	C.Y.	77.00
White marble chips, 1" deep	S.F.	1.09
Peat moss		
2" thick	S.Y.	4.45
4" thick	S.Y.	8.16
6" thick	S.Y.	12.11
Landscaping timbers, treated lumber		
4" x 4"	L.F.	2.84
6" x 6"	L.F.	4.29
8" x 8"	L.F.	6.26

	Unit	Total

03110.05 BEAM FORMWORK

Beam forms, job built
Beam bottoms

1 use	S.F.	13.68
4 uses	S.F.	9.95
5 uses	S.F.	9.57

Beam sides

1 use	S.F.	9.33
5 uses	S.F.	6.45

03110.15 COLUMN FORMWORK

Column, square forms, job built
8" x 8" columns

1 use	S.F.	15.06
5 uses	S.F.	11.08

12" x 12" columns

1 use	S.F.	13.50
5 uses	S.F.	10.10

Round fiber forms, 1 use

10" dia.	L.F.	16.15
12" dia.	L.F.	17.22

03110.18 CURB FORMWORK

Curb forms
Straight, 6" high

1 use	L.F.	7.82
5 uses	L.F.	5.53

Curved, 6" high

1 use	L.F.	9.42
5 uses	L.F.	6.75

03110.25 EQUIPMENT PAD FORMWORK

Equipment pad, job built

1 use	S.F.	10.82
3 uses	S.F.	8.11
5 uses	S.F.	6.80

03110.35 FOOTING FORMWORK

Wall footings, job built, continuous

1 use	S.F.	7.40
3 uses	S.F.	6.17
5 uses	S.F.	5.51

03110.50 GRADE BEAM FORMWORK

Grade beams, job built

1 use	S.F.	8.38
3 uses	S.F.	6.36
5 uses	S.F.	5.56

03110.53 PILE CAP FORMWORK

Pile cap forms, job built
Square

1 use	S.F.	10.17
5 uses	S.F.	6.72

03110.55 SLAB / MAT FORMWORK

Mat foundations, job built

1 use	S.F.	9.78
3 uses	S.F.	7.46
5 uses	S.F.	6.47

Edge forms
6" high

1 use	L.F.	7.85
3 uses	L.F.	5.88
5 uses	L.F.	5.15

	Unit	Total

03110.65 WALL FORMWORK

Wall forms, exterior, job built
Up to 8' high wall

1 use	S.F.	8.55
3 uses	S.F.	6.57
5 uses	S.F.	5.80

Retaining wall forms

1 use	S.F.	8.98
3 uses	S.F.	6.92
5 uses	S.F.	6.08

Column pier and pilaster

1 use	S.F.	14.63
5 uses	S.F.	9.55

03110.90 MISCELLANEOUS FORMWORK

Keyway forms (5 uses)

2 x 4	L.F.	3.10
2 x 6	L.F.	3.52

Bulkheads
Walls, with keyways

3 piece	L.F.	10.89

Ground slab, with keyway

2 piece	L.F.	8.93
3 piece	L.F.	10.32

Chamfer strips
Wood

1/2" wide	L.F.	1.51
3/4" wide	L.F.	1.58
1" wide	L.F.	1.68

PVC

1/2" wide	L.F.	2.31
3/4" wide	L.F.	2.40
1" wide	L.F.	2.91

03210.05 BEAM REINFORCING

Beam-girders

#3 - #4	TON	2,850
#5 - #6	TON	2,350

03210.15 COLUMN REINFORCING

Columns

#3 - #4	TON	3,050
#5 - #6	TON	2,500

03210.20 ELEVATED SLAB REINFORCING

Elevated slab

#3 - #4	TON	2,130
#5 - #6	TON	1,850

03210.25 EQUIP. PAD REINFORCING

Equipment pad

#3 - #4	TON	2,550
#5 - #6	TON	2,250

03210.35 FOOTING REINFORCING

Footings

#3 - #4	TON	2,370
#5 - #6	TON	2,030
#7 - #8	TON	1,880

Straight dowels, 24" long

3/4" dia. (#6)	EA.	9.68
5/8" dia. (#5)	EA.	8.18
1/2" dia. (#4)	EA.	6.67

	Unit	Total

03210.45 FOUNDATION REINFORCING

Foundations

#3 - #4	TON	2,370
#5 - #6	TON	2,030
#7 - #8	TON	1,880

03210.50 GRADE BEAM REINFORCING

Grade beams

#3 - #4	TON	2,300
#5 - #6	TON	1,980
#7 - #8	TON	1,840

03210.53 PILE CAP REINFORCING

Pile caps

#3 - #4	TON	2,850
#5 - #6	TON	2,500
#7 - #8	TON	2,300

03210.55 SLAB / MAT REINFORCING

Bars, slabs

#3 - #4	TON	2,370
#5 - #6	TON	2,030

Wire mesh, slabs
Galvanized
4x4

W1.4xW1.4	S.F.	.73
W2.0xW2.0	S.F.	.87
W2.9xW2.9	S.F.	1.08
W4.0xW4.0	S.F.	1.41

6x6

W1.4xW1.4	S.F.	.61
W2.0xW2.0	S.F.	.77
W2.9xW2.9	S.F.	.95
W4.0xW4.0	S.F.	1.04

03210.65 WALL REINFORCING

Walls

#3 - #4	TON	2,230
#5 - #6	TON	1,930

Masonry wall (horizontal)

#3 - #4	TON	3,750
#5 - #6	TON	3,150

Galvanized

#3 - #4	TON	4,700
#5 - #6	TON	4,200

Masonry wall (vertical)

#3 - #4	TON	4,300
#5 - #6	TON	3,550

Galvanized

#3 - #4	TON	5,250
#5 - #6	TON	4,600

03250.40 CONCRETE ACCESSORIES

Expansion joint, poured
Asphalt

1/2" x 1"	L.F.	1.65
1" x 2"	L.F.	3.34

Expansion joint, premolded, in slabs
Asphalt

1/2" x 6"	L.F.	2.06
1" x 12"	L.F.	3.05

Cork

1/2" x 6"	L.F.	2.99
1" x 12"	L.F.	8.55

Neoprene sponge

1/2" x 6"	L.F.	3.86

	Unit	Total

03250.40 CONCRETE ACCESSORIES (Cont.)

Expansion joint, premolded, in slabs
  Neoprene sponge

1" x 12"	L.F.	11.49

  Polyethylene foam

1/2" x 6"	L.F.	2.18
1" x 12"	L.F.	6.36

  Polyurethane foam

1/2" x 6"	L.F.	2.52
1" x 12"	L.F.	4.56

  Polyvinyl chloride foam

1/2" x 6"	L.F.	4.10
1" x 12"	L.F.	7.93

  Rubber, gray sponge

1/2" x 6"	L.F.	5.77
1" x 12"	L.F.	21.74

Asphalt felt control joints or bond breaker, screed joints

4" slab	L.F.	2.15
6" slab	L.F.	2.57
8" slab	L.F.	3.18

Waterstops
  Polyvinyl chloride
    Ribbed
      3/16" thick x

4" wide	L.F.	3.73
6" wide	L.F.	4.75

      1/2" thick x

9" wide	L.F.	8.81

    Ribbed with center bulb

3/16" thick x 9" wide	L.F.	7.85
3/8" thick x 9" wide	L.F.	8.74
Dumbbell type, 3/8" thick x 6" wide	L.F.	8.50
Plain, 3/8" thick x 9" wide	L.F.	10.79
Center bulb, 3/8" thick x 9" wide	L.F.	12.39

    Rubber
Vapor barrier

4 mil polyethylene	S.F.	.21
6 mil polyethylene	S.F.	.23
Gravel porous fill, under floor slabs, 3/4" stone	C.Y.	95.25

Reinforcing accessories
  Beam bolsters
    1-1/2" high, plain

1-1/2" high, plain	L.F.	1.14
Galvanized	L.F.	1.80

    3" high

Plain	L.F.	1.52
Galvanized	L.F.	2.69

  Slab bolsters
    1" high

Plain	L.F.	.88
Galvanized	L.F.	1.49

    2" high

Plain	L.F.	.98
Galvanized	L.F.	1.72

  Chairs, high chairs
    3" high

Plain	EA.	3.06
Galvanized	EA.	3.21

    8" high

Plain	EA.	4.35
Galvanized	EA.	6.23

  Continuous, high chair
    3" high

Plain	L.F.	2.60
Galvanized	L.F.	3.13

	Unit	Total

03300.10 CONCRETE ADMIXTURES

Concrete admixtures

Water reducing admixture	GAL	11.00
Set retarder	GAL	24.00
Air entraining agent	GAL	10.50

03350.10 CONCRETE FINISHES

Floor finishes

Broom	S.F.	.64
Screed	S.F.	.56
Darby	S.F.	.56
Steel float	S.F.	.74

Wall finishes

Burlap rub, with cement paste	S.F.	.85

03360.10 PNEUMATIC CONCRETE

Pneumatic applied concrete (gunite)

2" thick	S.F.	8.72
3" thick	S.F.	11.03
4" thick	S.F.	13.36

Finish surface

Minimum	S.F.	2.85
Maximum	S.F.	5.70

03370.10 CURING CONCRETE

Sprayed membrane

Slabs	S.F.	.15
Walls	S.F.	.19

Curing paper

Slabs	S.F.	.20
Walls	S.F.	.21

Burlap

7.5 oz.	S.F.	.22
12 oz.	S.F.	.25

03380.05 BEAM CONCRETE

Beams and girders

2500# or 3000# concrete

By crane	C.Y.	209.25
By pump	C.Y.	201.25
By hand buggy	C.Y.	164.75

3500# or 4000# concrete

By crane	C.Y.	209.25
By pump	C.Y.	201.25
By hand buggy	C.Y.	164.75

03380.15 COLUMN CONCRETE

Columns

2500# or 3000# concrete

By crane	C.Y.	201.25
By pump	C.Y.	194.50

3500# or 4000# concrete

By crane	C.Y.	201.25
By pump	C.Y.	194.50

03380.20 ELEVATED SLAB CONCRETE

Elevated slab

2500# or 3000# concrete

By crane	C.Y.	164.75
By pump	C.Y.	154.25
By hand buggy	C.Y.	164.75

	Unit	Total

03380.25 EQUIPMENT PAD CONCRETE

Equipment pad
   2500# or 3000# concrete

	Unit	Total
By chute	C.Y.	135.00
By pump	C.Y.	183.75
By crane	C.Y.	194.50

   3500# or 4000# concrete

	Unit	Total
By chute	C.Y.	135.00
By pump	C.Y.	183.75

03380.35 FOOTING CONCRETE

Continuous footing
   2500# or 3000# concrete

	Unit	Total
By chute	C.Y.	135.00
By pump	C.Y.	175.75
By crane	C.Y.	183.75

Spread footing
   2500# or 3000# concrete

	Unit	Total
By chute	C.Y.	125.00
By pump	C.Y.	169.50
By crane	C.Y.	178.75

03380.50 GRADE BEAM CONCRETE

Grade beam
   2500# or 3000# concrete

	Unit	Total
By chute	C.Y.	125.00
By crane	C.Y.	173.75
By pump	C.Y.	165.75
By hand buggy	C.Y.	154.75

   3500# or 4000# concrete

	Unit	Total
By chute	C.Y.	135.00
By crane	C.Y.	183.75
By pump	C.Y.	175.75
By hand buggy	C.Y.	164.75

03380.53 PILE CAP CONCRETE

Pile cap
   2500# or 3000 concrete

	Unit	Total
By chute	C.Y.	135.00
By crane	C.Y.	194.50
By pump	C.Y.	183.75
By hand buggy	C.Y.	164.75

03380.55 SLAB / MAT CONCRETE

Slab on grade
   2500# or 3000# concrete

	Unit	Total
By chute	C.Y.	131.25
By crane	C.Y.	157.25
By pump	C.Y.	152.00
By hand buggy	C.Y.	149.75

03380.58 SIDEWALKS

Walks, cast in place with wire mesh, base not incl.

	Unit	Total
4" thick	S.F.	3.16
5" thick	S.F.	4.05
6" thick	S.F.	5.00

03380.65 WALL CONCRETE

Walls
   2500# or 3000# concrete
    To 4'

	Unit	Total
By chute	C.Y.	132.75
By crane	C.Y.	194.50
By pump	C.Y.	188.75

    To 8'

	Unit	Total
By crane	C.Y.	201.25

	Unit	Total

03380.65 WALL CONCRETE (Cont.)

Walls
  2500# or 3000# concrete

	Unit	Total
By pump	C.Y.	194.50

Filled block (CMU)
  3000# concrete, by pump

	Unit	Total
4" wide	S.F.	3.64
6" wide	S.F.	4.72
8" wide	S.F.	6.02

03400.90 PRECAST SPECIALTIES

Precast concrete, coping, 4' to 8' long

	Unit	Total
12" wide	L.F.	15.16
10" wide	L.F.	15.05
Splash block, 30"x12"x4"	EA.	54.50
Stair unit, per riser	EA.	128.50

Sun screen and trellis, 8' long, 12" high

	Unit	Total
4" thick blades	EA.	127.00

03600.10 GROUTING

Grouting for bases
  Non-metallic grout

	Unit	Total
1" deep	S.F.	17.48
2" deep	S.F.	23.75

Portland cement grout (1 cement to 3 sand)
  1/2" joint thickness

	Unit	Total
6" wide joints	L.F.	2.15
8" wide joints	L.F.	2.57

1" joint thickness

	Unit	Total
4" wide joints	L.F.	2.05
6" wide joints	L.F.	2.38

	Unit	Total

04100.10 MASONRY GROUT

Grout, non shrink, non-metallic, trowelable	C.F.	6.99
Grout door frame, hollow metal		
Single	EA.	74.75
Double	EA.	83.25
Grout-filled concrete block (CMU)		
4" wide	S.F.	2.40
6" wide	S.F.	3.17
8" wide	S.F.	3.83
12" wide	S.F.	4.84
Grout-filled individual CMU cells		
4" wide	L.F.	1.53
6" wide	L.F.	1.63
8" wide	L.F.	1.77
10" wide	L.F.	2.07
12" wide	L.F.	2.21
Bond beams or lintels, 8" deep		
6" thick	L.F.	2.84
8" thick	L.F.	3.30
10" thick	L.F.	3.82
12" thick	L.F.	4.40
Cavity walls		
2" thick	S.F.	3.87
3" thick	S.F.	4.32
4" thick	S.F.	4.97
6" thick	S.F.	6.40

04150.10 MASONRY ACCESSORIES

Foundation vents	EA.	54.00
Bar reinforcing		
Horizontal		
#3 - #4	Lb.	2.81
#5 - #6	Lb.	2.45
Vertical		
#3 - #4	Lb.	3.36
#5 - #6	Lb.	2.81
Horizontal joint reinforcing		
Truss type		
4" wide, 6" wall	L.F.	.43
6" wide, 8" wall	L.F.	.44
8" wide, 10" wall	L.F.	.49
10" wide, 12" wall	L.F.	.50
12" wide, 14" wall	L.F.	.57
Ladder type		
4" wide, 6" wall	L.F.	.37
6" wide, 8" wall	L.F.	.40
8" wide, 10" wall	L.F.	.42
10" wide, 12" wall	L.F.	.46
Rectangular wall ties		
3/16" dia., galvanized		
2" x 6"	EA.	1.30
2" x 8"	EA.	1.32
2" x 10"	EA.	1.38
2" x 12"	EA.	1.44
4" x 6"	EA.	1.53
4" x 8"	EA.	1.59
4" x 10"	EA.	1.73
4" x 12"	EA.	1.83
1/4" dia., galvanized		
2" x 6"	EA.	1.63
2" x 8"	EA.	1.71
2" x 10"	EA.	1.82
2" x 12"	EA.	1.95
4" x 6"	EA.	1.91
4" x 8"	EA.	2.00

	Unit	Total

04150.10 MASONRY ACCESSORIES (Cont.)

Rectangular wall ties

4" x 10"	EA.	2.13
4" x 12"	EA.	2.18

"Z" type wall ties, galvanized
6" long

1/8" dia.	EA.	1.25
3/16" dia.	EA.	1.27
1/4" dia.	EA.	1.30

8" long

1/8" dia.	EA.	1.27
3/16" dia.	EA.	1.30
1/4" dia.	EA.	1.32

10" long

1/8" dia.	EA.	1.30
3/16" dia.	EA.	1.35
1/4" dia.	EA.	1.41

Dovetail anchor slots
Galvanized steel, filled

24 ga.	L.F.	2.38
20 ga.	L.F.	3.49
16 oz. copper, foam filled	L.F.	3.86

Dovetail anchors
16 ga.

3-1/2" long	EA.	1.22
5-1/2" long	EA.	1.29

12 ga.

3-1/2" long	EA.	1.32
5-1/2" long	EA.	1.59

Dovetail, triangular galvanized ties, 12 ga.

3" x 3"	EA.	1.60
5" x 5"	EA.	1.65
7" x 7"	EA.	1.75
7" x 9"	EA.	1.80

Brick anchors
Corrugated, 3-1/2" long

16 ga.	EA.	1.19
12 ga.	EA.	1.40

Non-corrugated, 3-1/2" long

16 ga.	EA.	1.30
12 ga.	EA.	1.61

Cavity wall anchors, corrugated, galvanized
5" long

16 ga.	EA.	1.78
12 ga.	EA.	2.20

7" long

28 ga.	EA.	1.86
24 ga.	EA.	2.11
22 ga.	EA.	2.14
16 ga.	EA.	2.29

Mesh ties, 16 ga., 3" wide

8" long	EA.	2.07
12" long	EA.	2.20
20" long	EA.	2.68
24" long	EA.	2.87

04150.20 MASONRY CONTROL JOINTS

Control joint, cross shaped PVC	L.F.	3.54

Closed cell joint filler

1/2"	L.F.	1.74
3/4"	L.F.	2.13

Rubber, for

4" wall	L.F.	3.87

PVC, for

4" wall	L.F.	2.67

	Unit	Total

04150.50 MASONRY FLASHING

Through-wall flashing
5 oz. coated copper	S.F.	8.22
0.030" elastomeric	S.F.	4.83

04210.10 BRICK MASONRY

Standard size brick, running bond
Face brick, red (6.4/sf)

Veneer	S.F.	14.45
Cavity wall	S.F.	13.16
9" solid wall	S.F.	26.25

Common brick (6.4/sf)

Select common for veneers	S.F.	12.58

Back-up

4" thick	S.F.	9.97
8" thick	S.F.	17.09

Glazed brick (7.4/sf)

Veneer	S.F.	24.63

Buff or gray face brick (6.4/sf)

Veneer	S.F.	15.33
Cavity wall	S.F.	14.04

Jumbo or oversize brick (3/sf)

4" veneer	S.F.	9.56
4" back-up	S.F.	8.65
8" back-up	S.F.	12.55

Norman brick, red face, (4.5/sf)

4" veneer	S.F.	12.74
Cavity wall	S.F.	11.98

Chimney, standard brick, including flue

16" x 16"	L.F.	84.75
16" x 20"	L.F.	105.75
16" x 24"	L.F.	109.00
20" x 20"	L.F.	110.75
20" x 24"	L.F.	126.00
20" x 32"	L.F.	142.50
Window sill, face brick on edge	L.F.	16.47

04210.60 PAVERS, MASONRY

Brick walk laid on sand, sand joints

Laid flat, (4.5 per sf)	S.F.	10.01
Laid on edge, (7.2 per sf)	S.F.	15.41

Precast concrete patio blocks
2" thick

Natural	S.F.	4.63
Colors	S.F.	5.74

Exposed aggregates, local aggregate

Natural	S.F.	10.30
Colors	S.F.	10.30
Granite or limestone aggregate	S.F.	10.68
White tumblestone aggregate	S.F.	8.16

Stone pavers, set in mortar
Bluestone
1" thick

Irregular	S.F.	19.96
Snapped rectangular	S.F.	20.57
1-1/2" thick, random rectangular	S.F.	24.75
2" thick, random rectangular	S.F.	28.75

Slate
Natural cleft

Irregular, 3/4" thick	S.F.	23.60

Random rectangular

1-1/4" thick	S.F.	31.00
1-1/2" thick	S.F.	34.75

Granite blocks
3" thick, 3" to 6" wide

4" to 12" long	S.F.	29.50

	Unit	Total

04210.60 PAVERS, MASONRY (Cont.)

Stone pavers, set in mortar
  Granite blocks

	Unit	Total
6" to 15" long	S.F.	23.02

04220.10 CONCRETE MASONRY UNITS

Hollow, load bearing

	Unit	Total
4"	S.F.	5.58
6"	S.F.	6.45
8"	S.F.	7.14
10"	S.F.	8.54
12"	S.F.	9.58

Solid, load bearing

	Unit	Total
4"	S.F.	6.46
6"	S.F.	6.91
8"	S.F.	8.26
10"	S.F.	8.91
12"	S.F.	11.34

Back-up block, 8" x 16"

	Unit	Total
2"	S.F.	4.74
4"	S.F.	4.90
6"	S.F.	5.89
8"	S.F.	6.47
10"	S.F.	7.82
12"	S.F.	8.70

Foundation wall, 8" x 16"

	Unit	Total
6"	S.F.	6.36
8"	S.F.	7.03
10"	S.F.	8.47
12"	S.F.	9.47

  Solid

	Unit	Total
6"	S.F.	7.18
8"	S.F.	8.62
10"	S.F.	9.30
12"	S.F.	11.91

Exterior, styrofoam inserts, std weight, 8" x 16"

	Unit	Total
6"	S.F.	8.54
8"	S.F.	9.24
10"	S.F.	11.03
12"	S.F.	13.80

  Lightweight

	Unit	Total
6"	S.F.	9.03
8"	S.F.	9.99
10"	S.F.	10.75
12"	S.F.	13.10

Acoustical slotted block

	Unit	Total
4"	S.F.	10.00
6"	S.F.	10.24
8"	S.F.	12.05

  Filled cavities

	Unit	Total
4"	S.F.	11.46
6"	S.F.	12.65
8"	S.F.	14.80

Hollow, split face

	Unit	Total
4"	S.F.	7.49
6"	S.F.	8.19
8"	S.F.	8.74
10"	S.F.	9.66
12"	S.F.	10.47

Split rib profile

	Unit	Total
4"	S.F.	9.15
6"	S.F.	9.83
8"	S.F.	10.76
10"	S.F.	11.27
12"	S.F.	11.76

	Unit	Total

04220.10 CONCRETE MASONRY UNITS (Cont.)

Solar screen concrete block
  4" thick

	Unit	Total
6" x 6"	S.F.	16.29
8" x 8"	S.F.	15.87
12" x 12"	S.F.	13.61

  8" thick

	Unit	Total
8" x 16"	S.F.	13.02

Vertical reinforcing
  4' o.c., add 5% to labor
  2'8" o.c., add 15% to labor
Interior partitions, add 10% to labor

04220.90 BOND BEAMS & LINTELS

Bond beam, no grout or reinforcement
  8" x 16" x

	Unit	Total
4" thick	L.F.	5.87
6" thick	L.F.	6.93
8" thick	L.F.	7.48
10" thick	L.F.	8.38
12" thick	L.F.	9.09

Beam lintel, no grout or reinforcement
  8" x 16" x

	Unit	Total
10" thick	L.F.	12.19
12" thick	L.F.	14.61

Precast masonry lintel
  6 lf, 8" high x

	Unit	Total
4" thick	L.F.	15.85
6" thick	L.F.	17.73
8" thick	L.F.	19.69
10" thick	L.F.	21.63

  10 lf, 8" high x

	Unit	Total
4" thick	L.F.	13.97
6" thick	L.F.	15.94
8" thick	L.F.	17.79
10" thick	L.F.	21.79

Steel angles and plates

	Unit	Total
Minimum	Lb.	1.88
Maximum	Lb.	2.98

Various size angle lintels
  1/4" stock

	Unit	Total
3" x 3"	L.F.	9.06
3" x 3-1/2"	L.F.	9.64

  3/8" stock

	Unit	Total
3" x 4"	L.F.	13.22
3-1/2" x 4"	L.F.	13.65
4" x 4"	L.F.	14.65
5" x 3-1/2"	L.F.	15.40
6" x 3-1/2"	L.F.	16.90

  1/2" stock

	Unit	Total
6" x 4"	L.F.	18.40

04270.10 GLASS BLOCK

Glass block, 4" thick

	Unit	Total
6" x 6"	S.F.	48.25
8" x 8"	S.F.	32.50
12" x 12"	S.F.	35.00

	Unit	Total

04295.10 PARGING / MASONRY PLASTER

Parging
1/2" thick	S.F.	3.95
3/4" thick	S.F.	4.94
1" thick	S.F.	6.00

04400.10 STONE

Rubble stone
Walls set in mortar
8" thick	S.F.	29.25
12" thick	S.F.	40.75
18" thick	S.F.	52.50
24" thick	S.F.	68.00

Dry set wall
8" thick	S.F.	26.81
12" thick	S.F.	33.50
18" thick	S.F.	45.75
24" thick	S.F.	55.50

Thresholds, 7/8" thick, 3' long, 4" to 6" wide
Plain	EA.	73.75
Beveled	EA.	76.75

Window sill
6" wide, 2" thick	L.F.	37.75

Stools
5" wide, 7/8" thick	L.F.	45.25

Granite veneer facing panels, polished
7/8" thick
Black	S.F.	72.50
Gray	S.F.	61.75

Slate, panels
1" thick	S.F.	46.75

Sills or stools
1" thick
6" wide	L.F.	33.50
10" wide	L.F.	42.75

04520.10 RESTORATION AND CLEANING

Masonry cleaning
Washing brick
Smooth surface	S.F.	1.17
Rough surface	S.F.	1.57

Steam clean masonry
Smooth face
Minimum	S.F.	.73
Maximum	S.F.	1.07

Rough face
Minimum	S.F.	.98
Maximum	S.F.	1.47

04550.10 REFRACTORIES

Flue liners
Rectangular
8" x 12"	L.F.	18.20
12" x 12"	L.F.	21.38
12" x 18"	L.F.	30.75
16" x 16"	L.F.	33.75
18" x 18"	L.F.	39.75
20" x 20"	L.F.	58.25
24" x 24"	L.F.	69.25

Round
18" dia.	L.F.	54.25
24" dia.	L.F.	97.00

	Unit	Total

05050.10 STRUCTURAL WELDING

Welding
  Single pass

1/8"	L.F.	3.48
3/16"	L.F.	4.75
1/4"	L.F.	6.02

05050.90 METAL ANCHORS

Anchor bolts
  3/8" x

8" long	EA.	1.01
12" long	EA.	1.20

  1/2" x

8" long	EA.	1.51
12" long	EA.	1.76

  5/8" x

8" long	EA.	1.40
12" long	EA.	1.65

  3/4" x

8" long	EA.	2.01
12" long	EA.	2.25

  Non-drilling anchor

1/4"	EA.	.65
3/8"	EA.	.80
1/2"	EA.	1.23

  Self-drilling anchor

1/4"	EA.	1.63
3/8"	EA.	2.44
1/2"	EA.	3.26

05050.95 METAL LINTELS

Lintels, steel

Plain	Lb.	2.90
Galvanized	Lb.	3.57

05120.10 STRUCTURAL STEEL

Beams and girders, A-36

Welded	TON	3,580
Bolted	TON	3,470

Columns
  Pipe

6" dia.	Lb.	2.35

Structural tube
  6" square

Light sections	TON	5,200

05410.10 METAL FRAMING

Furring channel, galvanized
Beams and columns, 3/4"

12" o.c.	S.F.	6.74
16" o.c.	S.F.	6.06

Walls, 3/4"

12" o.c.	S.F.	3.59
16" o.c.	S.F.	2.96
24" o.c.	S.F.	2.34

  1-1/2"

12" o.c.	S.F.	3.88
16" o.c.	S.F.	3.16
24" o.c.	S.F.	2.48

Stud, load bearing
  16" o.c.
    16 ga.

2-1/2"	S.F.	4.13
3-5/8"	S.F.	4.37
4"	S.F.	4.43

	Unit	Total

05410.10 METAL FRAMING (Cont.)

Stud, load bearing

16" o.c.

6"	S.F.	5.21

18 ga.

2-1/2"	S.F.	3.89
3-5/8"	S.F.	4.13
4"	S.F.	4.19
6"	S.F.	4.90
8"	S.F.	5.27

20 ga.

2-1/2"	S.F.	3.40
3-5/8"	S.F.	3.53
4"	S.F.	3.59
6"	S.F.	4.12
8"	S.F.	4.30

24" o.c.

16 ga.

2-1/2"	S.F.	3.33
3-5/8"	S.F.	3.51
4"	S.F.	3.57
6"	S.F.	4.01
8"	S.F.	4.37

18 ga.

2-1/2"	S.F.	3.15
3-5/8"	S.F.	3.27
4"	S.F.	3.33
6"	S.F.	3.77
8"	S.F.	4.01

20 ga.

2-1/2"	S.F.	2.86
3-5/8"	S.F.	2.92
4"	S.F.	2.97
6"	S.F.	3.34
8"	S.F.	3.50

05520.10 RAILINGS

Railing, pipe

1-1/4" diameter, welded steel

2-rail

Primed	L.F.	44.25
Galvanized	L.F.	53.25

3-rail

Primed	L.F.	56.50
Galvanized	L.F.	68.50

Wall mounted, single rail, welded steel

Primed	L.F.	30.94
Galvanized	L.F.	37.19

Wall mounted, single rail, welded steel

Primed	L.F.	31.69
Galvanized	L.F.	38.19

Wall mounted, single rail, welded steel

Primed	L.F.	34.25
Galvanized	L.F.	41.25

05700.10 ORNAMENTAL METAL

Railings, square bars, 6" o.c., shaped top rails

Steel	L.F.	124.00
Aluminum	L.F.	141.50
Bronze	L.F.	232.00
Stainless steel	L.F.	232.00

Laminated metal or wood handrails

2-1/2" round or oval shape	L.F.	311.50

	Unit	Total

05700.10 ORNAMENTAL METAL (Cont.)

Aluminum louvers
Residential use, fixed type, with screen

8" x 8"	EA.	49.25
12" x 12"	EA.	51.00
12" x 18"	EA.	55.00
14" x 24"	EA.	65.25
18" x 24"	EA.	69.25
30" x 24"	EA.	86.50

	Unit	Total
06050.10 ACCESSORIES		
Column/post base, cast aluminum		
4" x 4"	EA.	30.50
6" x 6"	EA.	36.75
Bridging, metal, per pair		
12" o.c.	EA.	7.90
16" o.c.	EA.	7.21
Anchors		
Bolts, threaded two ends, with nuts and washers		
1/2" dia.		
4" long	EA.	6.13
7-1/2" long	EA.	6.55
3/4" dia.		
7-1/2" long	EA.	9.23
15" long	EA.	12.09
Framing anchors		
10 gauge	EA.	5.76
Bolts, carriage		
1/4 x 4	EA.	6.37
5/16 x 6	EA.	7.51
3/8 x 6	EA.	9.06
1/2 x 6	EA.	10.26
Joist and beam hangers		
18 ga.		
2 x 4	EA.	6.90
2 x 6	EA.	7.14
2 x 8	EA.	7.38
2 x 10	EA.	8.14
2 x 12	EA.	9.46
16 ga.		
3 x 6	EA.	10.53
3 x 8	EA.	11.43
3 x 10	EA.	12.46
3 x 12	EA.	14.08
3 x 14	EA.	15.16
4 x 6	EA.	13.53
4 x 8	EA.	14.74
4 x 10	EA.	16.31
4 x 12	EA.	20.09
4 x 14	EA.	21.14
Rafter anchors, 18 ga., 1-1/2" wide		
5-1/4" long	EA.	5.66
10-3/4" long	EA.	6.09
Shear plates		
2-5/8" dia.	EA.	7.60
4" dia.	EA.	11.43
Sill anchors		
Embedded in concrete	EA.	8.06
Split rings		
2-1/2" dia.	EA.	8.27
4" dia.	EA.	10.70
Strap ties, 14 ga., 1-3/8" wide		
12" long	EA.	7.18
18" long	EA.	7.79
24" long	EA.	9.59
36" long	EA.	11.67
Toothed rings		
2-5/8" dia.	EA.	11.74
4" dia.	EA.	14.11

	Unit	Total

06110.10 BLOCKING

Steel construction
Walls

		Unit	Total
2x4		L.F.	4.25
2x6		L.F.	5.06
2x8		L.F.	5.64
2x10		L.F.	6.36
2x12		L.F.	7.23

Ceilings

		Unit	Total
2x4		L.F.	4.83
2x6		L.F.	5.86
2x8		L.F.	6.59
2x10		L.F.	7.51
2x12		L.F.	8.65

Wood construction
Walls

		Unit	Total
2x4		L.F.	3.66
2x6		L.F.	4.32
2x8		L.F.	4.80
2x10		L.F.	5.40
2x12		L.F.	6.10

Ceilings

		Unit	Total
2x4		L.F.	4.06
2x6		L.F.	4.83
2x8		L.F.	5.38
2x10		L.F.	6.08
2x12		L.F.	6.90

06110.20 CEILING FRAMING

Ceiling joists
12" o.c.

		Unit	Total
2x4		S.F.	2.10
2x6		S.F.	2.49
2x8		S.F.	3.07
2x10		S.F.	3.36
2x12		S.F.	4.96

16" o.c.

		Unit	Total
2x4		S.F.	1.70
2x6		S.F.	2.04
2x8		S.F.	2.46
2x10		S.F.	2.67
2x12		S.F.	3.97

24" o.c.

		Unit	Total
2x4		S.F.	1.33
2x6		S.F.	1.67
2x8		S.F.	2.07
2x10		S.F.	2.32
2x12		S.F.	4.34

Headers and nailers

		Unit	Total
2x4		L.F.	2.34
2x6		L.F.	2.66
2x8		L.F.	3.03
2x10		L.F.	3.52
2x12		L.F.	4.01

Sister joists for ceilings

		Unit	Total
2x4		L.F.	4.57
2x6		L.F.	5.51
2x8		L.F.	6.70
2x10		L.F.	8.45
2x12		L.F.	11.13

	Unit	Total
06110.30 FLOOR FRAMING		
Floor joists		
12" o.c.		
2x6	S.F.	2.05
2x8	S.F.	2.50
2x10	S.F.	3.04
2x12	S.F.	3.96
2x14	S.F.	5.33
3x6	S.F.	4.28
3x8	S.F.	5.24
3x10	S.F.	6.29
3x12	S.F.	7.36
3x14	S.F.	8.27
4x6	S.F.	5.19
4x8	S.F.	6.38
4x10	S.F.	7.86
4x12	S.F.	9.35
4x14	S.F.	10.69
16" o.c.		
2x6	S.F.	1.73
2x8	S.F.	2.07
2x10	S.F.	2.32
2x12	S.F.	2.69
2x14	S.F.	4.77
3x6	S.F.	3.55
3x8	S.F.	4.30
3x10	S.F.	5.19
3x12	S.F.	6.10
3x14	S.F.	7.06
4x6	S.F.	4.26
4x8	S.F.	5.52
4x10	S.F.	6.62
4x12	S.F.	7.67
4x14	S.F.	8.99
Sister joists for floors		
2x4	L.F.	4.06
2x6	L.F.	4.83
2x8	L.F.	5.75
2x10	L.F.	7.03
2x12	L.F.	8.84
3x6	L.F.	8.20
3x8	L.F.	9.40
3x10	L.F.	11.19
3x12	L.F.	13.06
4x6	L.F.	8.92
4x8	L.F.	10.61
4x10	L.F.	12.69
4x12	L.F.	14.34
06110.40 FURRING		
Furring, wood strips		
Walls		
On masonry or concrete walls		
1x2 furring		
12" o.c.	S.F.	2.18
16" o.c.	S.F.	1.97
24" o.c.	S.F.	1.83
1x3 furring		
12" o.c.	S.F.	2.28
16" o.c.	S.F.	2.08
24" o.c.	S.F.	1.85
On wood walls		
1x2 furring		
12" o.c.	S.F.	1.67
16" o.c.	S.F.	1.48
24" o.c.	S.F.	1.36

	Unit	Total

06110.40 FURRING (Cont.)

Walls
  On wood walls
    1x3 furring

12" o.c.	S.F.	1.78
16" o.c.	S.F.	1.57
24" o.c.	S.F.	1.39

Ceilings
  On masonry or concrete ceilings
    1x2 furring

12" o.c.	S.F.	3.56
16" o.c.	S.F.	3.19
24" o.c.	S.F.	2.91

    1x3 furring

12" o.c.	S.F.	3.66
16" o.c.	S.F.	3.28
24" o.c.	S.F.	2.94

  On wood ceilings
    1x2 furring

12" o.c.	S.F.	2.51
16" o.c.	S.F.	2.24
24" o.c.	S.F.	2.05

    1x3

12" o.c.	S.F.	2.61
16" o.c.	S.F.	2.33
24" o.c.	S.F.	2.08

06110.50 ROOF FRAMING

Roof framing
  Rafters, gable end
    0-2 pitch (flat to 2-in-12)
      12" o.c.

2x4	S.F.	1.91
2x6	S.F.	2.24
2x8	S.F.	2.72
2x10	S.F.	3.14
2x12	S.F.	4.70

      16" o.c.

2x6	S.F.	1.92
2x8	S.F.	2.31
2x10	S.F.	2.53
2x12	S.F.	3.78

      24" o.c.

2x6	S.F.	1.36
2x8	S.F.	1.94
2x10	S.F.	2.14
2x12	S.F.	3.09

    4-6 pitch (4-in-12 to 6-in-12)
      12" o.c.

2x4	S.F.	1.96
2x6	S.F.	2.36
2x8	S.F.	3.00
2x10	S.F.	3.27
2x12	S.F.	4.35

      16" o.c.

2x6	S.F.	1.95
2x8	S.F.	2.53
2x10	S.F.	2.78
2x12	S.F.	3.62

      24" o.c.

2x6	S.F.	1.61
2x8	S.F.	2.14
2x10	S.F.	2.26
2x12	S.F.	3.10

	Unit	Total
06110.50 ROOF FRAMING (Cont.)		
Rafters, gable end		
8-12 pitch (8-in-12 to 12-in-12), 12" o.c.		
2x4	S.F.	2.07
2x6	S.F.	2.58
2x8	S.F.	3.14
2x10	S.F.	3.50
2x12	S.F.	4.65
16" o.c.		
2x6	S.F.	2.10
2x8	S.F.	2.74
2x10	S.F.	2.97
2x12	S.F.	3.81
24" o.c.		
2x6	S.F.	1.70
2x8	S.F.	2.22
2x10	S.F.	2.41
2x12	S.F.	3.30
Ridge boards		
2x6	L.F.	3.61
2x8	L.F.	4.16
2x10	L.F.	4.89
2x12	L.F.	5.79
Hip rafters		
2x6	L.F.	2.79
2x8	L.F.	3.11
2x10	L.F.	3.52
2x12	L.F.	4.00
Jack rafters		
4-6 pitch (4-in-12 to 6-in-12)		
16" o.c.		
2x6	S.F.	2.61
2x8	S.F.	3.16
2x10	S.F.	3.48
2x12	S.F.	4.33
24" o.c.		
2x6	S.F.	2.01
2x8	S.F.	2.54
2x10	S.F.	2.82
2x12	S.F.	3.49
8-12 pitch (8-in-12 to 12-in-12)		
16" o.c.		
2x6	S.F.	3.21
2x8	S.F.	3.62
2x10	S.F.	4.47
2x12	S.F.	5.53
24" o.c.		
2x6	S.F.	2.50
2x8	S.F.	2.82
2x10	S.F.	3.70
2x12	S.F.	4.74
Sister rafters		
2x4	L.F.	4.57
2x6	L.F.	5.51
2x8	L.F.	6.70
2x10	L.F.	8.45
2x12	L.F.	11.21
Fascia boards		
2x4	L.F.	3.35
2x6	L.F.	3.61
2x8	L.F.	4.16
2x10	L.F.	4.49
2x12	L.F.	5.28

	Unit	Total

06110.50 ROOF FRAMING (Cont.)

Cant strips
Fiber

3x3	L.F.	2.03
4x4	L.F.	2.29

Wood

3x3	L.F.	3.80

06110.60 SLEEPERS

Sleepers, over concrete
12" o.c.

1x2	S.F.	1.53
1x3	S.F.	1.72
2x4	S.F.	2.36
2x6	S.F.	2.82

16" o.c.

1x2	S.F.	1.36
1x3	S.F.	1.45
2x4	S.F.	2.01
2x6	S.F.	2.38

06110.65 SOFFITS

Soffit framing

2x3	L.F.	4.41
2x4	L.F.	4.80
2x6	L.F.	5.37
2x8	L.F.	6.05

06110.70 WALL FRAMING

Framing wall, studs
12" o.c.

2x3	S.F.	1.49
2x4	S.F.	1.67
2x6	S.F.	2.04
2x8	S.F.	2.39

16" o.c.

2x3	S.F.	1.25
2x4	S.F.	1.39
2x6	S.F.	1.67
2x8	S.F.	2.11

24" o.c.

2x3	S.F.	1.05
2x4	S.F.	1.15
2x6	S.F.	1.41
2x8	S.F.	1.62

Plates, top or bottom

2x3	L.F.	2.02
2x4	L.F.	2.20
2x6	L.F.	2.52
2x8	L.F.	2.90

Headers, door or window
2x6
Single

3' long	EA.	30.52
6' long	EA.	39.54

Double

3' long	EA.	35.80
6' long	EA.	48.87

2x8
Single

4' long	EA.	39.20
8' long	EA.	51.15

Double

4' long	EA.	48.15
8' long	EA.	66.50

	Unit	Total

06110.70 WALL FRAMING (Cont.)

Headers, door or window, 2x10

Single

5' long	EA.	49.35
10' long	EA.	68.25

Double

5' long	EA.	58.75
10' long	EA.	79.50

2x12

Single

6' long	EA.	51.87
12' long	EA.	73.00

Double

6' long	EA.	67.75
12' long	EA.	95.00

06115.10 FLOOR SHEATHING

Sub-flooring, plywood, CDX

1/2" thick	S.F.	1.19
5/8" thick	S.F.	1.49
3/4" thick	S.F.	2.21

Structural plywood

1/2" thick	S.F.	1.46
5/8" thick	S.F.	2.01
3/4" thick	S.F.	2.14

Board type subflooring

1x6

Minimum	S.F.	2.41
Maximum	S.F.	2.87

1x8

Minimum	S.F.	2.46
Maximum	S.F.	2.82

1x10

Minimum	S.F.	2.90
Maximum	S.F.	3.16

Underlayment

Hardboard, 1/4" tempered ... S.F. 1.41

Plywood, CDX

3/8" thick	S.F.	1.44
1/2" thick	S.F.	1.63
5/8" thick	S.F.	1.82
3/4" thick	S.F.	2.14

06115.20 ROOF SHEATHING

Sheathing

Plywood, CDX

3/8" thick	S.F.	1.46
1/2" thick	S.F.	1.63
5/8" thick	S.F.	1.82
3/4" thick	S.F.	2.14

Structural plywood

3/8" thick	S.F.	1.20
1/2" thick	S.F.	1.36
5/8" thick	S.F.	1.54
3/4" thick	S.F.	1.76

06115.30 WALL SHEATHING

Sheathing

Plywood, CDX

3/8" thick	S.F.	1.57
1/2" thick	S.F.	1.75
5/8" thick	S.F.	1.96
3/4" thick	S.F.	2.30

Waferboard

3/8" thick	S.F.	1.31
1/2" thick	S.F.	1.48

	Unit	Total

06115.30 WALL SHEATHING (Cont.)

Waferboard

5/8" thick	S.F.	1.68
3/4" thick	S.F.	1.84

Structural plywood

3/8" thick	S.F.	1.57
1/2" thick	S.F.	1.75
5/8" thick	S.F.	1.96
3/4" thick	S.F.	1.91
Gypsum, 1/2" thick	S.F.	1.35
Asphalt impregnated fiberboard, 1/2" thick	S.F.	1.68

06125.10 WOOD DECKING

Decking, T&G solid

Cedar

3" thick	S.F.	10.28
4" thick	S.F.	12.52

Fir

3" thick	S.F.	5.30
4" thick	S.F.	6.23

Southern yellow pine

3" thick	S.F.	5.51
4" thick	S.F.	5.85

White pine

3" thick	S.F.	6.13
4" thick	S.F.	7.89

06130.10 HEAVY TIMBER

Mill framed structures

Beams to 20' long

Douglas fir

6x8	L.F.	13.79
6x10	L.F.	15.19
6x12	L.F.	17.23
6x14	L.F.	19.33
6x16	L.F.	20.68
8x10	L.F.	17.63
8x12	L.F.	20.02
8x14	L.F.	22.08
8x16	L.F.	24.43

Southern yellow pine

6x8	L.F.	12.47
6x10	L.F.	13.82
6x12	L.F.	16.10
6x14	L.F.	17.54
6x16	L.F.	18.86
8x10	L.F.	16.00
8x12	L.F.	18.27
8x14	L.F.	20.08
8x16	L.F.	22.18

Columns to 12' high

Douglas fir

6x6	L.F.	15.82
8x8	L.F.	19.08
10x10	L.F.	26.25
12x12	L.F.	29.50

Southern yellow pine

6x6	L.F.	15.18
8x8	L.F.	17.86
10x10	L.F.	22.75
12x12	L.F.	26.75

Posts, treated

4x4	L.F.	3.85
6x6	L.F.	7.42

	Unit	Total
06190.20 WOOD TRUSSES		
Truss, fink, 2x4 members		
3-in-12 slope		
24' span	EA.	157.50
26' span	EA.	162.00
28' span	EA.	177.75
30' span	EA.	177.75
34' span	EA.	182.00
38' span	EA.	192.00
5-in-12 slope		
24' span	EA.	164.25
28' span	EA.	177.75
30' span	EA.	179.75
32' span	EA.	189.75
40' span	EA.	234.50
Gable, 2x4 members		
5-in-12 slope		
24' span	EA.	175.75
26' span	EA.	185.75
28' span	EA.	207.75
30' span	EA.	219.75
32' span	EA.	219.75
36' span	EA.	232.00
40' span	EA.	244.50
King post type, 2x4 members		
4-in-12 slope		
16' span	EA.	129.00
18' span	EA.	136.75
24' span	EA.	145.75
26' span	EA.	151.50
30' span	EA.	179.75
34' span	EA.	189.75
38' span	EA.	212.00
42' span	EA.	247.00
06200.10 FINISH CARPENTRY		
Mouldings and trim		
Apron, flat		
9/16 x 2	L.F.	4.39
9/16 x 3-1/2	L.F.	6.55
Base		
Colonial		
7/16 x 2-1/4	L.F.	4.69
7/16 x 3	L.F.	5.23
7/16 x 3-1/4	L.F.	5.28
9/16 x 3	L.F.	5.38
9/16 x 3-1/4	L.F.	5.49
11/16 x 2-1/4	L.F.	5.77
Ranch		
7/16 x 2-1/4	L.F.	4.86
7/16 x 3-1/4	L.F.	5.23
9/16 x 2-1/4	L.F.	5.19
9/16 x 3	L.F.	5.38
9/16 x 3-1/4	L.F.	5.43
Casing		
11/16 x 2-1/2	L.F.	4.48
11/16 x 3-1/2	L.F.	4.84
Chair rail		
9/16 x 2-1/2	L.F.	4.86
9/16 x 3-1/2	L.F.	5.63
Closet pole		
1-1/8" dia.	L.F.	5.16
1-5/8" dia.	L.F.	5.81
Cove		
9/16 x 1-3/4	L.F.	4.39
11/16 x 2-3/4	L.F.	5.23

	Unit	Total

06200.10 FINISH CARPENTRY (Cont.)

Mouldings and trim

Crown

9/16 x 1-5/8	L.F.	5.81
9/16 x 2-5/8	L.F.	6.57
11/16 x 3-5/8	L.F.	7.13
11/16 x 4-1/4	L.F.	8.73
11/16 x 5-1/4	L.F.	9.67

Drip cap

1-1/16 x 1-5/8	L.F.	4.98

Glass bead

3/8 x 3/8	L.F.	4.33
1/2 x 9/16	L.F.	4.51
5/8 x 5/8	L.F.	4.57
3/4 x 3/4	L.F.	4.75

Half round

1/2	L.F.	3.17
5/8	L.F.	3.47
3/4	L.F.	3.89

Lattice

1/4 x 7/8	L.F.	3.00
1/4 x 1-1/8	L.F.	3.05
1/4 x 1-3/8	L.F.	3.10
1/4 x 1-3/4	L.F.	3.20
1/4 x 2	L.F.	3.35

Ogee molding

5/8 x 3/4	L.F.	4.27
11/16 x 1-1/8	L.F.	6.17
11/16 x 1-3/8	L.F.	5.46

Parting bead

3/8 x 7/8	L.F.	4.75

Quarter round

1/4 x 1/4	L.F.	2.70
3/8 x 3/8	L.F.	2.87
1/2 x 1/2	L.F.	3.05
11/16 x 11/16	L.F.	3.25
3/4 x 3/4	L.F.	3.90
1-1/16 x 1-1/16	L.F.	3.71

Railings, balusters

1-1/8 x 1-1/8	L.F.	9.50
1-1/2 x 1-1/2	L.F.	9.62

Screen moldings

1/4 x 3/4	L.F.	5.70
5/8 x 5/16	L.F.	5.94

Shoe

7/16 x 11/16	L.F.	3.47

Sash beads

1/2 x 3/4	L.F.	6.11
1/2 x 7/8	L.F.	6.29
1/2 x 1-1/8	L.F.	6.84
5/8 x 7/8	L.F.	6.84

Stop

5/8 x 1-5/8

Colonial	L.F.	4.38
Ranch	L.F.	4.38

Stools

11/16 x 2-1/4	L.F.	9.95
11/16 x 2-1/2	L.F.	10.13
11/16 x 5-1/4	L.F.	11.04

Exterior trim, casing, select pine, 1x3	L.F.	5.46

Douglas fir

1x3	L.F.	4.09
1x4	L.F.	4.39
1x6	L.F.	5.17
1x8	L.F.	6.34

	Unit	Total

06200.10 FINISH CARPENTRY (Cont.)

Exterior trim
  Cornices, white pine, #2 or better

1x2	L.F.	3.62
1x4	L.F.	3.80
1x6	L.F.	4.70
1x8	L.F.	5.24
1x10	L.F.	5.99
1x12	L.F.	6.82

  Shelving, pine

1x8	L.F.	5.74
1x10	L.F.	6.34
1x12	L.F.	7.01
Plywood shelf, 3/4", with edge band, 12" wide	L.F.	8.13

  Adjustable shelf, and rod, 12" wide

3' to 4' long	EA.	33.75
5' to 8' long	EA.	55.25

  Prefinished wood shelves with brackets and supports
  8" wide

3' long	EA.	71.25
4' long	EA.	79.50
6' long	EA.	109.00

  10" wide

3' long	EA.	77.25
4' long	EA.	105.50
6' long	EA.	114.25

06220.10 MILLWORK

Countertop, laminated plastic
  25" x 7/8" thick

Minimum	L.F.	29.50
Average	L.F.	47.75
Maximum	L.F.	65.00

  25" x 1-1/4" thick

Minimum	L.F.	37.50
Average	L.F.	59.50
Maximum	L.F.	83.75
Add for cutouts	EA.	35.50
Backsplash, 4" high, 7/8" thick	L.F.	31.75

Plywood, sanded, A-C

1/4" thick	S.F.	3.21
3/8" thick	S.F.	3.45
1/2" thick	S.F.	3.80

A-D

1/4" thick	S.F.	3.14
3/8" thick	S.F.	3.45
1/2" thick	S.F.	3.73

Base cab., 34-1/2" high, 24" deep, hardwood

Minimum	L.F.	222.75
Average	L.F.	258.50
Maximum	L.F.	288.00

Wall cabinets

Minimum	L.F.	79.50
Average	L.F.	104.50
Maximum	L.F.	128.50

	Unit	Total

06300.10 WOOD TREATMENT

Creosote preservative treatment
| 8 lb/cf | B.F. | .62 |
| 10 lb/cf | B.F. | .74 |

Salt preservative treatment
Oil borne
| Minimum | B.F. | .57 |
| Maximum | B.F. | .80 |

Water borne
| Minimum | B.F. | .40 |
| Maximum | B.F. | .62 |

Fire retardant treatment
| Minimum | B.F. | .80 |
| Maximum | B.F. | .97 |

Kiln dried, softwood, add to framing costs
1" thick	B.F.	.29
2" thick	B.F.	.40
3" thick	B.F.	.51
4" thick	B.F.	.62

06420.10 PANEL WORK

Hardboard, tempered, 1/4" thick
Natural faced	S.F.	2.37
Plastic faced	S.F.	3.05
Pegboard, natural	S.F.	2.61
Plastic faced	S.F.	3.05

Untempered, 1/4" thick
Natural faced	S.F.	2.31
Plastic faced	S.F.	3.17
Pegboard, natural	S.F.	2.37
Plastic faced	S.F.	2.99

Plywood unfinished, 1/4" thick
Birch
Natural	S.F.	2.91
Select	S.F.	3.38
Knotty pine	S.F.	3.86

Cedar (closet lining)
| Standard boards T&G | S.F. | 4.33 |
| Particle board | S.F. | 3.38 |

Plywood, prefinished, 1/4" thick, premium grade
Birch veneer	S.F.	5.83
Cherry veneer	S.F.	6.43
Chestnut veneer	S.F.	10.29
Lauan veneer	S.F.	3.82
Mahogany veneer	S.F.	6.37
Oak veneer (red)	S.F.	6.37
Pecan veneer	S.F.	7.44
Rosewood veneer	S.F.	10.29
Teak veneer	S.F.	7.56
Walnut veneer	S.F.	6.85

06430.10 STAIRWORK

Risers, 1x8, 42" wide
| White oak | EA. | 71.25 |
| Pine | EA. | 66.50 |

Treads, 1-1/16" x 9-1/2" x 42"
| White oak | EA. | 86.50 |

	Unit	Total
06440.10 COLUMNS		
Column, hollow, round wood		
12" diameter		
10' high	EA.	831.75
12' high	EA.	1,008
14' high	EA.	1,198
16' high	EA.	1,470
24" diameter		
16' high	EA.	3,220
18' high	EA.	3,680
20' high	EA.	4,480
22' high	EA.	4,740
24' high	EA.	5,140

	Unit	Total

07100.10 WATERPROOFING

Membrane waterproofing, elastomeric
Butyl

1/32" thick	S.F.	3.07
1/16" thick	S.F.	3.52

Neoprene

1/32" thick	S.F.	3.97
1/16" thick	S.F.	4.98

Plastic vapor barrier (polyethylene)

4 mil	S.F.	.24
6 mil	S.F.	.26
10 mil	S.F.	.34

Bituminous membrane, asphalt felt, 15 lb.

One ply	S.F.	1.92
Two ply	S.F.	2.29
Three ply	S.F.	2.75

Bentonite waterproofing, panels

3/16" thick	S.F.	2.81
1/4" thick	S.F.	3.04

07150.10 DAMPPROOFING

Silicone dampproofing, sprayed on
Concrete surface

1 coat	S.F.	.90
2 coats	S.F.	1.41

Concrete block

1 coat	S.F.	.95
2 coats	S.F.	1.48

Brick

1 coat	S.F.	1.09
2 coats	S.F.	1.61

07160.10 BITUMINOUS DAMPPROOFING

Building paper, asphalt felt

15 lb	S.F.	1.99
30 lb	S.F.	2.23

Asphalt, troweled, cold, primer plus

1 coat	S.F.	2.17
2 coats	S.F.	3.66
3 coats	S.F.	4.84

Fibrous asphalt, hot troweled, primer plus

1 coat	S.F.	2.47
2 coats	S.F.	3.91
3 coats	S.F.	5.24

Asphaltic paint dampproofing, per coat

Brush on	S.F.	.99
Spray on	S.F.	1.00

07190.10 VAPOR BARRIERS

Vapor barrier, polyethylene

2 mil	S.F.	.23
6 mil	S.F.	.29
8 mil	S.F.	.33
10 mil	S.F.	.34

07210.10 BATT INSULATION

Ceiling, fiberglass, unfaced

3-1/2" thick, R11	S.F.	.95
6" thick, R19	S.F.	1.16
9" thick, R30	S.F.	1.79

Suspended ceiling, unfaced

3-1/2" thick, R11	S.F.	.92
6" thick, R19	S.F.	1.12
9" thick, R30	S.F.	1.74

	Unit	Total

07210.10 BATT INSULATION (Cont.)

Crawl space, unfaced

3-1/2" thick, R11	S.F.	1.11
6" thick, R19	S.F.	1.30
9" thick, R30	S.F.	1.91

Wall, fiberglass
Paper backed

2" thick, R7	S.F.	.75
3" thick, R8	S.F.	.80
4" thick, R11	S.F.	1.03
6" thick, R19	S.F.	1.30

Foil backed, 1 side

2" thick, R7	S.F.	1.11
3" thick, R11	S.F.	1.18
4" thick, R14	S.F.	1.24
6" thick, R21	S.F.	1.49

Foil backed, 2 sides

2" thick, R7	S.F.	1.26
3" thick, R11	S.F.	1.48
4" thick, R14	S.F.	1.69
6" thick, R21	S.F.	1.81

Unfaced

2" thick, R7	S.F.	.88
3" thick, R9	S.F.	.96
4" thick, R11	S.F.	1.03
6" thick, R19	S.F.	1.20

Mineral wool batts
Paper backed

2" thick, R6	S.F.	.74
4" thick, R12	S.F.	1.08
6" thick, R19	S.F.	1.30

Fasteners, self adhering, attached to ceiling deck

2-1/2" long	EA.	.96
4-1/2" long	EA.	1.05
Capped, self-locking washers	EA.	.67

07210.20 BOARD INSULATION

Perlite board, roof

1.00" thick, R2.78	S.F.	.95
1.50" thick, R4.17	S.F.	1.29

Rigid urethane

1" thick, R6.67	S.F.	1.47
1.50" thick, R11.11	S.F.	1.88

Polystyrene

1.0" thick, R4.17	S.F.	.81
1.5" thick, R6.26	S.F.	1.07

07210.60 LOOSE FILL INSULATION

Blown-in type
Fiberglass

5" thick, R11	S.F.	.79
6" thick, R13	S.F.	.93
9" thick, R19	S.F.	1.22

Rockwool, attic application

6" thick, R13	S.F.	.83
8" thick, R19	S.F.	1.02
10" thick, R22	S.F.	1.23
12" thick, R26	S.F.	1.42
15" thick, R30	S.F.	1.71

Poured type
Fiberglass

1" thick, R4	S.F.	.74
2" thick, R8	S.F.	1.17
3" thick, R12	S.F.	1.61
4" thick, R16	S.F.	2.09

	Unit	Total

07210.60 LOOSE FILL INSULATION (Cont.)

Poured type, Mineral wool

1" thick, R3	S.F.	.78
2" thick, R6	S.F.	1.25
3" thick, R9	S.F.	1.78
4" thick, R12	S.F.	2.09

Vermiculite or perlite

2" thick, R4.8	S.F.	1.21
3" thick, R7.2	S.F.	1.63
4" thick, R9.6	S.F.	2.09

Masonry, poured vermiculite or perlite

4" block	S.F.	.68
6" block	S.F.	.96
8" block	S.F.	1.31
10" block	S.F.	1.65
12" block	S.F.	1.99

07210.70 SPRAYED INSULATION

Foam, sprayed on

Polystyrene

1" thick, R4	S.F.	1.22
2" thick, R8	S.F.	2.10

Urethane

1" thick, R4	S.F.	1.18
2" thick, R8	S.F.	1.99

07310.10 ASPHALT SHINGLES

Standard asphalt shingles, strip shingles

210 lb/square	SQ.	144.75
235 lb/square	SQ.	155.00
240 lb/square	SQ.	167.00
260 lb/square	SQ.	217.75
300 lb/square	SQ.	240.75
385 lb/square	SQ.	320.00

Roll roofing, mineral surface

90 lb	SQ.	94.00
110 lb	SQ.	137.00
140 lb	SQ.	149.00

07310.50 METAL SHINGLES

Aluminum, .020" thick

Plain	SQ.	370.00
Colors	SQ.	390.00

Steel, galvanized

26 ga.

Plain	SQ.	430.00
Colors	SQ.	510.00

24 ga.

Plain	SQ.	480.00
Colors	SQ.	580.00

Porcelain enamel, 22 ga.

Minimum	SQ.	940.00
Average	SQ.	1,060
Maximum	SQ.	1,190

07310.60 SLATE SHINGLES

Slate shingles

Pennsylvania

Ribbon	SQ.	900.00
Clear	SQ.	1,080

Vermont

Black	SQ.	1,010
Gray	SQ.	1,090
Green	SQ.	1,110
Red	SQ.	1,770

	Unit	Total
07310.70 WOOD SHINGLES		
Wood shingles, on roofs		
White cedar, #1 shingles		
4" exposure	SQ.	410.00
5" exposure	SQ.	350.00
#2 shingles		
4" exposure	SQ.	350.00
5" exposure	SQ.	280.00
Resquared and rebutted		
4" exposure	SQ.	390.00
5" exposure	SQ.	310.00
On walls		
White cedar, #1 shingles		
4" exposure	SQ.	500.00
5" exposure	SQ.	430.00
6" exposure	SQ.	350.00
#2 shingles		
4" exposure	SQ.	440.00
5" exposure	SQ.	360.00
6" exposure	SQ.	300.00
Add for fire retarding	SQ.	110.00
07310.80 WOOD SHAKES		
Shakes, hand split, 24" red cedar, on roofs		
5" exposure	SQ.	530.00
7" exposure	SQ.	470.00
9" exposure	SQ.	410.00
On walls		
6" exposure	SQ.	520.00
8" exposure	SQ.	460.00
10" exposure	SQ.	400.00
Add for fire retarding	SQ.	74.75
07460.10 METAL SIDING PANELS		
Aluminum siding panels		
Corrugated		
Plain finish		
.024"	S.F.	4.88
.032"	S.F.	5.29
Painted finish		
.024"	S.F.	5.45
.032"	S.F.	5.88
Steel siding panels		
Corrugated		
22 ga.	S.F.	6.68
24 ga.	S.F.	6.46
07460.50 PLASTIC SIDING		
Horizontal vinyl siding, solid		
8" wide		
Standard	S.F.	3.42
Insulated	S.F.	3.69
10" wide		
Standard	S.F.	3.31
Insulated	S.F.	3.56
Vinyl moldings for doors and windows	L.F.	3.07
07460.60 PLYWOOD SIDING		
Rough sawn cedar, 3/8" thick	S.F.	3.87
Fir, 3/8" thick	S.F.	2.99
Texture 1-11, 5/8" thick		
Cedar	S.F.	4.69
Fir	S.F.	3.89
Redwood	S.F.	4.80
Southern Yellow Pine	S.F.	3.54

	Unit	Total

07460.70 STEEL SIDING

Ribbed, sheets, galvanized

	Unit	Total
22 ga.	S.F.	5.02
24 ga.	S.F.	4.78

Primed

	Unit	Total
24 ga.	S.F.	5.47
26 ga.	S.F.	4.61

07460.80 WOOD SIDING

Beveled siding, cedar

A grade

	Unit	Total
1/2 x 8	S.F.	5.99
3/4 x 10	S.F.	6.68

Clear

	Unit	Total
1/2 x 6	S.F.	6.90
1/2 x 8	S.F.	6.42
3/4 x 10	S.F.	7.44

B grade

	Unit	Total
1/2 x 6	S.F.	6.77
1/2 x 8	S.F.	27.17
3/4 x 10	S.F.	6.06

Board and batten

Cedar

	Unit	Total
1x6	S.F.	8.23
1x8	S.F.	7.17
1x10	S.F.	6.45
1x12	S.F.	5.80

Pine

	Unit	Total
1x6	S.F.	4.21
1x8	S.F.	3.61
1x10	S.F.	3.31
1x12	S.F.	3.02

Redwood

	Unit	Total
1x6	S.F.	8.69
1x8	S.F.	7.72
1x10	S.F.	7.08
1x12	S.F.	6.50

Tongue and groove

Cedar

	Unit	Total
1x4	S.F.	8.21
1x6	S.F.	7.86
1x8	S.F.	7.40
1x10	S.F.	7.19

Pine

	Unit	Total
1x4	S.F.	4.68
1x6	S.F.	4.43
1x8	S.F.	4.19
1x10	S.F.	3.99

Redwood

	Unit	Total
1x4	S.F.	8.51
1x6	S.F.	8.15
1x8	S.F.	7.82
1x10	S.F.	7.45

07510.10 BUILT-UP ASPHALT ROOFING

Built-up roofing, asphalt felt, including gravel

	Unit	Total
2 ply	SQ.	227.75
3 ply	SQ.	300.00
4 ply	SQ.	390.00

Cant strip, 4" x 4"

	Unit	Total
Treated wood	L.F.	3.88
Foamglass	L.F.	3.36

	Unit	Total

07510.10 BUILT-UP ASPHALT ROOFING (Cont.)

New gravel for built-up roofing, 400 lb/sq .... SQ. | 145.00

07530.10 SINGLE-PLY ROOFING

Elastic sheet roofing
  Neoprene, 1/16" thick .... S.F. | 3.52
  PVC
    45 mil .... S.F. | 2.72
Flashing
  Pipe flashing, 90 mil thick
    1" pipe .... EA. | 46.50
  Neoprene flashing, 60 mil thick strip
    6" wide .... L.F. | 6.44
    12" wide .... L.F. | 10.56

07610.10 METAL ROOFING

Sheet metal roofing, copper, 16 oz, batten seam .... SQ. | 2,160
  Standing seam .... SQ. | 2,090
Aluminum roofing, natural finish
  Corrugated, on steel frame
    .0175" thick .... SQ. | 290.00
    .0215" thick .... SQ. | 330.00
    .024" thick .... SQ. | 370.00
    .032" thick .... SQ. | 410.00
  V-beam, on steel frame
    .032" thick .... SQ. | 420.00
    .040" thick .... SQ. | 440.00
    .050" thick .... SQ. | 510.00
  Ridge cap
    .019" thick .... L.F. | 5.85
Corrugated galvanized steel roofing, on steel frame
  28 ga. .... SQ. | 380.00
  26 ga. .... SQ. | 410.00
  24 ga. .... SQ. | 450.00
  22 ga. .... SQ. | 480.00
  26 ga., factory insulated with 1" polystyrene .... SQ. | 710.00
  Ridge roll
    10" wide .... L.F. | 4.01
    20" wide .... L.F. | 6.66

07620.10 FLASHING AND TRIM

Counter flashing
  Aluminum, .032" .... S.F. | 7.26
  Stainless steel, .015" .... S.F. | 11.26
  Copper
    16 oz. .... S.F. | 14.80
    20 oz. .... S.F. | 16.44
    24 oz. .... S.F. | 18.94
    32 oz. .... S.F. | 21.94
Valley flashing
  Aluminum, .032" .... S.F. | 4.98
  Stainless steel, .015 .... S.F. | 8.46
  Copper
    16 oz. .... S.F. | 12.76
    20 oz. .... S.F. | 15.53
    24 oz. .... S.F. | 16.90
    32 oz. .... S.F. | 19.90
Base flashing
  Aluminum, .040" .... S.F. | 7.14
  Stainless steel, .018" .... S.F. | 10.58
  Copper
    16 oz. .... S.F. | 13.89
    20 oz. .... S.F. | 14.40
    24 oz. .... S.F. | 18.03
    32 oz. .... S.F. | 21.03

	Unit	Total

07620.10 FLASHING AND TRIM (Cont.)

Flashing and trim, aluminum

	Unit	Total
.019" thick	S.F.	5.18
.032" thick	S.F.	5.46
.040" thick	S.F.	6.88
Neoprene sheet flashing, .060" thick	S.F.	5.54

Copper, paper backed

	Unit	Total
2 oz.	S.F.	8.19
5 oz.	S.F.	8.99

07620.20 GUTTERS AND DOWNSPOUTS

Copper gutter and downspout
Downspouts, 16 oz. copper
Round

	Unit	Total
3" dia.	L.F.	16.63
4" dia.	L.F.	19.88

Rectangular, corrugated

	Unit	Total
2" x 3"	L.F.	16.15
3" x 4"	L.F.	18.90

Rectangular, flat surface

	Unit	Total
2" x 3"	L.F.	18.13
3" x 4"	L.F.	24.13

Lead-coated copper downspouts
Round

	Unit	Total
3" dia.	L.F.	20.40
4" dia.	L.F.	24.64

Rectangular, corrugated

	Unit	Total
2" x 3"	L.F.	20.88
3" x 4"	L.F.	24.13

Rectangular, plain

	Unit	Total
2" x 3"	L.F.	15.63
3" x 4"	L.F.	17.63

Gutters, 16 oz. copper
Half round

	Unit	Total
4" wide	L.F.	17.19
5" wide	L.F.	20.29

Type K

	Unit	Total
4" wide	L.F.	18.44
5" wide	L.F.	19.79

Lead-coated copper gutters
Half round

	Unit	Total
4" wide	L.F.	19.69
6" wide	L.F.	25.54

Type K

	Unit	Total
4" wide	L.F.	21.19
5" wide	L.F.	26.29

Aluminum gutter and downspout
Downspouts

	Unit	Total
2" x 3"	L.F.	5.02
3" x 4"	L.F.	5.80
4" x 5"	L.F.	6.30

Round

	Unit	Total
3" dia.	L.F.	5.97
4" dia.	L.F.	6.89

Gutters, stock units

	Unit	Total
4" wide	L.F.	7.90
5" wide	L.F.	8.62

Galvanized steel gutter and downspout
Downspouts, round corrugated

	Unit	Total
3" dia.	L.F.	5.63
4" dia.	L.F.	6.32
5" dia.	L.F.	7.89
6" dia.	L.F.	9.20

Rectangular

	Unit	Total
2" x 3"	L.F.	5.44
3" x 4"	L.F.	5.99

	Unit	Total

07620.20 GUTTERS AND DOWNSPOUTS (Cont.)

Galvanized steel gutter and downspout
  Downspouts, round corrugated

4" x 4"	L.F.	6.65

  Gutters, stock units
    5" wide

Plain	L.F.	7.79
Painted	L.F.	7.94

    6" wide

Plain	L.F.	8.84
Painted	L.F.	9.14

07810.10 PLASTIC SKYLIGHTS

Single thickness, not including mounting curb

2' x 4'	EA.	438.00
4' x 4'	EA.	590.75
5' x 5'	EA.	810.00
6' x 8'	EA.	1,580

Double thickness, not including mounting curb

2' x 4'	EA.	558.00
4' x 4'	EA.	700.75
5' x 5'	EA.	1,040
6' x 8'	EA.	1,780

07920.10 CAULKING

Caulk exterior, two component

1/4 x 1/2	L.F.	3.27
3/8 x 1/2	L.F.	3.80
1/2 x 1/2	L.F.	4.43

Caulk interior, single component

1/4 x 1/2	L.F.	2.99
3/8 x 1/2	L.F.	3.39
1/2 x 1/2	L.F.	3.87

	Unit	Total

08110.10 METAL DOORS

Flush hollow metal, std. duty, 20 ga., 1-3/8" thick

	Unit	Total
2-6 x 6-8	EA.	363.25
2-8 x 6-8	EA.	403.25
3-0 x 6-8	EA.	423.25

1-3/4" thick

	Unit	Total
2-6 x 6-8	EA.	423.25
2-8 x 6-8	EA.	443.25
3-0 x 6-8	EA.	473.25
2-6 x 7-0	EA.	453.25
2-8 x 7-0	EA.	473.25
3-0 x 7-0	EA.	493.25

Heavy duty, 20 ga., unrated, 1-3/4"

	Unit	Total
2-8 x 6-8	EA.	453.25
3-0 x 6-8	EA.	483.25
2-8 x 7-0	EA.	513.25
3-0 x 7-0	EA.	493.25
3-4 x 7-0	EA.	513.25

18 ga., 1-3/4", unrated door

	Unit	Total
2-0 x 7-0	EA.	483.25
2-4 x 7-0	EA.	483.25
2-6 x 7-0	EA.	483.25
2-8 x 7-0	EA.	523.25
3-0 x 7-0	EA.	533.25
3-4 x 7-0	EA.	543.25

2", unrated door

	Unit	Total
2-0 x 7-0	EA.	531.25
2-4 x 7-0	EA.	531.25
2-6 x 7-0	EA.	531.25
2-8 x 7-0	EA.	571.25
3-0 x 7-0	EA.	591.25
3-4 x 7-0	EA.	601.25

08110.40 METAL DOOR FRAMES

Hollow metal, stock, 18 ga., 4-3/4" x 1-3/4"

	Unit	Total
2-0 x 7-0	EA.	211.25
2-4 x 7-0	EA.	231.25
2-6 x 7-0	EA.	231.25
2-8 x 7-0	EA.	231.25
3-0 x 7-0	EA.	231.25
4-0 x 7-0	EA.	275.00
5-0 x 7-0	EA.	285.00
6-0 x 7-0	EA.	325.00

16 ga., 6-3/4" x 1-3/4"

	Unit	Total
2-0 x 7-0	EA.	238.75
2-4 x 7-0	EA.	228.75
2-6 x 7-0	EA.	238.75
2-8 x 7-0	EA.	238.75
3-0 x 7-0	EA.	248.75
4-0 x 7-0	EA.	310.00
6-0 x 7-0	EA.	340.00

08210.10 WOOD DOORS

Solid core, 1-3/8" thick

Birch faced

	Unit	Total
2-4 x 7-0	EA.	221.25
2-8 x 7-0	EA.	231.25
3-0 x 7-0	EA.	231.25
3-4 x 7-0	EA.	381.25
2-4 x 6-8	EA.	221.25
2-6 x 6-8	EA.	221.25
2-8 x 6-8	EA.	231.25
3-0 x 6-8	EA.	231.25

Lauan faced

	Unit	Total
2-4 x 6-8	EA.	211.25

	Unit	Total
08210.10 WOOD DOORS (Cont.)		
Solid core, 1-3/8" thick, Lauan faced		
2-8 x 6-8	EA.	221.25
3-0 x 6-8	EA.	221.25
3-4 x 6-8	EA.	231.25
Tempered hardboard faced		
2-4 x 7-0	EA.	241.25
2-8 x 7-0	EA.	251.25
3-0 x 7-0	EA.	281.25
3-4 x 7-0	EA.	281.25
Hollow core, 1-3/8" thick		
Birch faced		
2-4 x 7-0	EA.	211.25
2-8 x 7-0	EA.	211.25
3-0 x 7-0	EA.	221.25
3-4 x 7-0	EA.	231.25
Lauan faced		
2-4 x 6-8	EA.	129.25
2-6 x 6-8	EA.	134.25
2-8 x 6-8	EA.	150.00
3-0 x 6-8	EA.	153.50
3-4 x 6-8	EA.	162.00
Tempered hardboard faced		
2-4 x 7-0	EA.	142.50
2-6 x 7-0	EA.	147.75
2-8 x 7-0	EA.	155.75
3-0 x 7-0	EA.	161.00
3-4 x 7-0	EA.	169.00
Solid core, 1-3/4" thick		
Birch faced		
2-4 x 7-0	EA.	301.25
2-6 x 7-0	EA.	311.25
2-8 x 7-0	EA.	321.25
3-0 x 7-0	EA.	301.25
3-4 x 7-0	EA.	311.25
Lauan faced		
2-4 x 7-0	EA.	231.25
2-6 x 7-0	EA.	251.25
2-8 x 7-0	EA.	271.25
3-4 x 7-0	EA.	271.25
3-0 x 7-0	EA.	291.25
Tempered hardboard faced		
2-4 x 7-0	EA.	281.25
2-6 x 7-0	EA.	311.25
2-8 x 7-0	EA.	331.25
3-0 x 7-0	EA.	341.25
3-4 x 7-0	EA.	361.25
Hollow core, 1-3/4" thick		
Birch faced		
2-4 x 7-0	EA.	231.25
2-6 x 7-0	EA.	231.25
2-8 x 7-0	EA.	241.25
3-0 x 7-0	EA.	241.25
3-4 x 7-0	EA.	251.25
Lauan faced		
2-4 x 6-8	EA.	168.50
2-6 x 6-8	EA.	181.25
2-8 x 6-8	EA.	168.50
3-0 x 6-8	EA.	171.25
3-4 x 6-8	EA.	181.25
Tempered hardboard		
2-4 x 7-0	EA.	160.00
2-6 x 7-0	EA.	164.50
2-8 x 7-0	EA.	168.50
3-0 x 7-0	EA.	171.25
3-4 x 7-0	EA.	181.25

	Unit	Total

08210.10 WOOD DOORS (Cont.)

Add-on, louver	EA.	92.00
Glass	EA.	167.00
Exterior doors, 3-0 x 7-0 x 2-1/2", solid core		
Carved		
One face	EA.	1,590
Two faces	EA.	2,140
Closet doors, 1-3/4" thick		
Bi-fold or bi-passing, includes frame and trim		
Paneled		
4-0 x 6-8	EA.	605.00
6-0 x 6-8	EA.	675.00
Louvered		
4-0 x 6-8	EA.	445.00
6-0 x 6-8	EA.	515.00
Flush		
4-0 x 6-8	EA.	355.00
6-0 x 6-8	EA.	425.00
Primed		
4-0 x 6-8	EA.	375.00
6-0 x 6-8	EA.	415.00

08210.90 WOOD FRAMES

Frame, interior, pine		
2-6 x 6-8	EA.	167.75
2-8 x 6-8	EA.	174.25
3-0 x 6-8	EA.	177.25
5-0 x 6-8	EA.	181.25
6-0 x 6-8	EA.	191.25
2-6 x 7-0	EA.	180.25
2-8 x 7-0	EA.	191.25
3-0 x 7-0	EA.	201.25
5-0 x 7-0	EA.	240.00
6-0 x 7-0	EA.	240.00
Exterior, custom, with threshold, including trim		
Walnut		
3-0 x 7-0	EA.	480.00
6-0 x 7-0	EA.	530.00
Oak		
3-0 x 7-0	EA.	450.00
6-0 x 7-0	EA.	500.00
Pine		
2-4 x 7-0	EA.	240.00
2-6 x 7-0	EA.	240.00
2-8 x 7-0	EA.	250.00
3-0 x 7-0	EA.	250.00
3-4 x 7-0	EA.	270.00
6-0 x 7-0	EA.	360.00

08300.10 SPECIAL DOORS

Sliding glass doors		
Tempered plate glass, 1/4" thick		
6' wide		
Economy grade	EA.	1,240
Premium grade	EA.	1,390
12' wide		
Economy grade	EA.	1,790
Premium grade	EA.	2,540
Insulating glass, 5/8" thick		
6' wide		
Economy grade	EA.	1,490
Premium grade	EA.	1,890
12' wide		
Economy grade	EA.	1,940
Premium grade	EA.	2,940

	Unit	Total

08300.10 SPECIAL DOORS (Cont.)

Insulating glass		
1" thick		
6' wide		
Economy grade	EA.	1,840
Premium grade	EA.	2,090
12' wide		
Economy grade	EA.	2,840
Premium grade	EA.	4,040
Added costs		
Custom quality, add to material, 30%		
Tempered glass, 6' wide, add	S.F.	4.62
Residential storm door		
Minimum	EA.	265.00
Average	EA.	325.00
Maximum	EA.	650.00

08520.10 ALUMINUM WINDOWS

Jalousie		
3-0 x 4-0	EA.	418.75
3-0 x 5-0	EA.	468.75
Fixed window		
6 sf to 8 sf	S.F.	25.74
12 sf to 16 sf	S.F.	21.75
Projecting window		
6 sf to 8 sf	S.F.	52.50
12 sf to 16 sf	S.F.	43.75
Horizontal sliding		
6 sf to 8 sf	S.F.	31.87
12 sf to 16 sf	S.F.	28.30
Double hung		
6 sf to 8 sf	S.F.	45.75
10 sf to 12 sf	S.F.	40.00
Storm window, 0.5 cfm, up to		
60 u.i. (united inches)	EA.	109.00
70 u.i.	EA.	110.75
80 u.i.	EA.	120.00
90 u.i.	EA.	125.25
100 u.i.	EA.	127.00
2.0 cfm, up to		
60 u.i.	EA.	131.00
70 u.i.	EA.	131.50
80 u.i.	EA.	131.50
90 u.i.	EA.	145.00
100 u.i.	EA.	145.00

08600.10 WOOD WINDOWS

Double hung		
24" x 36"		
Minimum	EA.	287.00
Average	EA.	411.25
Maximum	EA.	545.00
24" x 48"		
Minimum	EA.	327.00
Average	EA.	461.25
Maximum	EA.	645.00
30" x 48"		
Minimum	EA.	343.25
Average	EA.	471.25
Maximum	EA.	680.00
30" x 60"		
Minimum	EA.	373.25
Average	EA.	571.25
Maximum	EA.	710.00

	Unit	Total

08600.10 WOOD WINDOWS (Cont.)

Casement
  1 leaf, 22" x 38" high

	Unit	Total
Minimum	EA.	397.00
Average	EA.	481.25
Maximum	EA.	575.00

  2 leaf, 50" x 50" high

	Unit	Total
Minimum	EA.	971.25
Average	EA.	1,245
Maximum	EA.	1,490

  3 leaf, 71" x 62" high

	Unit	Total
Minimum	EA.	1,571
Average	EA.	1,595
Maximum	EA.	1,940

  4 leaf, 95" x 75" high

	Unit	Total
Minimum	EA.	2,031
Average	EA.	2,360
Maximum	EA.	3,040

  5 leaf, 119" x 75" high

	Unit	Total
Minimum	EA.	2,631
Average	EA.	2,860
Maximum	EA.	3,690

Picture window, fixed glass, 54" x 54" high

	Unit	Total
Minimum	EA.	601.25
Average	EA.	671.25
Maximum	EA.	1,145

  68" x 55" high

	Unit	Total
Minimum	EA.	1,021
Average	EA.	1,181
Maximum	EA.	1,495

Sliding, 40" x 31" high

	Unit	Total
Minimum	EA.	367.00
Average	EA.	551.25
Maximum	EA.	665.00

  52" x 39" high

	Unit	Total
Minimum	EA.	461.25
Average	EA.	661.25
Maximum	EA.	715.00

  64" x 72" high

	Unit	Total
Minimum	EA.	671.25
Average	EA.	1,055
Maximum	EA.	1,160

Awning windows
  34" x 21" high

	Unit	Total
Minimum	EA.	377.00
Average	EA.	431.25
Maximum	EA.	515.00

  40" x 21" high

	Unit	Total
Minimum	EA.	433.25
Average	EA.	491.25
Maximum	EA.	570.00

  48" x 27" high

	Unit	Total
Minimum	EA.	453.25
Average	EA.	551.25
Maximum	EA.	650.00

  60" x 36" high

	Unit	Total
Minimum	EA.	481.25
Average	EA.	825.00
Maximum	EA.	930.00

Window frame, milled

	Unit	Total
Minimum	L.F.	17.31
Average	L.F.	20.72
Maximum	L.F.	28.74

	Unit	Total

08710.10 HINGES

Hinges

3 x 3 butts, steel, interior, plain bearing	PAIR	20.75
4 x 4 butts, steel, standard	PAIR	30.50
5 x 4-1/2 butts, bronze/s. steel, heavy duty	PAIR	79.25

08710.20 LOCKSETS

Latchset, heavy duty

Cylindrical	EA.	225.50
Mortise	EA.	257.00

Lockset, heavy duty

Cylindrical	EA.	345.50
Mortise	EA.	407.00

Lockset

Privacy (bath or bedroom)	EA.	267.50
Entry lock	EA.	287.50

08710.30 CLOSERS

Door closers

Standard	EA.	311.25
Heavy duty	EA.	351.25

08710.40 DOOR TRIM

Panic device

Mortise	EA.	920.00
Vertical rod	EA.	1,290
Labeled, rim type	EA.	950.00
Mortise	EA.	1,190
Vertical rod	EA.	1,290

08710.60 WEATHERSTRIPPING

Weatherstrip, head and jamb, metal strip, neoprene bulb

Standard duty	L.F.	8.11
Heavy duty	L.F.	9.06

Spring type

Metal doors	EA.	194.50
Wood doors	EA.	244.50
Sponge type with adhesive backing	EA.	108.25

Thresholds

Bronze	L.F.	67.50

Aluminum

Plain	L.F.	52.75
Vinyl insert	L.F.	53.50
Aluminum with grit	L.F.	51.75

Steel

Plain	L.F.	44.00
Interlocking	L.F.	87.00

08810.10 GLAZING

Sheet glass, 1/8" thick	S.F.	11.20
Plate glass, bronze or grey, 1/4" thick	S.F.	16.97
Clear	S.F.	14.52
Polished	S.F.	16.22

Plexiglass

1/8" thick	S.F.	10.67
1/4" thick	S.F.	12.41

Float glass, clear

3/16" thick	S.F.	11.25
1/4" thick	S.F.	11.82
3/8" thick	S.F.	20.12

Tinted glass, polished plate, twin ground

3/16" thick	S.F.	13.50
1/4" thick	S.F.	13.97
3/8" thick	S.F.	21.12

	Unit	Total

08810.10 GLAZING (Cont.)

Insulating glass, two lites, clear float glass

1/2" thick	S.F.	22.50
5/8" thick	S.F.	26.25
3/4" thick	S.F.	31.00
7/8" thick	S.F.	34.00
1" thick	S.F.	42.25

Glass seal edge

3/8" thick	S.F.	20.50

Tinted glass

1/2" thick	S.F.	31.00
1" thick	S.F.	43.00

Tempered, clear

1" thick	S.F.	61.25

Plate mirror glass

1/4" thick

15 sf	S.F.	16.80
Over 15 sf	S.F.	15.40

08910.10 GLAZED CURTAIN WALLS

Curtain wall, aluminum system, framing sections

2" x 3"

Jamb	L.F.	19.00
Horizontal	L.F.	19.25
Mullion	L.F.	24.00

2" x 4"

Jamb	L.F.	26.62
Horizontal	L.F.	27.12
Mullion	L.F.	26.62

3" x 5-1/2"

Jamb	L.F.	32.62
Horizontal	L.F.	35.37
Mullion	L.F.	32.87
4" corner mullion	L.F.	43.50

Coping sections

1/8" x 8"	L.F.	45.00
1/8" x 9"	L.F.	45.25
1/8" x 12-1/2"	L.F.	48.25

Sill section

1/8" x 6"	L.F.	40.30
1/8" x 7"	L.F.	40.80
1/8" x 8-1/2"	L.F.	41.55

Column covers, aluminum

1/8" x 26"	L.F.	49.75
1/8" x 34"	L.F.	51.00
1/8" x 38"	L.F.	51.25

Doors

Aluminum framed, standard hardware

Narrow stile

2-6 x 7-0	EA.	980.00
3-0 x 7-0	EA.	990.00
3-6 x 7-0	EA.	1,010

	Unit	Total

09110.10 METAL STUDS

Studs, non load bearing, galvanized
2-1/2", 20 ga.

12" o.c.	S.F.	1.91
16" o.c.	S.F.	1.50

25 ga.

12" o.c.	S.F.	1.67
16" o.c.	S.F.	1.33
24" o.c.	S.F.	1.09

3-5/8", 20 ga.

12" o.c.	S.F.	2.28
16" o.c.	S.F.	1.80
24" o.c.	S.F.	1.45

25 ga.

12" o.c.	S.F.	1.99
16" o.c.	S.F.	1.60
24" o.c.	S.F.	1.30

4", 20 ga.

12" o.c.	S.F.	2.36
16" o.c.	S.F.	1.86
24" o.c.	S.F.	1.50

25 ga.

12" o.c.	S.F.	2.06
16" o.c.	S.F.	1.64
24" o.c.	S.F.	1.32

6", 20 ga.

12" o.c.	S.F.	2.98
16" o.c.	S.F.	2.30
24" o.c.	S.F.	1.91

25 ga.

12" o.c.	S.F.	2.56
16" o.c.	S.F.	2.04
24" o.c.	S.F.	1.65

Load bearing studs, galvanized
3-5/8", 16 ga.

12" o.c.	S.F.	2.97
16" o.c.	S.F.	2.57

18 ga.

12" o.c.	S.F.	2.06
16" o.c.	S.F.	2.35

4", 16 ga.

12" o.c.	S.F.	3.05
16" o.c.	S.F.	2.62

6", 16 ga.

12" o.c.	S.F.	3.86
16" o.c.	S.F.	3.29

Furring
On beams and columns

7/8" channel	L.F.	4.35
1-1/2" channel	L.F.	5.04

On ceilings
3/4" furring channels

12" o.c.	S.F.	2.77
16" o.c.	S.F.	2.59
24" o.c.	S.F.	2.25

1-1/2" furring channels

12" o.c.	S.F.	3.25
16" o.c.	S.F.	2.87
24" o.c.	S.F.	2.53

On walls
3/4" furring channels

12" o.c.	S.F.	2.30
16" o.c.	S.F.	2.09
24" o.c.	S.F.	1.90

	Unit	Total

09110.10 METAL STUDS (Cont.)

Furring
  On walls, 1-1/2" furring channels

12" o.c.	S.F.	2.69
16" o.c.	S.F.	2.40
24" o.c.	S.F.	2.12

09205.10 GYPSUM LATH

Gypsum lath, 1/2" thick

Clipped	S.Y.	10.36
Nailed	S.Y.	10.76

09205.20 METAL LATH

Diamond expanded, galvanized
  2.5 lb., on walls

Nailed	S.Y.	11.34
Wired	S.Y.	12.36

  On ceilings

Nailed	S.Y.	12.36
Wired	S.Y.	13.71

  3.4 lb., on walls

Nailed	S.Y.	12.85
Wired	S.Y.	13.87

  On ceilings

Nailed	S.Y.	13.87
Wired	S.Y.	15.22

Flat rib
  2.75 lb., on walls

Nailed	S.Y.	11.11
Wired	S.Y.	12.13

  On ceilings

Nailed	S.Y.	12.13
Wired	S.Y.	13.48

  3.4 lb., on walls

Nailed	S.Y.	11.92
Wired	S.Y.	12.94

  On ceilings

Nailed	S.Y.	12.94
Wired	S.Y.	14.29

Stucco lath

1.8 lb.	S.Y.	12.08
3.6 lb.	S.Y.	12.69

Paper backed

Minimum	S.Y.	9.55
Maximum	S.Y.	14.36

09205.60 PLASTER ACCESSORIES

Expansion joint, 3/4", 26 ga., galv.	L.F.	2.90
Plaster corner beads, 3/4", galvanized	L.F.	2.05
Casing bead, expanded flange, galvanized	L.F.	1.98
Expanded wing, 1-1/4" wide, galvanized	L.F.	2.08
Joint clips for lath	EA.	.46
Metal base, galvanized, 2-1/2" high	L.F.	2.66
Stud clips for gypsum lath	EA.	.46
Tie wire galvanized, 18 ga., 25 lb. hank	EA.	47.00
Sound deadening board, 1/4"	S.F.	1.27

09210.10 PLASTER

Gypsum plaster, trowel finish, 2 coats

Ceilings	S.Y.	23.32
Walls	S.Y.	22.32

  3 coats

Ceilings	S.Y.	32.46
Walls	S.Y.	29.96

	Unit	Total

09210.10 PLASTER (Cont.)

Vermiculite plaster
  2 coats
    Ceilings ....S.Y.   33.02
    Walls ....S.Y.   30.77
  3 coats
    Ceilings ....S.Y.   43.50
    Walls ....S.Y.   40.25
Keenes cement plaster
  2 coats
    Ceilings ....S.Y.   35.75
    Walls ....S.Y.   33.00
  3 coats
    Ceilings ....S.Y.   43.00
    Walls ....S.Y.   40.50
On columns, add to installation, 50% ....S.Y.   .00
Chases, fascia, and soffits, add to installation, 50% ...........................S.Y.   .00
Beams, add to installation, 50% ....S.Y.   .00
Patch holes, average size holes
  1 sf to 5 sf
    Minimum ....S.F.   11.33
    Average ....S.F.   12.98
    Maximum ....S.F.   15.73
  Over 5 sf
    Minimum ....S.F.   7.79
    Average ....S.F.   10.07
    Maximum ....S.F.   11.33
Patch cracks
    Minimum ....S.F.   4.25
    Average ....S.F.   5.14
    Maximum ....S.F.   7.79

09220.10 PORTLAND CEMENT PLASTER

Stucco, portland, gray, 3 coat, 1" thick
  Sand finish ....S.Y.   31.92
  Trowel finish ....S.Y.   33.17
  White cement
    Sand finish ....S.Y.   34.50
    Trowel finish ....S.Y.   36.75
Scratch coat
  For ceramic tile ....S.Y.   8.55
  For quarry tile ....S.Y.   8.55
Portland cement plaster
  2 coats, 1/2" ....S.Y.   16.93
  3 coats, 7/8" ....S.Y.   20.92

09250.10 GYPSUM BOARD

Drywall, plasterboard, 3/8" clipped to
  Metal furred ceiling ....S.F.   1.00
  Columns and beams ....S.F.   1.79
  Walls ....S.F.   .94
  Nailed or screwed to
    Wood or metal framed ceiling ....S.F.   .94
    Columns and beams ....S.F.   1.64
    Walls ....S.F.   .89
  1/2", clipped to
    Metal furred ceiling ....S.F.   1.01
    Columns and beams ....S.F.   1.77
    Walls ....S.F.   .92
  Nailed or screwed to
    Wood or metal framed ceiling ....S.F.   .92
    Columns and beams ....S.F.   1.62
    Walls ....S.F.   .87
  5/8", clipped to
    Metal furred ceiling ....S.F.   1.09
    Columns and beams ....S.F.   1.96

	Unit	Total

09250.10 GYPSUM BOARD (Cont.)

Drywall, plasterboard
  5/8", clipped to

Walls	S.F.	1.01

  Nailed or screwed to

Wood or metal framed ceiling	S.F.	1.09
Columns and beams	S.F.	1.96
Walls	S.F.	1.01

  Vinyl faced, clipped to metal studs

1/2"	S.F.	1.80
5/8"	S.F.	1.74

Add for

Fire resistant	S.F.	.11
Water resistant	S.F.	.18
Water and fire resistant	S.F.	.22

Taping and finishing joints

Minimum	S.F.	.42
Average	S.F.	.54
Maximum	S.F.	.67

Casing bead

Minimum	L.F.	1.78
Average	L.F.	2.06
Maximum	L.F.	3.06

Corner bead

Minimum	L.F.	1.79
Average	L.F.	2.11
Maximum	L.F.	3.10

09310.10 CERAMIC TILE

Glazed wall tile, 4-1/4" x 4-1/4"

Minimum	S.F.	6.20
Average	S.F.	8.21
Maximum	S.F.	18.69

  Base, 4-1/4" high

Minimum	L.F.	10.83
Average	L.F.	11.49
Maximum	L.F.	12.99

Unglazed floor tile
  Portland cem., cushion edge, face mtd

1" x 1"	S.F.	13.82
2" x 2"	S.F.	13.92
4" x 4"	S.F.	13.26

  Adhesive bed, with white grout

1" x 1"	S.F.	12.32
4" x 4"	S.F.	12.33

  Organic adhesive bed, thin set, back mounted

1" x 1"	S.F.	12.32
2" x 2"	S.F.	13.12

  For group 2 colors, add to material, 10%
  For group 3 colors, add to material, 20%
  For abrasive surface, add to material, 25%
Unglazed wall tile
  Organic adhesive, face mounted cushion edge
  1" x 1"

Minimum	S.F.	8.11
Average	S.F.	9.62
Maximum	S.F.	12.42

  2" x 2"

Minimum	S.F.	8.30
Average	S.F.	9.21
Maximum	S.F.	12.58

  Back mounted
  1" x 1"

Minimum	S.F.	8.11
Average	S.F.	9.62
Maximum	S.F.	12.42

	Unit	Total

09310.10 CERAMIC TILE (Cont.)

Unglazed wall tile
  Back mounted
    2" x 2"

	Unit	Total
Minimum	S.F.	8.30
Average	S.F.	9.21
Maximum	S.F.	12.58

For glazed finish, add to material, 25%
For glazed mosaic, add to material, 100%
For metallic colors, add to material, 125%
For exterior wall use, add to total, 25%
For exterior soffit, add to total, 25%
For portland cement bed, add to total, 25%
For dry set portland cement bed, add to total, 10%
Ceramic accessories
  Towel bar, 24" long

	Unit	Total
Minimum	EA.	38.00
Average	EA.	47.50
Maximum	EA.	90.25

Soap dish

	Unit	Total
Minimum	EA.	43.95
Average	EA.	55.75
Maximum	EA.	81.75

09330.10 QUARRY TILE

Floor

	Unit	Total
4 x 4 x 1/2"	S.F.	13.22
6 x 6 x 1/2"	S.F.	12.65
6 x 6 x 3/4"	S.F.	14.07

Wall, applied to 3/4" portland cement bed

	Unit	Total
4 x 4 x 1/2"	S.F.	15.37
6 x 6 x 3/4"	S.F.	14.23

Cove base

	Unit	Total
5 x 6 x 1/2" straight top	L.F.	15.11
6 x 6 x 3/4" round top	L.F.	14.69
Stair treads 6 x 6 x 3/4"	L.F.	21.79
Window sill 6 x 8 x 3/4"	L.F.	18.31

For abrasive surface, add to material, 25%

09410.10 TERRAZZO

Floors on concrete, 1-3/4" thick, 5/8" topping

	Unit	Total
Gray cement	S.F.	11.83
White cement	S.F.	12.21

Sand cushion, 3" thick, 5/8" top, 1/4"

	Unit	Total
Gray cement	S.F.	13.85
White cement	S.F.	14.41
Monolithic terrazzo, 3-1/2" base slab, 5/8" topping	S.F.	10.61
Terrazzo wainscot, cast-in-place, 1/2" thick	S.F.	20.73
Base, cast in place, terrazzo cove type, 6" high	L.F.	16.46
Curb, cast in place, 6" wide x 6" high, polished top	L.F.	36.35

For venetian type terrazzo, add to material, 10%
For abrasive heavy duty terrazzo, add to material, 15%
Divider strips

	Unit	Total
Zinc	L.F.	1.51
Brass	L.F.	2.80

Stairs, cast-in-place, topping on concrete or metal

	Unit	Total
1-1/2" thick treads, 12" wide	L.F.	32.41
Combined tread and riser	L.F.	75.37

Precast terrazzo, thin set
  Terrazzo tiles, non-slip surface

	Unit	Total
9" x 9" x 1" thick	S.F.	26.34

12" x 12"

	Unit	Total
1" thick	S.F.	27.33
1-1/2" thick	S.F.	28.59
18" x 18" x 1-1/2" thick	S.F.	35.09
24" x 24" x 1-1/2" thick	S.F.	41.75

	Unit	Total

09410.10 TERRAZZO (Cont.)

Precast terrazzo, thin set
  Terrazzo tiles, non-slip surface
    For white cement, add to material, 10%
    For venetian type terrazzo, add to material, 25%

	Unit	Total
Terrazzo wainscot		
12" x 12" x 1" thick	S.F.	22.55
18" x 18" x 1-1/2" thick	S.F.	30.50
Base		
6" high		
Straight	L.F.	17.34
Coved	L.F.	19.84
8" high		
Straight	L.F.	19.43
Coved	L.F.	21.93
Terrazzo curbs		
8" wide x 8" high	L.F.	56.00
6" wide x 6" high	L.F.	49.00
Precast terrazzo stair treads, 12" wide		
1-1/2" thick		
Diamond pattern	L.F.	51.41
Non-slip surface	L.F.	53.66
2" thick		
Diamond pattern	L.F.	53.66
Non-slip surface	L.F.	56.75
Stair risers, 1" thick to 6" high		
Straight sections	L.F.	19.31
Cove sections	L.F.	21.81
Combined tread and riser		
Straight sections		
1-1/2" tread, 3/4" riser	L.F.	75.75
3" tread, 1" riser	L.F.	87.50
Curved sections		
2" tread, 1" riser	L.F.	95.00
3" tread, 1" riser	L.F.	97.50
Stair stringers, notched for treads and risers		
1" thick	L.F.	49.75
2" thick	L.F.	55.50
Landings, structural, nonslip		
1-1/2" thick	S.F.	43.35
3" thick	S.F.	58.50

09510.10 CEILINGS AND WALLS

Acoustical panels, suspension system not included
  Fiberglass panels

	Unit	Total
5/8" thick		
2' x 2'	S.F.	2.26
2' x 4'	S.F.	1.84
3/4" thick		
2' x 2'	S.F.	2.75
2' x 4'	S.F.	2.51
Glass cloth faced fiberglass panels		
3/4" thick	S.F.	3.71
1" thick	S.F.	4.02
Mineral fiber panels		
5/8" thick		
2' x 2'	S.F.	2.04
2' x 4'	S.F.	1.86
3/4" thick		
2' x 2'	S.F.	2.75
2' x 4'	S.F.	2.51
Wood fiber panels		
1/2" thick		
2' x 2'	S.F.	2.49
2' x 4'	S.F.	2.31

	Unit	Total

09510.10 CEILINGS AND WALLS (Cont.)

Wood fiber panels, 5/8" thick

	Unit	Total
2' x 2'	S.F.	2.75
2' x 4'	S.F.	2.57

Acoustical tiles, suspension system not included

Fiberglass tile, 12" x 12"

	Unit	Total
5/8" thick	S.F.	2.44
3/4" thick	S.F.	2.89

Glass cloth faced fiberglass tile

	Unit	Total
3/4" thick	S.F.	4.51
3" thick	S.F.	5.05

Mineral fiber tile, 12" x 12"

5/8" thick

	Unit	Total
Standard	S.F.	2.05
Vinyl faced	S.F.	2.96

3/4" thick

	Unit	Total
Standard	S.F.	2.47
Vinyl faced	S.F.	3.46

Ceiling suspension systems

T bar system

	Unit	Total
2' x 4'	S.F.	1.73
2' x 2'	S.F.	1.88
Concealed Z bar suspension system, 12" module	S.F.	2.03
For 1-1/2" carrier channels, 4' o.c., add	S.F.	.38
Carrier channel for recessed light fixtures	S.F.	.69

09550.10 WOOD FLOORING

Wood strip flooring, unfinished

Fir floor

C and better

	Unit	Total
Vertical grain	S.F.	5.42
Flat grain	S.F.	5.22

Oak floor

	Unit	Total
Minimum	S.F.	6.43
Average	S.F.	7.84
Maximum	S.F.	10.13

Maple floor

25/32" x 2-1/4"

	Unit	Total
Minimum	S.F.	6.53
Maximum	S.F.	8.29

33/32" x 3-1/4"

	Unit	Total
Minimum	S.F.	8.83
Maximum	S.F.	9.63

Added costs

For factory finish, add to material, 10%

For random width floor, add to total, 20%

For simulated pegs, add to total, 10%

Wood block industrial flooring

Creosoted

	Unit	Total
2" thick	S.F.	6.10
2-1/2" thick	S.F.	6.56
3" thick	S.F.	6.86

Parquet, 5/16", white oak

	Unit	Total
Finished	S.F.	11.98
Unfinished	S.F.	7.25
Gym floor, 2 ply felt, 25/32" maple, finished, in mastic	S.F.	10.92
Over wood sleepers	S.F.	12.25
Finishing, sand, fill, finish, and wax	S.F.	2.08
Refinish sand, seal, and 2 coats of polyurethane	S.F.	3.06
Clean and wax floors	S.F.	.52

	Unit	Total

09630.10 UNIT MASONRY FLOORING

Clay brick
  9 x 4-1/2 x 3" thick

	Unit	Total
Glazed	S.F.	12.78
Unglazed	S.F.	12.45

  8 x 4 x 3/4" thick

	Unit	Total
Glazed	S.F.	12.21
Unglazed	S.F.	12.81

For herringbone pattern, add to labor, 15%

09660.10 RESILIENT TILE FLOORING

Solid vinyl tile, 1/8" thick, 12" x 12"

	Unit	Total
Marble patterns	S.F.	6.32
Solid colors	S.F.	7.77
Travertine patterns	S.F.	8.56

Conductive resilient flooring, vinyl tile

	Unit	Total
1/8" thick, 12" x 12"	S.F.	8.34

09665.10 RESILIENT SHEET FLOORING

Vinyl sheet flooring

	Unit	Total
Minimum	S.F.	4.60
Average	S.F.	7.18
Maximum	S.F.	11.95
Cove, to 6"	L.F.	3.54

Fluid applied resilient flooring

	Unit	Total
Polyurethane, poured in place, 3/8" thick	S.F.	15.25

Vinyl sheet goods, backed

	Unit	Total
0.070" thick	S.F.	4.81
0.093" thick	S.F.	7.06
0.125" thick	S.F.	8.04
0.250" thick	S.F.	9.14

09678.10 RESILIENT BASE AND ACCESSORIES

Wall base, vinyl

	Unit	Total
4" high	L.F.	3.12
6" high	L.F.	3.57

09682.10 CARPET PADDING

Carpet padding

	Unit	Total
Foam rubber, waffle type, 0.3" thick	S.Y.	8.72

Jute padding

	Unit	Total
Minimum	S.Y.	6.57
Average	S.Y.	8.04
Maximum	S.Y.	10.96

Sponge rubber cushion

	Unit	Total
Minimum	S.Y.	7.30
Average	S.Y.	9.14
Maximum	S.Y.	12.06

Urethane cushion, 3/8" thick

	Unit	Total
Minimum	S.Y.	7.30
Average	S.Y.	8.35
Maximum	S.Y.	10.34

09685.10 CARPET

Carpet, acrylic

	Unit	Total
24 oz., light traffic	S.Y.	22.33
28 oz., medium traffic	S.Y.	25.58

Nylon

	Unit	Total
15 oz., light traffic	S.Y.	28.83
28 oz., medium traffic	S.Y.	35.33

Nylon

	Unit	Total
28 oz., medium traffic	S.Y.	34.08
35 oz., heavy traffic	S.Y.	40.33

Wool

	Unit	Total
30 oz., medium traffic	S.Y.	52.33
36 oz., medium traffic	S.Y.	54.83

	Unit	Total

09685.10 CARPET (Cont.)

42 oz., heavy traffic	S.Y.	70.58
Carpet tile		
Foam backed		
Minimum	S.F.	4.85
Average	S.F.	5.56
Maximum	S.F.	8.22
Tufted loop or shag		
Minimum	S.F.	5.15
Average	S.F.	6.11
Maximum	S.F.	9.21
Clean and vacuum carpet		
Minimum	S.Y.	.58
Average	S.Y.	.94
Maximum	S.Y.	1.34

09905.10 PAINTING PREPARATION

Dropcloths		
Minimum	S.F.	.06
Average	S.F.	.10
Maximum	S.F.	.12
Masking		
Paper and tape		
Minimum	L.F.	.50
Average	L.F.	.63
Maximum	L.F.	.84
Doors		
Minimum	EA.	6.00
Average	EA.	7.99
Maximum	EA.	10.57
Windows		
Minimum	EA.	6.00
Average	EA.	7.99
Maximum	EA.	10.57
Sanding		
Walls and flat surfaces		
Minimum	S.F.	.32
Average	S.F.	.40
Maximum	S.F.	.48
Doors and windows		
Minimum	EA.	7.93
Average	EA.	12.00
Maximum	EA.	15.75
Trim		
Minimum	L.F.	.60
Average	L.F.	.79
Maximum	L.F.	1.06
Puttying		
Minimum	S.F.	.74
Average	S.F.	.97
Maximum	S.F.	1.22

09910.05 EXT. PAINTING, SITEWORK

Concrete Block		
Roller		
First Coat		
Minimum	S.F.	.41
Average	S.F.	.49
Maximum	S.F.	.65
Second Coat		
Minimum	S.F.	.37
Average	S.F.	.43
Maximum	S.F.	.57
Spray		
First Coat		
Minimum	S.F.	.27

	Unit	Total

09910.05 EXT. PAINTING, SITEWORK (Cont.)

Concrete Block
  Spray, First Coat

	Unit	Total
Average	S.F.	.30
Maximum	S.F.	.32

  Second Coat

	Unit	Total
Minimum	S.F.	.22
Average	S.F.	.25
Maximum	S.F.	.29

Fences, Chain Link
  Roller
   First Coat

	Unit	Total
Minimum	S.F.	.45
Average	S.F.	.51
Maximum	S.F.	.56

   Second Coat

	Unit	Total
Minimum	S.F.	.31
Average	S.F.	.35
Maximum	S.F.	.41

  Spray
   First Coat

	Unit	Total
Minimum	S.F.	.24
Average	S.F.	.26
Maximum	S.F.	.29

   Second Coat

	Unit	Total
Minimum	S.F.	.20
Average	S.F.	.22
Maximum	S.F.	.24

Fences, Wood or Masonry
  Brush
   First Coat

	Unit	Total
Minimum	S.F.	.67
Average	S.F.	.77
Maximum	S.F.	.96

   Second Coat

	Unit	Total
Minimum	S.F.	.47
Average	S.F.	.54
Maximum	S.F.	.65

  Roller
   First Coat

	Unit	Total
Minimum	S.F.	.43
Average	S.F.	.49
Maximum	S.F.	.54

   Second Coat

	Unit	Total
Minimum	S.F.	.35
Average	S.F.	.40
Maximum	S.F.	.47

  Spray
   First Coat

	Unit	Total
Minimum	S.F.	.31
Average	S.F.	.36
Maximum	S.F.	.44

   Second Coat

	Unit	Total
Minimum	S.F.	.26
Average	S.F.	.29
Maximum	S.F.	.34

	Unit	Total

09910.15 EXT. PAINTING, BUILDINGS

Decks, Wood, Stained
  Brush
    First Coat
      Minimum .... S.F. .38
      Average .... S.F. .40
      Maximum .... S.F. .44
    Second Coat
      Minimum .... S.F. .31
      Average .... S.F. .32
      Maximum .... S.F. .34
  Roller
    First Coat
      Minimum .... S.F. .31
      Average .... S.F. .32
      Maximum .... S.F. .34
    Second Coat
      Minimum .... S.F. .29
      Average .... S.F. .30
      Maximum .... S.F. .32
  Spray
    First Coat
      Minimum .... S.F. .26
      Average .... S.F. .27
      Maximum .... S.F. .29
    Second Coat
      Minimum .... S.F. .24
      Average .... S.F. .25
      Maximum .... S.F. .27
Doors, Wood
  Brush
    First Coat
      Minimum .... S.F. .87
      Average .... S.F. 1.09
      Maximum .... S.F. 1.33
    Second Coat
      Minimum .... S.F. .74
      Average .... S.F. .82
      Maximum .... S.F. .93
  Roller
    First Coat
      Minimum .... S.F. .46
      Average .... S.F. .54
      Maximum .... S.F. .74
    Second Coat
      Minimum .... S.F. .38
      Average .... S.F. .40
      Maximum .... S.F. .54
  Spray
    First Coat
      Minimum .... S.F. .26
      Average .... S.F. .29
      Maximum .... S.F. .35
    Second Coat
      Minimum .... S.F. .23
      Average .... S.F. .25
      Maximum .... S.F. .27
Gutters and Downspouts
  Brush
    First Coat
      Minimum .... L.F. .77
      Average .... L.F. .85
      Maximum .... L.F. .96
    Second Coat
      Minimum .... L.F. .57
      Average .... L.F. .65

	Unit	Total

09910.15 EXT. PAINTING, BUILDINGS (Cont.)

Gutters and Downspouts
  Brush, Second Coat

	Unit	Total
Maximum	L.F.	.77

Siding, Wood
  Roller
    First Coat

	Unit	Total
Minimum	S.F.	.28
Average	S.F.	.31
Maximum	S.F.	.33

    Second Coat

	Unit	Total
Minimum	S.F.	.31
Average	S.F.	.33
Maximum	S.F.	.35

  Spray
    First Coat

	Unit	Total
Minimum	S.F.	.27
Average	S.F.	.28
Maximum	S.F.	.29

    Second Coat

	Unit	Total
Minimum	S.F.	.23
Average	S.F.	.27
Maximum	S.F.	.35

Stucco
  Roller
    First Coat

	Unit	Total
Minimum	S.F.	.39
Average	S.F.	.42
Maximum	S.F.	.47

    Second Coat

	Unit	Total
Minimum	S.F.	.35
Average	S.F.	.37
Maximum	S.F.	.41

  Spray
    First Coat

	Unit	Total
Minimum	S.F.	.29
Average	S.F.	.31
Maximum	S.F.	.34

    Second Coat

	Unit	Total
Minimum	S.F.	.26
Average	S.F.	.28
Maximum	S.F.	.30

Trim
  Brush
    First Coat

	Unit	Total
Minimum	L.F.	.37
Average	L.F.	.41
Maximum	L.F.	.47

    Second Coat

	Unit	Total
Minimum	L.F.	.32
Average	L.F.	.37
Maximum	L.F.	.47

Walls
  Roller
    First Coat

	Unit	Total
Minimum	S.F.	.31
Average	S.F.	.32
Maximum	S.F.	.33

    Second Coat

	Unit	Total
Minimum	S.F.	.29
Average	S.F.	.30
Maximum	S.F.	.32

  Spray
    First Coat

	Unit	Total
Minimum	S.F.	.17
Average	S.F.	.20

	Unit	Total

09910.15 EXT. PAINTING, BUILDINGS (Cont.)

Walls
  Spray, First Coat

	Unit	Total
Maximum	S.F.	.22

  Second Coat

	Unit	Total
Minimum	S.F.	.16
Average	S.F.	.18
Maximum	S.F.	.21

Windows
  Brush
   First Coat

	Unit	Total
Minimum	S.F.	.90
Average	S.F.	1.06
Maximum	S.F.	1.30

   Second Coat

	Unit	Total
Minimum	S.F.	.79
Average	S.F.	.90
Maximum	S.F.	1.06

09910.25 EXT. PAINTING, MISC.

Shakes
  Spray
   First Coat

	Unit	Total
Minimum	S.F.	.33
Average	S.F.	.35
Maximum	S.F.	.37

   Second Coat

	Unit	Total
Minimum	S.F.	.31
Average	S.F.	.33
Maximum	S.F.	.35

Shingles, Wood
  Roller
   First Coat

	Unit	Total
Minimum	S.F.	.40
Average	S.F.	.44
Maximum	S.F.	.48

   Second Coat

	Unit	Total
Minimum	S.F.	.32
Average	S.F.	.34
Maximum	S.F.	.36

  Spray
   First Coat

	Unit	Total
Minimum	L.F.	.29
Average	L.F.	.31
Maximum	L.F.	.33

   Second Coat

	Unit	Total
Minimum	L.F.	.25
Average	L.F.	.26
Maximum	L.F.	.27

Shutters and Louvres
  Brush
   First Coat

	Unit	Total
Minimum	EA.	9.69
Average	EA.	12.17
Maximum	EA.	15.92

   Second Coat

	Unit	Total
Minimum	EA.	6.12
Average	EA.	7.49
Maximum	EA.	9.69

  Spray
   First Coat

	Unit	Total
Minimum	EA.	3.30
Average	EA.	3.94
Maximum	EA.	4.89

   Second Coat

	Unit	Total
Minimum	EA.	2.51

	Unit	Total

09910.25 EXT. PAINTING, MISC. (Cont.)

Shutters and Louvres
Spray

		Unit	Total
Average		EA.	3.30
Maximum		EA.	3.94

Stairs, metal
Brush
First Coat

	Unit	Total
Minimum	S.F.	.70
Average	S.F.	.77
Maximum	S.F.	.85

Second Coat

	Unit	Total
Minimum	S.F.	.47
Average	S.F.	.51
Maximum	S.F.	.57

Spray
First Coat

	Unit	Total
Minimum	S.F.	.39
Average	S.F.	.47
Maximum	S.F.	.50

Second Coat

	Unit	Total
Minimum	S.F.	.33
Average	S.F.	.37
Maximum	S.F.	.43

09910.35 INT. PAINTING, BUILDINGS

Acoustical Ceiling
Roller
First Coat

	Unit	Total
Minimum	S.F.	.47
Average	S.F.	.57
Maximum	S.F.	.77

Second Coat

	Unit	Total
Minimum	S.F.	.41
Average	S.F.	.47
Maximum	S.F.	.57

Spray
First Coat

	Unit	Total
Minimum	S.F.	.27
Average	S.F.	.30
Maximum	S.F.	.34

Second Coat

	Unit	Total
Minimum	S.F.	.25
Average	S.F.	.26
Maximum	S.F.	.28

Cabinets and Casework
Brush
First Coat

	Unit	Total
Minimum	S.F.	.65
Average	S.F.	.70
Maximum	S.F.	.77

Second Coat

	Unit	Total
Minimum	S.F.	.57
Average	S.F.	.60
Maximum	S.F.	.65

Spray
First Coat

	Unit	Total
Minimum	S.F.	.38
Average	S.F.	.42
Maximum	S.F.	.48

Second Coat

	Unit	Total
Minimum	S.F.	.33
Average	S.F.	.35
Maximum	S.F.	.40

	Unit	Total

09910.35 INT. PAINTING, BUILDINGS (Cont.)

Ceilings
  Roller
    First Coat

	Unit	Total
Minimum	S.F.	.34
Average	S.F.	.36
Maximum	S.F.	.38

    Second Coat

	Unit	Total
Minimum	S.F.	.30
Average	S.F.	.32
Maximum	S.F.	.34

  Spray
    First Coat

	Unit	Total
Minimum	S.F.	.23
Average	S.F.	.24
Maximum	S.F.	.26

    Second Coat

	Unit	Total
Minimum	S.F.	.20
Average	S.F.	.21
Maximum	S.F.	.23

Doors, Wood
  Brush
    First Coat

	Unit	Total
Minimum	S.F.	.85
Average	S.F.	1.04
Maximum	S.F.	1.23

    Second Coat

	Unit	Total
Minimum	S.F.	.66
Average	S.F.	.73
Maximum	S.F.	.81

  Spray
    First Coat

	Unit	Total
Minimum	S.F.	.27
Average	S.F.	.30
Maximum	S.F.	.35

    Second Coat

	Unit	Total
Minimum	S.F.	.24
Average	S.F.	.26
Maximum	S.F.	.28

Trim
  Brush
    First Coat

	Unit	Total
Minimum	L.F.	.36
Average	L.F.	.39
Maximum	L.F.	.43

    Second Coat

	Unit	Total
Minimum	L.F.	.31
Average	L.F.	.35
Maximum	L.F.	.43

Walls
  Roller
    First Coat

	Unit	Total
Minimum	S.F.	.31
Average	S.F.	.32
Maximum	S.F.	.34

    Second Coat

	Unit	Total
Minimum	S.F.	.29
Average	S.F.	.30
Maximum	S.F.	.32

  Spray
    First Coat

	Unit	Total
Minimum	S.F.	.18
Average	S.F.	.20
Maximum	S.F.	.23

    Second Coat

	Unit	Total
Minimum	S.F.	.18

	Unit	Total

09910.35 INT. PAINTING, BUILDINGS (Cont.)

Walls
  Spray, Second Coat

Average	S.F.	.19
Maximum	S.F.	.22

09955.10 WALL COVERING

Vinyl wall covering

Medium duty	S.F.	1.54
Heavy duty	S.F.	2.56

Over pipes and irregular shapes

Lightweight, 13 oz.	S.F.	2.44
Medium weight, 25 oz.	S.F.	2.83
Heavy weight, 34 oz.	S.F.	3.36

Cork wall covering
  1' x 1' squares

1/4" thick	S.F.	5.82
1/2" thick	S.F.	7.08
3/4" thick	S.F.	7.83

Wall fabrics
  Natural fabrics, grass cloths

Minimum	S.F.	2.22
Average	S.F.	2.45
Maximum	S.F.	6.50
Flexible gypsum coated wall fabric, fire resistant	S.F.	2.15

Vinyl corner guards

3/4" x 3/4" x 8'	EA.	13.79
2-3/4" x 2-3/4" x 4'	EA.	10.58

09980.15 PAINT

Paint, enamel

600 sf per gal.	GAL	51.50
550 sf per gal.	GAL	48.00
500 sf per gal.	GAL	34.25
450 sf per gal.	GAL	32.00
350 sf per gal.	GAL	31.00
Filler, 60 sf per gal.	GAL	36.50
Latex, 400 sf per gal.	GAL	34.25

Aluminum

400 sf per gal.	GAL	45.75
500 sf per gal.	GAL	73.25
Red lead, 350 sf per gal.	GAL	64.00

Primer

400 sf per gal.	GAL	31.00
300 sf per gal.	GAL	31.00
Latex base, interior, white	GAL	34.25

Sealer and varnish

400 sf per gal.	GAL	32.00
425 sf per gal.	GAL	45.75
600 sf per gal.	GAL	59.50

	Unit	Total
10185.10 SHOWER STALLS		
Shower receptors		
Precast, terrazzo		
32" x 32"	EA.	662.25
32" x 48"	EA.	712.50
Concrete		
32" x 32"	EA.	302.25
48" x 48"	EA.	349.50
Shower door, trim and hardware		
Economy, 24" wide, chrome, tempered glass	EA.	342.50
Porcelain enameled steel, flush	EA.	562.50
Baked enameled steel, flush	EA.	362.50
Aluminum, tempered glass, 48" wide, sliding	EA.	698.25
Folding	EA.	668.25
Aluminum and tempered glass, molded plastic		
Complete with receptor and door		
32" x 32"	EA.	910.00
36" x 36"	EA.	1,010
40" x 40"	EA.	1,060
10210.10 VENTS AND WALL LOUVERS		
Block vent, 8"x16"x4" alum., w/screen, mill finish	EA.	171.00
Standard	EA.	104.75
Vents w/screen, 4" deep, 8" wide, 5" high		
Modular	EA.	118.25
Aluminum gable louvers	S.F.	28.50
Vent screen aluminum, 4" wide, continuous	L.F.	7.35
10290.10 PEST CONTROL		
Termite control		
Under slab spraying		
Minimum	S.F.	1.25
Average	S.F.	1.36
Maximum	S.F.	2.11
10350.10 FLAGPOLES		
Installed in concrete base		
Fiberglass		
25' high	EA.	1,780
50' high	EA.	4,700
Aluminum		
25' high	EA.	1,780
50' high	EA.	3,700
Bonderized steel		
25' high	EA.	1,990
50' high	EA.	4,250
Freestanding tapered, fiberglass		
30' high	EA.	2,110
40' high	EA.	2,720
10800.10 BATH ACCESSORIES		
Grab bar, 1-1/2" dia., stainless steel, wall mounted		
24" long	EA.	74.50
36" long	EA.	81.75
1" dia., stainless steel		
12" long	EA.	53.50
24" long	EA.	67.50
36" long	EA.	83.50
Medicine cabinet, 16 x 22, baked enamel, lighted	EA.	152.75
With mirror, lighted	EA.	228.00
Mirror, 1/4" plate glass, up to 10 sf	S.F.	15.70
Mirror, stainless steel frame		
18"x24"	EA.	96.00
18"x32"	EA.	111.00
24"x30"	EA.	122.50

	Unit	Total

10800.10 BATH ACCESSORIES (Cont.)

Mirror, stainless steel frame		
24"x60"	EA.	407.00
Soap dish, stainless steel, wall mounted	EA.	168.00
Toilet tissue dispenser, stainless, wall mounted		
Single roll	EA.	78.75
Towel bar, stainless steel		
18" long	EA.	102.00
24" long	EA.	136.00
30" long	EA.	138.50
36" long	EA.	151.75
Toothbrush and tumbler holder	EA.	69.25

	Unit	Total
11010.10 MAINTENANCE EQUIPMENT		
Vacuum cleaning system		
3 valves		
1.5 hp	EA.	1,570
2.5 hp	EA.	1,960
5 valves	EA.	2,900
7 valves	EA.	3,750
11450.10 RESIDENTIAL EQUIPMENT		
Compactor, 4 to 1 compaction	EA.	1,500
Dishwasher, built-in		
2 cycles	EA.	960.00
4 or more cycles	EA.	2,090
Disposal		
Garbage disposer	EA.	370.00
Heaters, electric, built-in		
Ceiling type	EA.	570.00
Wall type		
Minimum	EA.	340.00
Maximum	EA.	860.00
Hood for range, 2-speed, vented		
30" wide	EA.	720.00
42" wide	EA.	1,170
Ice maker, automatic		
30 lb per day	EA.	1,883
50 lb per day	EA.	2,540
Folding access stairs, disappearing metal stair		
8' long	EA.	1,023
11' long	EA.	1,063
12' long	EA.	1,133
Wood frame, wood stair		
22" x 54" x 8'9" long	EA.	238.00
25" x 54" x 10' long	EA.	278.00
Ranges electric		
Built-in, 30", 1 oven	EA.	2,140
2 oven	EA.	2,440
Counter top, 4 burner, standard	EA.	1,300
With grill	EA.	3,000
Free standing, 21", 1 oven	EA.	1,190
30", 1 oven	EA.	2,120
2 oven	EA.	3,370
Water softener		
30 grains per gallon	EA.	1,290
70 grains per gallon	EA.	1,690

	Unit	Total

12302.10 CASEWORK

Kitchen base cabinet, standard, 24" deep, 35" high

	Unit	Total
12"wide	EA.	257.00
18" wide	EA.	287.00
24" wide	EA.	363.25
27" wide	EA.	393.25
36" wide	EA.	471.25
48" wide	EA.	551.25

Drawer base, 24" deep, 35" high

	Unit	Total
15"wide	EA.	307.00
18" wide	EA.	327.00
24" wide	EA.	493.25
27" wide	EA.	553.25
30" wide	EA.	633.25

Sink-ready, base cabinet

	Unit	Total
30" wide	EA.	333.25
36" wide	EA.	343.25
42" wide	EA.	373.25
60" wide	EA.	431.25
Corner cabinet, 36" wide	EA.	571.25

Wall cabinet, 12" deep, 12" high

	Unit	Total
30" wide	EA.	307.00
36" wide	EA.	327.00

15" high

	Unit	Total
30" wide	EA.	363.25
36" wide	EA.	513.25

24" high

	Unit	Total
30" wide	EA.	393.25
36" wide	EA.	403.25

30" high

	Unit	Total
12" wide	EA.	261.25
18" wide	EA.	291.25
24" wide	EA.	311.25
27" wide	EA.	351.25
30" wide	EA.	391.25
36" wide	EA.	401.25

Corner cabinet, 30" high

	Unit	Total
24" wide	EA.	445.00
30" wide	EA.	515.00
36" wide	EA.	555.00
Wardrobe	EA.	1,070

Vanity with top, laminated plastic

	Unit	Total
24" wide	EA.	910.00
30" wide	EA.	1,000
36" wide	EA.	1,180
48" wide	EA.	1,330

12390.10 COUNTER TOPS

	Unit	Total
Stainless steel, counter top, with backsplash	S.F.	254.25
Acid-proof, kemrock surface	S.F.	105.24

12500.10 WINDOW TREATMENT

Drapery tracks, wall or ceiling mounted

Basic traverse rod

	Unit	Total
50 to 90"	EA.	79.50
84 to 156"	EA.	100.00
136 to 250"	EA.	130.75
165 to 312"	EA.	185.50

Traverse rod with stationary curtain rod

	Unit	Total
30 to 50"	EA.	105.50
50 to 90"	EA.	116.50
84 to 156"	EA.	151.75
136 to 250"	EA.	185.50

Double traverse rod

	Unit	Total
30 to 50"	EA.	118.75

	Unit	Total

12500.10 WINDOW TREATMENT (Cont.)

Drapery tracks, wall or ceiling mounted, double traverse rod

	Unit	Total
50 to 84"	EA.	148.50
84 to 156"	EA.	151.75
136 to 250"	EA.	195.50

12510.10 BLINDS

Venetian blinds

	Unit	Total
2" slats	S.F.	37.42
1" slats	S.F.	39.92

	Unit	Total

13056.10 VAULTS

Floor safes
1.0 cf	EA.	897.50
1.3 cf	EA.	1,011

13121.10 PRE-ENGINEERED BUILDINGS

Pre-engineered metal building, 40'x100'
14' eave height	S.F.	12.42
16' eave height	S.F.	14.18

13200.10 STORAGE TANKS

Oil storage tank, underground, single wall, no excv.
Steel
500 gals	EA.	3,860
1,000 gals	EA.	5,260

Fiberglass, double wall
550 gals	EA.	10,410
1,000 gals	EA.	13,310

Above ground
Steel, single wall
275 gals	EA.	2,250
500 gals	EA.	5,460
1,000 gals	EA.	7,390
Fill cap	EA.	182.50
Vent cap	EA.	182.50
Level indicator	EA.	252.50

	Unit	Total

14410.10 PERSONNEL LIFTS

Electrically operated, 1 or 2 person lift
 With attached foot platforms
  3 stops .... EA.   10,400
Residential stair climber, per story .... EA.   5,380

	Unit	Total

15100.10 SPECIALTIES

Wall penetration
Concrete wall, 6" thick

2" dia.	EA.	15.00
4" dia.	EA.	22.25

12" thick

2" dia.	EA.	20.25
4" dia.	EA.	32.00

15120.10 BACKFLOW PREVENTERS

Backflow preventer, flanged, cast iron, with valves

3" pipe	EA.	3,960
4" pipe	EA.	5,050

Threaded

3/4" pipe	EA.	789.00
2" pipe	EA.	1,363

15140.11 PIPE HANGERS, LIGHT

A band, black iron

1/2"	EA.	5.47
1"	EA.	5.71
1-1/4"	EA.	6.01
1-1/2"	EA.	6.46
2"	EA.	7.01
2-1/2"	EA.	8.24
3"	EA.	9.36
4"	EA.	10.99

Copper

1/2"	EA.	6.10
3/4"	EA.	6.52
1"	EA.	6.52
1-1/4"	EA.	6.83
1-1/2"	EA.	7.39
2"	EA.	8.00
2-1/2"	EA.	10.91
3"	EA.	11.80
4"	EA.	13.17

2 hole clips, galvanized

3/4"	EA.	4.43
1"	EA.	4.61
1-1/4"	EA.	4.85
1-1/2"	EA.	5.10
2"	EA.	5.43
2-1/2"	EA.	6.11
3"	EA.	6.83
4"	EA.	9.15

Perforated strap
3/4"

Galvanized, 20 ga.	L.F.	3.56
Copper, 22 ga.	L.F.	3.80

J-Hooks

1/2"	EA.	3.61
3/4"	EA.	3.66
1"	EA.	3.83
1-1/4"	EA.	3.94
1-1/2"	EA.	4.04
2"	EA.	4.08
3"	EA.	4.38
4"	EA.	4.47

PVC coated hangers, galvanized, 28 ga.

1-1/2" x 12"	EA.	5.43
2" x 12"	EA.	5.85
3" x 12"	EA.	6.35
4" x 12"	EA.	6.91

	Unit	Total

15140.11 PIPE HANGERS, LIGHT (Cont.)

PVC coated hangers, copper, 30 ga.

1-1/2" x 12"	EA.	6.11
2" x 12"	EA.	6.77
3" x 12"	EA.	7.35
4" x 12"	EA.	7.99

Wire hook hangers
Black wire, 1/2" x

4"	EA.	3.56
6"	EA.	3.79

Copper wire hooks
1/2" x

4"	EA.	3.69
6"	EA.	3.93

15240.10 VIBRATION CONTROL

Vibration isolator, in-line, stainless connector

1/2"	EA.	128.00
3/4"	EA.	146.75
1"	EA.	149.00
1-1/4"	EA.	191.75
1-1/2"	EA.	214.75
2"	EA.	258.00
2-1/2"	EA.	362.25
3"	EA.	416.75
4"	EA.	522.50

15290.10 DUCTWORK INSULATION

Fiberglass duct insulation, plain blanket

1-1/2" thick	S.F.	.99
2" thick	S.F.	1.32

With vapor barrier

1-1/2" thick	S.F.	1.02
2" thick	S.F.	1.35

Rigid with vapor barrier

2" thick	S.F.	3.41

15410.05 C.I. PIPE, ABOVE GROUND

No hub pipe

1-1/2" pipe	L.F.	12.32
2" pipe	L.F.	12.16
3" pipe	L.F.	15.87
4" pipe	L.F.	23.00

No hub fittings, 1-1/2" pipe

1/4 bend	EA.	29.20
1/8 bend	EA.	27.82
Sanitary tee	EA.	43.00
Sanitary cross	EA.	47.00
Plug	EA.	4.66
Coupling	EA.	16.75
Wye	EA.	46.00
Tapped tee	EA.	36.25
P-trap	EA.	34.00
Tapped cross	EA.	38.25

2" pipe

1/4 bend	EA.	34.77
1/8 bend	EA.	32.88
Sanitary tee	EA.	55.00
Sanitary cross	EA.	64.25
Plug	EA.	4.66
Coupling	EA.	14.75
Wye	EA.	64.75
Double wye	EA.	71.50
2x1-1/2" wye & 1/8 bend	EA.	62.25
Double wye & 1/8 bend	EA.	71.50
Test tee less 2" plug	EA.	37.00

	Unit	Total

15410.05 C.I. PIPE, ABOVE GROUND (Cont.)

No hub pipe

No hub fittings, 2" pipe

Tapped tee

2"x2"	EA.	40.75
2"x1-1/2"	EA.	39.75

P-trap

2"x2"	EA.	39.25

Tapped cross

2"x1-1/2"	EA.	45.00

3" pipe

1/4 bend	EA.	44.75
1/8 bend	EA.	42.50
Sanitary tee	EA.	55.25
3"x2" sanitary tee	EA.	53.75
3"x1-1/2" sanitary tee	EA.	54.50
Sanitary cross	EA.	87.00
3x2" sanitary cross	EA.	83.25
Plug	EA.	6.92
Coupling	EA.	16.75
Wye	EA.	70.00
3x2" wye	EA.	65.50
Double wye	EA.	88.00
3x2" double wye	EA.	82.50
3x2" wye & 1/8 bend	EA.	61.50
3x1-1/2" wye & 1/8 bend	EA.	61.50
Double wye & 1/8 bend	EA.	88.00
3x2" double wye & 1/8 bend	EA.	82.50
3x2" reducer	EA.	35.25
Test tee, less 3" plug	EA.	49.75
Plug	EA.	6.92
3x3" tapped tee	EA.	73.75
3x2" tapped tee	EA.	54.25
3x1-1/2" tapped tee	EA.	51.00
P-trap	EA.	62.50
3x2" tapped cross	EA.	60.25
3x1-1/2" tapped cross	EA.	58.50
Closet flange, 3-1/2" deep	EA.	35.50

4" pipe

1/4 bend	EA.	50.50
1/8 bend	EA.	45.50
Sanitary tee	EA.	77.50
4x3" sanitary tee	EA.	75.50
4x2" sanitary tee	EA.	71.50
Sanitary cross	EA.	128.25
4x3" sanitary cross	EA.	115.75
4x2" sanitary cross	EA.	106.75
Plug	EA.	10.75
Coupling	EA.	16.50
Wye	EA.	81.25
4x3" wye	EA.	77.50
4x2" wye	EA.	70.75
Double wye	EA.	135.25
4x3" double wye	EA.	108.00
4x2" double wye	EA.	102.75
Wye & 1/8 bend	EA.	91.75
4x3" wye & 1/8 bend	EA.	81.00
4x2" wye & 1/8 bend	EA.	74.50
Double wye & 1/8 bend	EA.	162.50
4x3" double wye & 1/8 bend	EA.	129.00
4x2" double wye & 1/8 bend	EA.	126.00
4x3" reducer	EA.	41.75
4x2" reducer	EA.	41.75
Test tee, less 4" plug	EA.	62.75
Plug	EA.	10.75
4x2" tapped tee	EA.	54.25

	Unit	Total

15410.05 C.I. PIPE, ABOVE GROUND (Cont.)

No hub pipe
  No hub fittings, 4" pipe

	Unit	Total
4x1-1/2" tapped tee	EA.	51.50
P-trap	EA.	85.50
4x2" tapped cross	EA.	72.75
4x1-1/2" tapped cross	EA.	63.50
Closet flange		
3" deep	EA.	52.75
8" deep	EA.	86.75

15410.06 C.I. PIPE, BELOW GROUND

No hub pipe

	Unit	Total
1-1/2" pipe	L.F.	10.55
2" pipe	L.F.	11.10
3" pipe	L.F.	14.41
4" pipe	L.F.	18.96
Fittings, 1-1/2"		
1/4 bend	EA.	26.61
1/8 bend	EA.	25.15
Plug	EA.	4.66
Wye	EA.	37.50
Wye & 1/8 bend	EA.	31.00
P-trap	EA.	32.50
2"		
1/4 bend	EA.	30.49
1/8 bend	EA.	29.03
Plug	EA.	4.66
Double wye	EA.	58.25
Wye & 1/8 bend	EA.	44.75
Double wye & 1/8 bend	EA.	72.25
P-trap	EA.	35.00
3"		
1/4 bend	EA.	38.25
1/8 bend	EA.	36.25
Plug	EA.	6.92
Wye	EA.	56.75
3x2" wye	EA.	52.25
Wye & 1/8 bend	EA.	60.50
Double wye & 1/8 bend	EA.	90.00
3x2" double wye & 1/8 bend	EA.	77.75
3x2" reducer	EA.	31.75
P-trap	EA.	56.25
4"		
1/4 bend	EA.	44.25
1/8 bend	EA.	39.25
Plug	EA.	10.75
Wye	EA.	68.00
4x3" wye	EA.	64.25
4x2" wye	EA.	57.50
Double wye	EA.	125.00
4x3" double wye	EA.	97.75
4x2" double wye	EA.	92.50
Wye & 1/8 bend	EA.	78.50
4x3" wye & 1/8 bend	EA.	67.75
4x2" wye & 1/8 bend	EA.	61.25
Double wye & 1/8 bend	EA.	152.25
4x3" double wye & 1/8 bend	EA.	118.75
4x2" double wye & 1/8 bend	EA.	115.75
4x3" reducer	EA.	35.50
4x2" reducer	EA.	35.50

	Unit	Total
15410.10 COPPER PIPE		
Type "K" copper		
1/2"	L.F.	5.69
3/4"	L.F.	9.04
1"	L.F.	11.33
DWV, copper		
1-1/4"	L.F.	12.61
1-1/2"	L.F.	15.84
2"	L.F.	19.88
3"	L.F.	31.98
4"	L.F.	53.91
6"	L.F.	194.47
Refrigeration tubing, copper, sealed		
1/8"	L.F.	3.23
3/16"	L.F.	3.46
1/4"	L.F.	3.73
Type "L" copper		
1/4"	L.F.	3.35
3/8"	L.F.	4.15
1/2"	L.F.	4.64
3/4"	L.F.	6.37
1"	L.F.	8.67
Type "M" copper		
1/2"	L.F.	3.85
3/4"	L.F.	5.17
1"	L.F.	7.23
Type "K" tube, coil		
1/4" x 60'	EA.	110.00
1/2" x 60'	EA.	230.00
1/2" x 100'	EA.	390.00
3/4" x 60'	EA.	430.00
3/4" x 100'	EA.	720.00
1" x 60'	EA.	560.00
1" x 100'	EA.	940.00
Type "L" tube, coil		
1/4" x 60'	EA.	120.00
3/8" x 60'	EA.	190.00
1/2" x 60'	EA.	250.00
1/2" x 100'	EA.	420.00
3/4" x 60'	EA.	400.00
3/4" x 100'	EA.	670.00
1" x 60'	EA.	580.00
1" x 100'	EA.	960.00
15410.11 COPPER FITTINGS		
Coupling, with stop		
1/4"	EA.	21.66
3/8"	EA.	26.19
1/2"	EA.	28.20
5/8"	EA.	34.00
3/4"	EA.	36.64
1"	EA.	40.64
Reducing coupling		
1/4" x 1/8"	EA.	27.43
3/8" x 1/4"	EA.	29.92
1/2" x		
3/8"	EA.	33.26
1/4"	EA.	33.68
1/8"	EA.	33.93
3/4" x		
3/8"	EA.	39.06
1/2"	EA.	38.17
1" x		
3/8"	EA.	46.73
1" x 1/2"	EA.	46.49
1" x 3/4"	EA.	45.31

	Unit	Total

15410.11 COPPER FITTINGS (Cont.)

Coupling
  Slip coupling

1/4"	EA.	21.50
1/2"	EA.	26.26
3/4"	EA.	33.88
1"	EA.	40.32

  Coupling with drain

1/2"	EA.	40.85
3/4"	EA.	48.75
1"	EA.	56.50

  Reducer

3/8" x 1/4"	EA.	27.73
1/2" x 3/8"	EA.	27.20
3/4" x		
1/4"	EA.	32.96
3/8"	EA.	33.15
1/2"	EA.	33.35
1" x		
1/2"	EA.	37.94
3/4"	EA.	36.38

  Female adapters

1/4"	EA.	32.08
3/8"	EA.	35.76
1/2"	EA.	34.70
3/4"	EA.	39.48
1"	EA.	45.75

  Increasing female adapters

1/8" x		
3/8"	EA.	31.96
1/2"	EA.	31.49
1/4" x 1/2"	EA.	34.05
3/8" x 1/2"	EA.	35.79
1/2" X		
3/4"	EA.	38.98
1"	EA.	46.75
3/4" X		
1"	EA.	51.25
1-1/4"	EA.	62.75
1" x		
1-1/4"	EA.	64.50
1-1/2"	EA.	67.25

  Reducing female adapters

3/8" x 1/4"	EA.	34.78
1/2" x		
1/4"	EA.	36.65
3/8"	EA.	36.65
3/4" x 1/2"	EA.	42.27
1" x		
1/2"	EA.	55.00
3/4"	EA.	51.00

  Female fitting adapters

1/2"	EA.	40.86
3/4"	EA.	43.75
3/4" x 1/2"	EA.	47.75
1"	EA.	51.25

  Male adapters

1/4"	EA.	39.50
3/8"	EA.	33.90

  Increasing male adapters

3/8" x 1/2"	EA.	35.85
1/2" x		
3/4"	EA.	37.63
1"	EA.	45.50

	Unit	Total

15410.11 COPPER FITTINGS (Cont.)

Increasing male adapters, 3/4" x

1"	EA.	47.00
1-1/4"	EA.	51.00
1" x 1-1/4"	EA.	52.75

Reducing male adapters

1/2" x

1/4"	EA.	40.59
3/8"	EA.	39.01
3/4" x 1/2"	EA.	41.86

1" x

1/2"	EA.	59.00
3/4"	EA.	54.25

Fitting x male adapters

1/2"	EA.	44.75
3/4"	EA.	50.25
1"	EA.	52.25

90 ells

1/8"	EA.	27.04
1/4"	EA.	28.23
3/8"	EA.	31.57
1/2"	EA.	32.27
3/4"	EA.	35.30
1"	EA.	40.40

Reducing 90 ell

3/8" x 1/4"	EA.	33.76

1/2" x

1/4"	EA.	38.77
3/8"	EA.	38.77
3/4" x 1/2"	EA.	39.61

1" x

1/2"	EA.	46.25
3/4"	EA.	45.50

Street ells, copper

1/4"	EA.	30.46
3/8"	EA.	32.25
1/2"	EA.	32.77
3/4"	EA.	36.19
1"	EA.	43.01

Female, 90 ell

1/2"	EA.	32.28
3/4"	EA.	35.32
1"	EA.	40.46

Female increasing, 90 ell

3/8" x 1/2"	EA.	40.00

1/2" x

3/4"	EA.	39.23
1"	EA.	47.50
3/4" x 1"	EA.	47.50
1" x 1-1/4"	EA.	72.00

Female reducing, 90 ell

1/2" x 3/8"	EA.	44.00
3/4" x 1/2"	EA.	47.00

1" x

1/2"	EA.	54.50
3/4"	EA.	56.25

Male, 90 ell

1/4"	EA.	34.76
3/8"	EA.	39.00
1/2"	EA.	36.67
3/4"	EA.	45.25
1"	EA.	49.00

Male, increasing 90 ell

1/2" x

3/4"	EA.	50.50

	Unit	Total

15410.11 COPPER FITTINGS (Cont.)

Male, increasing 90 ell, 1/2" x

1"	EA.	69.50
3/4" x 1"	EA.	69.25
1" x 1-1/4"	EA.	68.25

Male, reducing 90 ell

1/2" x 3/8"	EA.	42.25
3/4" x 1/2"	EA.	52.25
1" x		
1/2"	EA.	71.25
3/4"	EA.	69.50

Drop ear ells

1/2"	EA.	38.25

Female drop ear ells

1/2"	EA.	38.25
1/2" x 3/8"	EA.	43.50
3/4"	EA.	53.50

Female flanged sink ell

1/2"	EA.	44.00

45 ells

1/4"	EA.	30.84
3/8"	EA.	33.24

45 street ell

1/4"	EA.	31.60
3/8"	EA.	35.63
1/2"	EA.	33.37
3/4"	EA.	36.19
1"	EA.	43.16

Tee

1/8"	EA.	29.96
1/4"	EA.	30.22
3/8"	EA.	32.49

Caps

1/4"	EA.	25.90
3/8"	EA.	29.94

Test caps

1/2"	EA.	32.10
3/4"	EA.	33.95
1"	EA.	36.45

Flush bushing

1/4" x 1/8"	EA.	26.72
1/2" x		
1/4"	EA.	33.58
3/8"	EA.	33.31
3/4" x		
3/8"	EA.	37.32
1/2"	EA.	36.82
1" x		
1/2"	EA.	41.34
3/4"	EA.	40.60

Female flush bushing

1/2" x		
1/2" x 1/8"	EA.	36.45
1/4"	EA.	36.72

Union

1/4"	EA.	57.50
3/8"	EA.	73.00

Female

1/2"	EA.	46.75
3/4"	EA.	48.50

Male

1/2"	EA.	48.00
3/4"	EA.	55.25
1"	EA.	83.25

	Unit	Total

15410.11 COPPER FITTINGS (Cont.)

Union, male
1/2"	EA.	52.00
3/4"	EA.	62.75
1"	EA.	75.00
1" x 3/4" x 3/4"	EA.	90.50

Twin ells
1" x 3/4" x 3/4"	EA.	49.25
1" x 1" x 1"	EA.	49.25

90 union ells, male
1/2"	EA.	53.75
3/4"	EA.	70.50
1"	EA.	90.75

DWV fittings, coupling with stop
1-1/4"	EA.	41.62
1-1/2"	EA.	45.07
1-1/2" x 1-1/4"	EA.	48.82
2"	EA.	50.15
2" x 1-1/4"	EA.	53.25
2" x 1-1/2"	EA.	53.00
3"	EA.	68.50
3" x 1-1/2"	EA.	91.25
3" x 2"	EA.	89.25
4"	EA.	114.25

Slip coupling
1-1/2"	EA.	48.44
2"	EA.	53.00
3"	EA.	72.75

90 degree ells
1-1/2"	EA.	50.50
1-1/2" x 1-1/4"	EA.	70.50
2"	EA.	62.75
2" x 1-1/2"	EA.	84.25
3"	EA.	108.25
4"	EA.	252.50

Street, 90 elbows
1-1/2"	EA.	53.75
2"	EA.	73.75
3"	EA.	133.75
4"	EA.	262.50

Female, 90 elbows
1-1/2"	EA.	53.50
2"	EA.	69.75

Male, 90 elbows
1-1/2"	EA.	64.75
2"	EA.	94.50

90 with side inlet
3" x 3" x 1"	EA.	129.50
3" x 3" x 1-1/2"	EA.	132.00
3" x 3" x 2"	EA.	132.00

45 degree ells
1-1/4"	EA.	46.33
1-1/2"	EA.	46.91
2"	EA.	60.00
3"	EA.	91.00
4"	EA.	242.50

Street, 45 degree ell
1-1/2"	EA.	51.75
2"	EA.	64.50
3"	EA.	117.50

60 degree ell
1-1/2"	EA.	58.75
2"	EA.	78.50
3"	EA.	134.25

22-1/2 degree ell
1-1/2"	EA.	63.25

	Unit	Total

15410.11 COPPER FITTINGS (Cont.)

DWV fittings

22-1/2 degree ell

2"	EA.	72.75
3"	EA.	106.50

11-1/4 degree ell

1-1/2"	EA.	65.75
2"	EA.	79.50
3"	EA.	127.75

Wye

1-1/4"	EA.	77.25
1-1/2"	EA.	83.25
2"	EA.	99.25
2" x 1-1/2" x 1-1/2"	EA.	105.75
2" x 1-1/2" x 2"	EA.	112.75
2" x 1-1/2" x 2"	EA.	112.75
3"	EA.	192.25
3" x 3" x 1-1/2"	EA.	182.25
3" x 3" x 2"	EA.	182.25
4"	EA.	342.50
4" x 4" x 2"	EA.	262.50
4" x 4" x 3"	EA.	262.50

Sanitary tee

1-1/4"	EA.	57.25
1-1/2"	EA.	64.50
2"	EA.	71.50
2" x 1-1/2" x 1-1/2"	EA.	89.25
2" x 1-1/2" x 2"	EA.	90.50
2" x 2" x 1-1/2"	EA.	70.00
3"	EA.	162.25
3" x 3" x 1-1/2"	EA.	137.25
3" x 3" x 2"	EA.	137.25
4"	EA.	342.50
4" x 4" x 3"	EA.	292.50

Female sanitary tee

1-1/2"	EA.	88.75

Long turn tee

1-1/2"	EA.	88.25
2"	EA.	151.75
3" x 1-1/2"	EA.	192.25

Double wye

1-1/2"	EA.	111.75
2"	EA.	171.75
2" x 2" x 1-1/2" x 1-1/2"	EA.	141.75
3"	EA.	262.25
3" x 3" x 1-1/2" x 1-1/2"	EA.	262.25
3" x 3" x 2" x 2"	EA.	262.25
4" x 4" x 1-1/2" x 1-1/2"	EA.	282.50

Double sanitary tee

1-1/2"	EA.	89.25
2"	EA.	161.75
2" x 2" x 1-1/2"	EA.	141.75
3"	EA.	182.25
3" x 3" x 1-1/2" x 1-1/2"	EA.	232.25
3" x 3" x 2" x 2"	EA.	202.25
4" x 4" x 1-1/2" x 1-1/2"	EA.	372.50

Long

2" x 1-1/2"	EA.	171.75

Twin elbow

1-1/2"	EA.	104.50
2"	EA.	141.75
2" x 1-1/2" x 1-1/2"	EA.	133.00

Spigot adapter, manoff

1-1/2" x 2"	EA.	82.25
1-1/2" x 3"	EA.	91.25
2"	EA.	63.00

	Unit	Total

15410.11 COPPER FITTINGS (Cont.)

DWV fittings
  Spigot adapter, manoff

	Unit	Total
2" x 3"	EA.	92.00
2" x 4"	EA.	113.00
3"	EA.	125.75
3" x 4"	EA.	182.25
4"	EA.	172.50

No-hub adapters

1-1/2" x 2"	EA.	65.25
2"	EA.	66.50
2" x 3"	EA.	98.50
3"	EA.	102.00
3" x 4"	EA.	152.25
4"	EA.	172.50

Fitting reducers

1-1/2" x 1-1/4"	EA.	48.20
2" x 1-1/2"	EA.	56.25
3" x 1-1/2"	EA.	93.00
3" x 2"	EA.	88.75

Slip joint (Desanco)

1-1/4"	EA.	52.25
1-1/2"	EA.	55.25
1-1/2" x 1-1/4"	EA.	55.75

Street x slip joint (Desanco)

1-1/2"	EA.	59.00
1-1/2" x 1-1/4"	EA.	60.25

Flush bushing

1-1/2" x 1-1/4"	EA.	50.50
2" x 1-1/2"	EA.	61.50
3" x 1-1/2"	EA.	87.75
3" x 2"	EA.	87.75

Male hex trap bushing

1-1/4" x 1-1/2"	EA.	53.50
1-1/2"	EA.	51.25
1-1/2" x 2"	EA.	57.50
2"	EA.	56.25

Round trap bushing

1-1/2"	EA.	53.25
2"	EA.	57.00

Female adapter

1-1/4"	EA.	53.25
1-1/2"	EA.	65.00
1-1/2" x 2"	EA.	105.00
2"	EA.	77.00
2" x 1-1/2"	EA.	99.25
3"	EA.	192.25

Fitting x female adapter

1-1/2"	EA.	74.00
2"	EA.	88.25

Male adapters

1-1/4"	EA.	51.25
1-1/4" x 1-1/2"	EA.	70.50
1-1/2"	EA.	55.75
1-1/2" x 2"	EA.	102.00
2"	EA.	69.75
2" x 1-1/2"	EA.	106.75
3"	EA.	192.25

Male x slip joint adapters

1-1/2" x 1-1/4"	EA.	65.50

Dandy cleanout

1-1/2"	EA.	85.75
2"	EA.	97.00
3"	EA.	252.25

End cleanout, flush pattern

1-1/2" x 1"	EA.	67.50

	Unit	Total

15410.11 COPPER FITTINGS (Cont.)

DWV fittings
  End cleanout, flush pattern

	Unit	Total
2" x 1-1/2"	EA.	75.75
3" x 2-1/2"	EA.	124.50

Copper caps

1-1/2"	EA.	48.67
2"	EA.	59.50

Closet flanges

3"	EA.	94.50
4"	EA.	137.00

Drum traps, with cleanout

1-1/2" x 3" x 6"	EA.	199.00

P-trap, swivel, with cleanout

1-1/2"	EA.	138.75

P-trap, solder union

1-1/2"	EA.	80.75
2"	EA.	115.00

With cleanout

1-1/2"	EA.	85.00
2"	EA.	123.25
2" x 1-1/2"	EA.	123.25

Swivel joint, with cleanout

1-1/2" x 1-1/4"	EA.	97.75
1-1/2"	EA.	114.25
2" x 1-1/2"	EA.	133.50

Estabrook TY, with inlets

3", with 1-1/2" inlet	EA.	182.25

Fine thread adapters

1/2"	EA.	34.63
1/2" x 1/2" IPS	EA.	35.06
1/2" x 3/4" IPS	EA.	37.45
1/2" x male	EA.	33.59
1/2" x female	EA.	36.03

Copper pipe fittings
  1/2"

90 deg ell	EA.	15.48
45 deg ell	EA.	15.88
Tee	EA.	20.25
Cap	EA.	7.96
Coupling	EA.	15.09
Union	EA.	23.30

3/4"

90 deg ell	EA.	18.99
45 deg ell	EA.	19.55
Tee	EA.	26.18
Cap	EA.	9.34
Coupling	EA.	17.96
Union	EA.	28.75

1"

90 deg ell	EA.	28.30
45 deg ell	EA.	30.57
Tee	EA.	37.25
Cap	EA.	14.17
Coupling	EA.	26.18
Union	EA.	35.25

	Unit	Total

15410.14 BRASS I.P.S. FITTINGS

Fittings, iron pipe size, 45 deg ell

1/8"	EA.	35.75
1/4"	EA.	35.75
3/8"	EA.	39.25
1/2"	EA.	42.00
3/4"	EA.	48.25
1"	EA.	61.00

90 deg ell

1/8"	EA.	35.25
1/4"	EA.	35.25
3/8"	EA.	38.75
1/2"	EA.	41.50
3/4"	EA.	45.25
1"	EA.	56.50

90 deg ell, reducing

1/4" x 1/8"	EA.	37.25
3/8" x 1/8"	EA.	40.75
3/8" x 1/4"	EA.	40.75
1/2" x 1/4"	EA.	43.50
1/2" x 3/8"	EA.	43.50
3/4" x 1/2"	EA.	50.50
1" x 3/8"	EA.	59.75
1" x 1/2"	EA.	59.75
1" x 3/4"	EA.	59.75

Street ell, 45 deg

1/2"	EA.	43.50
3/4"	EA.	50.50

90 deg

1/8"	EA.	37.00
1/4"	EA.	37.00
3/8"	EA.	40.50
1/2"	EA.	43.25
3/4"	EA.	47.75
1"	EA.	54.25

Tee, 1/8"

Tee, 1/8"	EA.	35.25
1/4"	EA.	35.25
3/8"	EA.	38.75
1/2"	EA.	41.50
3/4"	EA.	47.00
1"	EA.	55.50

Tee, reducing, 3/8" x

1/4"	EA.	42.75
1/2"	EA.	42.75

1/2" x

1/4"	EA.	45.50
3/8"	EA.	45.50
3/4"	EA.	48.00

3/4" x

1/4"	EA.	49.75
1/2"	EA.	49.75
1"	EA.	66.75

1" x

1/2"	EA.	68.25
3/4"	EA.	68.25

Tee, reducing

1/2" x 3/8" x 1/2"	EA.	44.25
3/4" x 1/2" x 1/2"	EA.	51.75
3/4" x 1/2" x 3/4"	EA.	50.50
1" x 1/2" x 1/2"	EA.	67.25
1" x 1/2" x 3/4"	EA.	67.25
1" x 3/4" x 1/2"	EA.	74.50
1" x 3/4" x 3/4"	EA.	67.25

	Unit	Total

15410.14 BRASS I.P.S. FITTINGS (Cont.)

		Unit	Total
Union			
1/8"		EA.	52.00
1/4"		EA.	52.00
3/8"		EA.	55.50
1/2"		EA.	58.25
3/4"		EA.	70.00
1"		EA.	84.25
Brass face bushing			
3/8" x 1/4"		EA.	37.83
1/2" x 3/8"		EA.	40.58
3/4" x 1/2"		EA.	44.50
1" x 3/4"		EA.	54.50
Hex bushing, 1/4" x 1/8"		EA.	31.60
1/2" x			
1/4"		EA.	37.28
3/8"		EA.	37.28
5/8" x			
1/8"		EA.	37.28
1/4"		EA.	37.28
3/4" x			
1/8"		EA.	41.74
1/4"		EA.	41.74
3/8"		EA.	40.59
1/2"		EA.	40.59
1" x			
1/4"		EA.	46.50
3/8"		EA.	46.50
1/2"		EA.	45.50
3/4"		EA.	45.50
Caps			
1/8"		EA.	31.02
1/4"		EA.	31.49
3/8"		EA.	34.99
1/2"		EA.	37.74
3/4"		EA.	39.84
1"		EA.	47.25
Couplings			
1/8"		EA.	32.00
1/4"		EA.	32.00
3/8"		EA.	35.50
1/2"		EA.	38.25
3/4"		EA.	42.60
1"		EA.	50.00
Couplings, reducing, 1/4" x 1/8"		EA.	33.17
3/8" x			
1/8"		EA.	36.67
1/4"		EA.	36.67
1/2" x			
1/8"		EA.	41.25
1/4"		EA.	40.18
3/8"		EA.	40.18
3/4" x			
1/4"		EA.	47.00
3/8"		EA.	44.50
1/2"		EA.	44.50
1" x			
1/2"		EA.	49.25
3/4"		EA.	49.25
Square head plug, solid			
1/8"		EA.	31.84
1/4"		EA.	31.84
3/8"		EA.	35.34
1/2"		EA.	38.09
3/4"		EA.	41.17

	Unit	Total

15410.14 BRASS I.P.S. FITTINGS (Cont.)

Square head plug

Cored

	Unit	Total
1/2"	EA.	36.68
3/4"	EA.	39.84
1"	EA.	45.75

Countersunk

	Unit	Total
1/2"	EA.	38.83
3/4"	EA.	41.10

Locknut

	Unit	Total
3/4"	EA.	39.84
1"	EA.	43.27
Close standard red nipple, 1/8"	EA.	27.22

1/8" x

	Unit	Total
1-1/2"	EA.	29.11
2"	EA.	29.54
2-1/2"	EA.	30.15
3"	EA.	30.81
3-1/2"	EA.	31.96
4"	EA.	32.45
4-1/2"	EA.	32.81
5"	EA.	33.23
5-1/2"	EA.	34.56
6"	EA.	35.25
1/4" x close	EA.	29.54

1/4" x

	Unit	Total
1-1/2"	EA.	31.72
2"	EA.	32.14
2-1/2"	EA.	32.45
3"	EA.	32.81
3-1/2"	EA.	33.71
4"	EA.	34.07
4-1/2"	EA.	34.68
5"	EA.	34.99
5-1/2"	EA.	36.00
6"	EA.	36.25
3/8" x close	EA.	33.04

3/8" x

	Unit	Total
1-1/2"	EA.	33.82
2"	EA.	34.35
2-1/2"	EA.	35.55
3"	EA.	37.08
3-1/2"	EA.	37.88
4"	EA.	40.50
4-1/2"	EA.	41.00
5"	EA.	41.75
5-1/2"	EA.	42.50
6"	EA.	44.25
1/2" x close	EA.	37.25

1/2" x

	Unit	Total
1-1/2"	EA.	37.97
2"	EA.	39.43
2-1/2"	EA.	40.63
3"	EA.	42.00
3-1/2"	EA.	43.00
4"	EA.	43.75
4-1/2"	EA.	44.50
5"	EA.	44.75
5-1/2"	EA.	45.25
6"	EA.	46.50
7-1/2"	EA.	77.75
8"	EA.	77.75
3/4" x close	EA.	49.50

3/4" x

	Unit	Total
1-1/2"	EA.	42.25
2"	EA.	43.75

	Unit	Total
15410.14 BRASS I.P.S. FITTINGS (Cont.)		
Close standard red nipple		
3/4" x		
2-1/2"	EA.	44.75
3"	EA.	45.75
3-1/2"	EA.	47.00
4"	EA.	48.00
4-1/2"	EA.	49.00
5"	EA.	49.75
5-1/2"	EA.	51.75
6"	EA.	52.50
1" x close	EA.	48.00
1" x		
2"	EA.	54.00
2-1/2"	EA.	54.25
3"	EA.	55.00
3-1/2"	EA.	56.00
4"	EA.	57.75
4-1/2"	EA.	58.25
5"	EA.	62.00
5-1/2"	EA.	62.75
6"	EA.	65.75
15410.15 BRASS FITTINGS		
Compression fittings, union		
3/8"	EA.	14.39
1/2"	EA.	16.90
5/8"	EA.	17.85
Union elbow		
3/8"	EA.	13.20
1/2"	EA.	14.23
5/8"	EA.	15.43
Union tee		
3/8"	EA.	13.81
1/2"	EA.	15.08
5/8"	EA.	16.38
Male connector		
3/8"	EA.	13.24
1/2"	EA.	12.70
5/8"	EA.	12.44
Female connector		
3/8"	EA.	12.99
1/2"	EA.	13.64
5/8"	EA.	14.16
Brass flare fittings, union		
3/8"	EA.	12.19
1/2"	EA.	13.00
5/8"	EA.	13.23
90 deg elbow union		
3/8"	EA.	14.26
1/2"	EA.	16.94
5/8"	EA.	20.25
Three way tee		
3/8"	EA.	21.73
1/2"	EA.	23.27
5/8"	EA.	27.50
Cross		
3/8"	EA.	32.25
1/2"	EA.	43.75
5/8"	EA.	67.25
Male connector, half union		
3/8"	EA.	11.48
1/2"	EA.	12.60
5/8"	EA.	13.63
Female connector, half union		
3/8"	EA.	12.04

	Unit	Total

15410.15 BRASS FITTINGS (Cont.)

Brass flare fittings

Female connector, half union

1/2"	EA.	11.89
5/8"	EA.	13.63

Long forged nut

3/8"	EA.	11.61
1/2"	EA.	12.33
5/8"	EA.	18.06

Short forged nut

3/8"	EA.	11.30
1/2"	EA.	11.77
5/8"	EA.	12.26

Nut

1/8"	EA.	.29
1/4"	EA.	.29
5/16"	EA.	.33
3/8"	EA.	.44
1/2"	EA.	.64
5/8"	EA.	1.33

Sleeve

1/8"	EA.	12.71
1/4"	EA.	12.58
5/16"	EA.	12.71
3/8"	EA.	12.81
1/2"	EA.	12.88
5/8"	EA.	13.06

Tee

1/4"	EA.	21.09
5/16"	EA.	22.75

Male tee

5/16" x 1/8"	EA.	24.64

Female union

1/8" x 1/8"	EA.	17.42
1/4" x 3/8"	EA.	18.95
3/8" x 1/4"	EA.	18.39
3/8" x 1/2"	EA.	19.09
5/8" x 1/2"	EA.	22.96

Male union, 1/4"

1/4" x 1/4"	EA.	17.33
3/8"	EA.	17.84
1/2"	EA.	18.89

5/16" x

1/8"	EA.	17.28
1/4"	EA.	17.70
3/8"	EA.	18.73

3/8" x

1/8"	EA.	17.55
1/4"	EA.	17.84
1/2"	EA.	18.62

5/8" x

3/8"	EA.	21.91
1/2"	EA.	21.34

Female elbow, 1/4" x 1/4"	EA.	21.69

5/16" x

1/8"	EA.	22.06
1/4"	EA.	23.38

3/8" x

3/8"	EA.	21.23
1/2"	EA.	20.53

Male elbow, 1/8" x 1/8"	EA.	21.48
3/16" x 1/4"	EA.	21.31

1/4" x

1/8"	EA.	19.95
1/4"	EA.	20.33
3/8"	EA.	19.99

	Unit	Total

15410.15 BRASS FITTINGS (Cont.)

Brass flare fittings
Male elbow
5/16" x

1/8"	EA.	20.06
1/4"	EA.	20.45
3/8"	EA.	21.70

3/8" x

1/8"	EA.	19.96
1/4"	EA.	20.80
3/8"	EA.	20.06
1/2"	EA.	20.83

1/2" x

1/4"	EA.	25.59
3/8"	EA.	25.05
1/2"	EA.	24.49

5/8" x

3/8"	EA.	25.62
1/2"	EA.	25.90
3/4"	EA.	31.25

Union

1/8"	EA.	19.97
3/16"	EA.	19.97
1/4"	EA.	19.64
5/16"	EA.	19.91
3/8"	EA.	20.18

Reducing union

3/8" x 1/4"	EA.	23.41

5/8" x

3/8"	EA.	24.96
1/2"	EA.	25.37

15410.17 CHROME PLATED FITTINGS

Fittings
90 ell

3/8"	EA.	43.25
1/2"	EA.	51.25

45 ell

3/8"	EA.	51.25
1/2"	EA.	62.50

Tee

3/8"	EA.	54.75
1/2"	EA.	61.25

Coupling

3/8"	EA.	37.25
1/2"	EA.	37.25

Union

3/8"	EA.	51.25
1/2"	EA.	52.50

Tee

1/2" x 3/8" x 3/8"	EA.	61.25
1/2" x 3/8" x 1/2"	EA.	62.00

15410.30 PVC/CPVC PIPE

PVC schedule 40

1/2" pipe	L.F.	3.09
3/4" pipe	L.F.	3.50
1" pipe	L.F.	3.97
1-1/4" pipe	L.F.	4.56
1-1/2" pipe	L.F.	5.53
2" pipe	L.F.	6.52
2-1/2" pipe	L.F.	8.51
3" pipe	L.F.	10.46
4" pipe	L.F.	13.83

	Unit	Total

15410.30 PVC/CPVC PIPE (Cont.)

Fittings, 1/2"

90 deg ell	EA.	8.28
45 deg ell	EA.	8.45
Tee	EA.	9.41
Reducing insert	EA.	10.98
Threaded	EA.	8.95
Male adapter	EA.	10.95
Female adapter	EA.	8.30
Coupling	EA.	8.17
Union	EA.	16.26
Cap	EA.	10.94
Flange	EA.	20.44

3/4"

90 deg elbow	EA.	10.95
45 deg elbow	EA.	11.57
Tee	EA.	13.12
Reducing insert	EA.	9.39
Threaded	EA.	11.18

1"

90 deg elbow	EA.	13.28
45 deg elbow	EA.	13.66
Tee	EA.	15.04
Reducing insert	EA.	13.28
Threaded	EA.	15.04
Male adapter	EA.	16.49
Female adapter	EA.	16.38
Coupling	EA.	16.32
Union	EA.	26.39
Cap	EA.	13.13
Flange	EA.	28.75

1-1/4"

90 deg elbow	EA.	19.11
45 deg elbow	EA.	19.37
Tee	EA.	22.32
Reducing insert	EA.	21.70
Threaded	EA.	22.32
Female adapter	EA.	21.74
Coupling	EA.	21.59
Union	EA.	38.00
Cap	EA.	21.64
Flange	EA.	33.10

1-1/2"

90 deg elbow	EA.	19.27
45 deg elbow	EA.	19.99
Tee	EA.	22.84
Reducing insert	EA.	21.79
Threaded	EA.	22.63
Male adapter	EA.	22.00
Female adapter	EA.	22.00
Coupling	EA.	21.70
Union	EA.	49.00
Cap	EA.	21.74
Flange	EA.	45.00

2"

90 deg elbow	EA.	23.16
45 deg elbow	EA.	23.79
Tee	EA.	28.19
Reducing insert	EA.	27.04
Threaded	EA.	27.72
Male adapter	EA.	26.67
Female adapter	EA.	26.73
Coupling	EA.	26.41
Union	EA.	63.25
Cap	EA.	26.31
Flange	EA.	53.50

	Unit	Total

15410.30 PVC/CPVC PIPE (Cont.)

Fittings
2-1/2"
   90 deg elbow .... EA. 46.26
   45 deg elbow .... EA. 49.50
   Tee .... EA. 51.10
   Reducing insert .... EA. 44.68
    Threaded .... EA. 45.93
   Male adapter .... EA. 46.61
   Female adapter .... EA. 45.78
   Coupling .... EA. 44.65
   Union .... EA. 84.50
   Cap .... EA. 42.87
   Flange .... EA. 71.75
3"
   90 deg elbow .... EA. 60.09
   45 deg elbow .... EA. 62.50
   Tee .... EA. 69.25
   Reducing insert .... EA. 56.01
    Threaded .... EA. 57.11
   Male adapter .... EA. 58.21
   Female adapter .... EA. 57.06
   Coupling .... EA. 56.69
   Union .... EA. 96.25
   Cap .... EA. 56.12
   Flange .... EA. 80.25
4"
   90 deg elbow .... EA. 76.50
   45 deg elbow .... EA. 80.75
   Tee .... EA. 90.25
   Reducing insert .... EA. 71.01
    Threaded .... EA. 73.50
   Male adapter .... EA. 70.08
   Female adapter .... EA. 70.65
   Coupling .... EA. 68.98
   Union .... EA. 119.75
   Cap .... EA. 71.28
   Flange .... EA. 102.25
PVC schedule 80 pipe
   1-1/2" pipe .... L.F. 6.07
   2" pipe .... L.F. 7.39
   3" pipe .... L.F. 12.27
   4" pipe .... L.F. 15.66
Fittings, 1-1/2"
   90 deg elbow .... EA. 27.45
   45 deg elbow .... EA. 35.50
   Tee .... EA. 54.25
   Reducing insert .... EA. 25.00
    Threaded .... EA. 25.81
   Male adapter .... EA. 28.81
   Female adapter .... EA. 29.46
   Coupling .... EA. 30.06
   Union .... EA. 48.00
   Cap .... EA. 25.49
   Flange .... EA. 42.25
2"
   90 deg elbow .... EA. 33.11
   45 deg elbow .... EA. 44.00
   Tee .... EA. 67.75
   Reducing insert .... EA. 31.04
    Threaded .... EA. 31.09
   Male adapter .... EA. 36.00
   Female adapter .... EA. 40.25
2-1/2"
   90 deg elbow .... EA. 58.00

	Unit	Total

15410.30 PVC/CPVC PIPE (Cont.)

PVC schedule 80 pipe
  Fittings, 2-1/2"

45 deg elbow	EA.	79.00
Tee	EA.	83.50
Reducing insert	EA.	49.50
Threaded	EA.	52.00
Male adapter	EA.	52.25
Female adapter	EA.	63.00
Coupling	EA.	52.00
Union	EA.	88.25
Cap	EA.	54.25
Flange	EA.	71.50

  3"

90 deg elbow	EA.	69.25
45 deg elbow	EA.	101.00
Tee	EA.	101.75
Reducing insert	EA.	69.00
Threaded	EA.	76.50
Male adapter	EA.	67.00
Female adapter	EA.	79.25
Coupling	EA.	67.00
Union	EA.	108.50
Cap	EA.	71.50
Flange	EA.	84.50

  4"

90 deg elbow	EA.	106.00
45 deg elbow	EA.	150.25
Tee	EA.	123.50
Reducing insert	EA.	85.50
Threaded	EA.	99.75
Male adapter	EA.	88.50
Coupling	EA.	81.00
Union	EA.	121.75
Cap	EA.	86.00
Flange	EA.	108.25

CPVC schedule 40

1/2" pipe	L.F.	3.23
3/4" pipe	L.F.	3.66
1" pipe	L.F.	4.33
1-1/4" pipe	L.F.	5.05
1-1/2" pipe	L.F.	5.81
2" pipe	L.F.	7.00

  Fittings, CPVC, schedule 80

1/2", 90 deg ell	EA.	9.70
Tee	EA.	21.00
3/4", 90 deg ell	EA.	10.75
Tee	EA.	26.00
1", 90 deg ell	EA.	14.05
Tee	EA.	27.75
1-1/4", 90 deg ell	EA.	19.95
Tee	EA.	26.75
1-1/2", 90 deg ell	EA.	26.75
Tee	EA.	33.25
2", 90 deg ell	EA.	28.00
Tee	EA.	35.50

	Unit	Total

15410.33 ABS DWV PIPE

Schedule 40 ABS

1-1/2" pipe	L.F.	4.51
2" pipe	L.F.	5.32
3" pipe	L.F.	8.23
4" pipe	L.F.	11.58

Fittings

1/8 bend

1-1/2"	EA.	14.50
2"	EA.	18.70
3"	EA.	27.83
4"	EA.	37.50

Tee, sanitary

1-1/2"	EA.	23.65
2"	EA.	29.48
3"	EA.	43.50
4"	EA.	61.25

Tee, sanitary reducing

2 x 1-1/2 x 1-1/2	EA.	29.11
2 x 1-1/2 x 2	EA.	30.24
2 x 2 x 1-1/2	EA.	32.44
3 x 3 x 1-1/2	EA.	38.39
3 x 3 x 2	EA.	43.65
4 x 4 x 1-1/2	EA.	61.25
4 x 4 x 2	EA.	65.50
4 x 4 x 3	EA.	66.00

Wye

1-1/2"	EA.	21.99
2"	EA.	30.93
3"	EA.	44.75
4"	EA.	68.25

Reducer

2 x 1-1/2	EA.	18.60
3 x 1-1/2	EA.	28.08
3 x 2	EA.	26.99
4 x 2	EA.	37.50
4 x 3	EA.	38.00

P-trap

1-1/2"	EA.	27.35
2"	EA.	32.15
3"	EA.	61.25
4"	EA.	101.00

Double sanitary, tee

1-1/2"	EA.	31.41
2"	EA.	40.57
3"	EA.	64.50
4"	EA.	93.00

Long sweep, 1/4 bend

1-1/2"	EA.	15.83
2"	EA.	19.99
3"	EA.	31.00
4"	EA.	50.00

Wye, standard

1-1/2"	EA.	25.03
2"	EA.	30.93
3"	EA.	44.75
4"	EA.	68.25

Wye, reducing

2 x 1-1/2 x 1-1/2	EA.	28.68
2 x 2 x 1-1/2	EA.	32.57
4 x 4 x 2	EA.	55.00
4 x 4 x 3	EA.	63.75

Double wye

1-1/2"	EA.	34.68
2"	EA.	42.75
3"	EA.	68.75

	Unit	Total

15410.33 ABS DWV PIPE (Cont.)

Schedule 40 ABS
Fittings, Double wye

4"	EA.	112.50
2 x 2 x 1-1/2 x 1-1/2	EA.	42.75
3 x 3 x 2 x 2	EA.	63.25
4 x 4 x 3 x 3	EA.	109.00

Combination wye and 1/8 bend

1-1/2"	EA.	27.53
2"	EA.	33.17
3"	EA.	48.75
4"	EA.	75.00
2 x 2 x 1-1/2	EA.	32.02
3 x 3 x 1-1/2	EA.	48.00
3 x 3 x 2	EA.	43.00
4 x 4 x 2	EA.	62.25
4 x 4 x 3	EA.	67.50

15410.80 STEEL PIPE

Black steel, extra heavy pipe, threaded

1/2" pipe	L.F.	4.83
3/4" pipe	L.F.	5.51

Fittings, malleable iron, threaded, 1/2" pipe

90 deg ell	EA.	23.68
45 deg ell	EA.	24.70
Tee	EA.	34.43
Reducing tee	EA.	38.38
Cap	EA.	14.98
Coupling	EA.	28.30
Union	EA.	34.50
Nipple, 4" long	EA.	23.35

3/4" pipe

90 deg ell	EA.	24.17
45 deg ell	EA.	36.67
Tee	EA.	35.85
Reducing tee	EA.	28.70
Cap	EA.	15.80
Coupling	EA.	24.64
Union	EA.	36.50
Nipple, 4" long	EA.	23.75

Cast iron fittings
1/2" pipe

90 deg. ell	EA.	24.60
45 deg. ell	EA.	28.56
Tee	EA.	36.33
Reducing tee	EA.	40.82

3/4" pipe

90 deg. ell	EA.	24.86
45 deg. ell	EA.	25.83
Tee	EA.	37.61
Reducing tee	EA.	39.48

15410.82 GALVANIZED STEEL PIPE

Galvanized pipe

1/2" pipe	L.F.	9.43
3/4" pipe	L.F.	11.96

90 degree ell, 150 lb malleable iron, galvanized

1/2"	EA.	14.63
3/4"	EA.	18.58

45 degree ell, 150 lb m.i., galv.

1/2"	EA.	15.90
3/4"	EA.	20.37

Tees, straight, 150 lb m.i., galv.

1/2"	EA.	18.58
3/4"	EA.	22.46

	Unit	Total

15410.82 GALVANIZED STEEL PIPE (Cont.)

Tees, reducing, out, 150 lb m.i., galv.

1/2"	EA.	20.63
3/4"	EA.	23.41

Couplings, straight, 150 lb m.i., galv.

1/2"	EA.	15.12
3/4"	EA.	17.14

Couplings, reducing, 150 lb m.i., galv

1/2"	EA.	15.55
3/4"	EA.	17.40

Caps, 150 lb m.i., galv.

1/2"	EA.	8.44
3/4"	EA.	9.46

Unions, 150 lb m.i., galv.

1/2"	EA.	27.75
3/4"	EA.	31.50

Nipples, galvanized steel, 4" long

1/2"	EA.	10.96
3/4"	EA.	12.52

90 degree reducing ell, 150 lb m.i., galv.

3/4" x 1/2"	EA.	15.90
1" x 3/4"	EA.	18.62

Square head plug (C.I.)

1/2"	EA.	9.11
3/4"	EA.	12.62

15430.23 CLEANOUTS

Cleanout, wall

2"	EA.	251.75
3"	EA.	331.75
4"	EA.	352.25

Floor

2"	EA.	242.25
3"	EA.	302.25
4"	EA.	322.50

15430.25 HOSE BIBBS

Hose bibb

1/2"	EA.	29.82
3/4"	EA.	30.37

15430.60 VALVES

Gate valve, 125 lb, bronze, soldered

1/2"	EA.	44.25
3/4"	EA.	49.75

Threaded

1/4", 125 lb	EA.	57.75

1/2"

125 lb	EA.	56.25
150 lb	EA.	66.75
300 lb	EA.	103.75

3/4"

125 lb	EA.	61.75
150 lb	EA.	74.75
300 lb	EA.	119.50

Check valve, bronze, soldered, 125 lb

1/2"	EA.	69.75
3/4"	EA.	82.50

Threaded

1/2"

125 lb	EA.	83.25
150 lb	EA.	79.00
200 lb	EA.	81.25

3/4"

125 lb	EA.	71.50
150 lb	EA.	97.50

	Unit	Total

15430.60 VALVES (Cont.)

Check valve, bronze
  Threaded, 3/4"

200 lb	EA.	105.50

Vertical check valve, bronze, 125 lb, threaded

1/2"	EA.	96.50
3/4"	EA.	128.50

Globe valve, bronze, soldered, 125 lb

1/2"	EA.	84.00
3/4"	EA.	101.50

  Threaded
  1/2"

125 lb	EA.	81.25
150 lb	EA.	100.50
300 lb	EA.	170.75

  3/4"

125 lb	EA.	111.25
150 lb	EA.	121.75
300 lb	EA.	205.00

Ball valve, bronze, 250 lb, threaded

1/2"	EA.	43.50
3/4"	EA.	52.75

Angle valve, bronze, 150 lb, threaded

1/2"	EA.	108.75
3/4"	EA.	145.00

Balancing valve, meter connections, circuit setter

1/2"	EA.	107.00
3/4"	EA.	114.75

Balancing valve, straight type

1/2"	EA.	47.25
3/4"	EA.	52.00

Angle type

1/2"	EA.	55.00
3/4"	EA.	66.50

Square head cock, 125 lb, bronze body

1/2"	EA.	38.25
3/4"	EA.	46.00

Radiator temp control valve, with control and sensor

1/2" valve	EA.	159.00

Pressure relief valve, 1/2", bronze

Low pressure	EA.	53.00
High pressure	EA.	57.75

Pressure and temperature relief valve

Bronze, 3/4"	EA.	125.00

  Cast iron, 3/4"

High pressure	EA.	73.50
Temperature relief	EA.	90.50
Pressure & temp relief valve	EA.	103.00

Pressure reducing valve, bronze, threaded, 250 lb

1/2"	EA.	209.00
3/4"	EA.	209.00

Solar water temperature regulating valve

3/4"	EA.	692.25

Tempering valve, threaded

3/4"	EA.	370.75

Thermostatic mixing valve, threaded

1/2"	EA.	142.25
3/4"	EA.	145.00

  Sweat connection

1/2"	EA.	152.25
3/4"	EA.	195.00

Mixing valve, sweat connection

1/2"	EA.	94.50
3/4"	EA.	97.25

	Unit	Total

15430.60 VALVES (Cont.)

Liquid level gauge, aluminum body
| 3/4" | EA. | 385.00 |

125 psi, pvc body
| 3/4" | EA. | 455.00 |

150 psi, crs body
| 3/4" | EA. | 365.00 |
| 175 psi, bronze body, 1/2" | EA. | 712.25 |

15430.65 VACUUM BREAKERS

Vacuum breaker, atmospheric, threaded connection
| 3/4" | EA. | 70.75 |

Anti-siphon, brass
| 3/4" | EA. | 74.50 |

15430.68 STRAINERS

Strainer, Y pattern, 125 psi, cast iron body, threaded
| 3/4" | EA. | 33.75 |

250 psi, brass body, threaded
| 3/4" | EA. | 54.75 |

Cast iron body, threaded
| 3/4" | EA. | 42.50 |

15430.70 DRAINS, ROOF & FLOOR

Floor drain, cast iron, with cast iron top
2"	EA.	202.25
3"	EA.	202.25
4"	EA.	372.25

Roof drain, cast iron
2"	EA.	282.25
3"	EA.	292.25
4"	EA.	352.25

15430.80 TRAPS

Bucket trap, threaded
| 3/4" | EA. | 249.00 |

Inverted bucket steam trap, threaded
| 3/4" | EA. | 289.00 |

With stainless interior
| 1/2" | EA. | 199.00 |
| 3/4" | EA. | 219.00 |

Brass interior
| 3/4" | EA. | 319.00 |

Cast steel body, threaded, high temperature
| 3/4" | EA. | 769.00 |

Float trap, 15 psi
| 3/4" | EA. | 219.00 |

Float and thermostatic trap, 15 psi
| 3/4" | EA. | 229.00 |

Steam trap, cast iron body, threaded, 125 psi
| 3/4" | EA. | 269.00 |

Thermostatic trap, low pressure, angle type, 25 psi
| 1/2" | EA. | 109.25 |
| 3/4" | EA. | 159.00 |

Cast iron body, threaded, 125 psi
| 3/4" | EA. | 199.00 |

15440.10 BATHS

Bath tub, 5' long
Minimum	EA.	740.00
Average	EA.	1,460
Maximum	EA.	3,280

6' long
Minimum	EA.	800.00
Average	EA.	1,510
Maximum	EA.	4,030

	Unit	Total

15440.10 BATHS (Cont.)

Square tub, whirlpool, 4'x4'

Minimum	EA.	2,110
Average	EA.	3,180
Maximum	EA.	8,630

5'x5'

Minimum	EA.	2,110
Average	EA.	3,180
Maximum	EA.	8,780

6'x6'

Minimum	EA.	2,510
Average	EA.	3,880
Maximum	EA.	10,030

For trim and rough-in

Minimum	EA.	400.00
Average	EA.	590.00
Maximum	EA.	1,410

15440.12 DISPOSALS & ACCESSORIES

Continuous feed

Minimum	EA.	201.50
Average	EA.	360.00
Maximum	EA.	600.00

Batch feed, 1/2 hp

Minimum	EA.	410.00
Average	EA.	710.00
Maximum	EA.	1,160

Hot water dispenser

Minimum	EA.	330.00
Average	EA.	480.00
Maximum	EA.	720.00
Epoxy finish faucet	EA.	420.00
Lock stop assembly	EA.	138.75
Mounting gasket	EA.	59.29
Tailpipe gasket	EA.	53.28
Stopper assembly	EA.	86.50
Switch assembly, on/off	EA.	127.50
Tailpipe gasket washer	EA.	32.35
Stop gasket	EA.	37.17
Tailpipe flange	EA.	31.53
Tailpipe	EA.	42.14

15440.15 FAUCETS

Kitchen

Minimum	EA.	182.50
Average	EA.	360.00
Maximum	EA.	450.00

Bath

Minimum	EA.	182.50
Average	EA.	370.00
Maximum	EA.	530.00

Lavatory, domestic

Minimum	EA.	188.00
Average	EA.	410.00
Maximum	EA.	620.00

Washroom

Minimum	EA.	210.00
Average	EA.	410.00
Maximum	EA.	670.00

Handicapped

Minimum	EA.	250.00
Average	EA.	520.00
Maximum	EA.	770.00

	Unit	Total

15440.15 FAUCETS (Cont.)

Shower
Minimum	EA.	210.00
Average	EA.	450.00
Maximum	EA.	670.00

For trim and rough-in
Minimum	EA.	207.00
Average	EA.	280.00
Maximum	EA.	510.00

15440.18 HYDRANTS

Wall hydrant
8" thick	EA.	460.00
12" thick	EA.	560.00

15440.20 LAVATORIES

Lavatory, counter top, porcelain enamel on cast iron
Minimum	EA.	320.00
Average	EA.	450.00
Maximum	EA.	730.00

Wall hung, china
Minimum	EA.	390.00
Average	EA.	470.00
Maximum	EA.	980.00

Handicapped
Minimum	EA.	590.00
Average	EA.	710.00
Maximum	EA.	1,140

For trim and rough-in
Minimum	EA.	380.00
Average	EA.	580.00
Maximum	EA.	770.00

15440.30 SHOWERS

Shower, fiberglass, 36"x34"x84"
Minimum	EA.	1,020
Average	EA.	1,430
Maximum	EA.	1,780

Steel, 1 piece, 36"x36"
Minimum	EA.	980.00
Average	EA.	1,430
Maximum	EA.	1,580

Receptor, molded stone, 36"x36"
Minimum	EA.	430.00
Average	EA.	680.00
Maximum	EA.	1,090

For trim and rough-in
Minimum	EA.	500.00
Average	EA.	720.00
Maximum	EA.	1,090

15440.40 SINKS

Service sink, 24"x29"
Minimum	EA.	800.00
Average	EA.	1,000
Maximum	EA.	1,460

Kitchen sink, single, stainless steel, single bowl
Minimum	EA.	410.00
Average	EA.	480.00
Maximum	EA.	790.00

Double bowl
Minimum	EA.	480.00
Average	EA.	570.00
Maximum	EA.	930.00

Porcelain enamel, cast iron, single bowl
Minimum	EA.	330.00

	Unit	Total

15440.40 SINKS (Cont.)

Kitchen sink
  Porcelain enamel, cast iron, single bowl

Average	EA.	420.00
Maximum	EA.	620.00

  Double bowl

Minimum	EA.	440.00
Average	EA.	600.00
Maximum	EA.	860.00

Mop sink, 24"x36"x10"

Minimum	EA.	610.00
Average	EA.	740.00
Maximum	EA.	990.00

Washing machine box

Minimum	EA.	340.00
Average	EA.	460.00
Maximum	EA.	620.00

For trim and rough-in

Minimum	EA.	500.00
Average	EA.	750.00
Maximum	EA.	980.00

15440.60 WATER CLOSETS

Water closet flush tank, floor mounted

Minimum	EA.	490.00
Average	EA.	860.00
Maximum	EA.	1,310

Handicapped

Minimum	EA.	580.00
Average	EA.	980.00
Maximum	EA.	1,930

For trim and rough-in

Minimum	EA.	370.00
Average	EA.	460.00
Maximum	EA.	640.00

15440.70 WATER HEATERS

Water heater, electric

6 gal	EA.	510.00
10 gal	EA.	520.00
15 gal	EA.	510.00
20 gal	EA.	710.00
30 gal	EA.	730.00
40 gal	EA.	780.00
52 gal	EA.	890.00

Oil fired

20 gal	EA.	1,610
50 gal	EA.	2,450

15450.40 STORAGE TANKS

Hot water storage tank, cement lined

10 gallon	EA.	700.00
70 gallon	EA.	1,860

15555.10 BOILERS

Cast iron, gas fired, hot water

115 mbh	EA.	4,650
175 mbh	EA.	5,350
235 mbh	EA.	6,400

Steam

115 mbh	EA.	4,900
175 mbh	EA.	5,700
235 mbh	EA.	6,550

	Unit	Total

15555.10 BOILERS (Cont.)

Electric, hot water
115 mbh	EA.	5,900
175 mbh	EA.	6,400
235 mbh	EA.	7,100

Steam
115 mbh	EA.	7,100
175 mbh	EA.	8,450
235 mbh	EA.	9,100

Oil fired, hot water
115 mbh	EA.	5,100
175 mbh	EA.	6,250
235 mbh	EA.	8,250

Steam
115 mbh	EA.	5,100
175 mbh	EA.	6,250
235 mbh	EA.	7,800

15610.10 FURNACES

Electric, hot air
40 mbh	EA.	1,120
60 mbh	EA.	1,210
80 mbh	EA.	1,310
100 mbh	EA.	1,470
125 mbh	EA.	1,680

Gas fired hot air
40 mbh	EA.	1,120
60 mbh	EA.	1,200
80 mbh	EA.	1,350
100 mbh	EA.	1,420
125 mbh	EA.	1,530

Oil fired hot air
40 mbh	EA.	1,410
60 mbh	EA.	2,130
80 mbh	EA.	2,150
100 mbh	EA.	2,220
125 mbh	EA.	2,280

15670.10 CONDENSING UNITS

Air cooled condenser, single circuit
3 ton	EA.	1,750
5 ton	EA.	2,700

With low ambient dampers
3 ton	EA.	2,060
5 ton	EA.	3,110

15780.20 ROOFTOP UNITS

Packaged, single zone rooftop unit, with roof curb
2 ton	EA.	4,380
3 ton	EA.	4,580
4 ton	EA.	5,080

15830.10 RADIATION UNITS

Baseboard radiation unit
1.7 mbh/lf	L.F.	110.50
2.1 mbh/lf	L.F.	141.25

15830.70 UNIT HEATERS

Steam unit heater, horizontal
12,500 btuh, 200 cfm	EA.	640.00
17,000 btuh, 300 cfm	EA.	810.00

	Unit	Total

15855.10 AIR HANDLING UNITS

Air handling unit, medium pressure, single zone

1500 cfm	EA.	4,390
3000 cfm	EA.	5,950

Rooftop air handling units

4950 cfm	EA.	12,200
7370 cfm	EA.	15,490

15870.20 EXHAUST FANS

Belt drive roof exhaust fans

640 cfm, 2618 fpm	EA.	1,128
940 cfm, 2604 fpm	EA.	1,428

15890.10 METAL DUCTWORK

Rectangular duct
Galvanized steel

Minimum	Lb.	6.57
Average	Lb.	8.05
Maximum	Lb.	12.18

Aluminum

Minimum	Lb.	14.80
Average	Lb.	18.81
Maximum	Lb.	24.55

Fittings

Minimum	EA.	28.01
Average	EA.	42.25
Maximum	EA.	78.50

15890.30 FLEXIBLE DUCTWORK

Flexible duct, 1.25" fiberglass

5" dia.	L.F.	6.44
6" dia.	L.F.	7.16
7" dia.	L.F.	8.22
8" dia.	L.F.	8.67
10" dia.	L.F.	10.82
12" dia.	L.F.	11.74
Flexible duct connector, 3" wide fabric	L.F.	12.81

15910.10 DAMPERS

Horizontal parallel aluminum backdraft damper

12" x 12"	EA.	70.75
16" x 16"	EA.	74.50

15940.10 DIFFUSERS

Ceiling diffusers, round, baked enamel finish

6" dia.	EA.	57.25
8" dia.	EA.	70.00
10" dia.	EA.	74.75
12" dia.	EA.	88.50

Rectangular

6x6"	EA.	59.75
9x9"	EA.	78.50
12x12"	EA.	100.25
15x15"	EA.	117.50
18x18"	EA.	141.25

15940.40 REGISTERS AND GRILLES

Lay in flush mounted, perforated face, return

6x6/24x24	EA.	73.50
8x8/24x24	EA.	73.50
9x9/24x24	EA.	77.75
10x10/24x24	EA.	81.75
12x12/24x24	EA.	81.75

	Unit	Total

15940.40 REGISTERS AND GRILLES (Cont.)

Rectangular, ceiling return, single deflection

10x10	EA.	60.50
12x12	EA.	65.25
14x14	EA.	72.75
16x8	EA.	65.25
16x16	EA.	65.25

Wall, return air register

12x12	EA.	64.25
16x16	EA.	87.25
18x18	EA.	100.25

Ceiling, return air grille

6x6	EA.	48.75
8x8	EA.	60.00
10x10	EA.	68.25

Ceiling, exhaust grille, aluminum egg crate

6x6	EA.	40.00
8x8	EA.	44.25
10x10	EA.	46.25
12x12	EA.	57.50

	Unit	Total

16050.30 BUS DUCT

Bus duct, 100a, plug-in
10', 600v	EA.	520.00
With ground	EA.	740.00

Circuit breakers, with enclosure
1 pole
15a-60a	EA.	392.50
70a-100a	EA.	460.75

2 pole
15a-60a	EA.	560.00
70a-100a	EA.	664.50

Circuit breaker, adapter cubicle
225a	EA.	5,310
400a	EA.	6,220

Fusible switches, 240v, 3 phase
30a	EA.	632.50
60a	EA.	780.75
100a	EA.	1,030
200a	EA.	1,750

16110.20 CONDUIT SPECIALTIES

Rod beam clamp, 1/2"	EA.	10.24

Hanger rod
3/8"	L.F.	4.30
1/2"	L.F.	7.11

All thread rod
1/4"	L.F.	2.64
3/8"	L.F.	3.41
1/2"	L.F.	4.58
5/8"	L.F.	7.49

Hanger channel, 1-1/2"
No holes	EA.	6.59
Holes	EA.	7.63

Channel strap
1/2"	EA.	5.00
3/4"	EA.	5.47

Conduit penetrations, roof and wall, 8" thick
1/2"	EA.	44.75
3/4"	EA.	44.75
1"	EA.	58.00

Threaded rod couplings
1/4"	EA.	5.09
3/8"	EA.	5.17
1/2"	EA.	5.37
5/8"	EA.	6.30
3/4"	EA.	6.56

Hex nuts
1/4"	EA.	3.80
3/8"	EA.	3.88
1/2"	EA.	4.18
5/8"	EA.	4.80
3/4"	EA.	5.18

Square nuts
1/4"	EA.	3.78
3/8"	EA.	3.92
3/8"	EA.	4.11
5/8"	EA.	4.27
3/4"	EA.	4.75

Flat washers
1/4"	EA.	.17
3/8"	EA.	.23
1/2"	EA.	.32
5/8"	EA.	.64
3/4"	EA.	.89

	Unit	Total

16110.20 CONDUIT SPECIALTIES (Cont.)

Lockwashers
1/4"	EA.	.10
3/8"	EA.	.18
1/2"	EA.	.22
5/8"	EA.	.38
3/4"	EA.	.64

16110.21 ALUMINUM CONDUIT

Aluminum conduit
1/2"	L.F.	4.29
3/4"	L.F.	5.62
1"	L.F.	7.43

90 deg. elbow
1/2"	EA.	30.00
3/4"	EA.	40.50
1"	EA.	53.00

Coupling
1/2"	EA.	6.95
3/4"	EA.	9.33
1"	EA.	12.45

16110.22 EMT CONDUIT

EMT conduit
1/2"	L.F.	2.75
3/4"	L.F.	3.91
1"	L.F.	5.32

90 deg. elbow
1/2"	EA.	11.67
3/4"	EA.	12.99
1"	EA.	16.57

Connector, steel compression
1/2"	EA.	8.13
3/4"	EA.	9.65
1"	EA.	11.28

Coupling, steel, compression
1/2"	EA.	7.15
3/4"	EA.	8.18
1"	EA.	10.16

1 hole strap, steel
1/2"	EA.	3.09
3/4"	EA.	3.14
1"	EA.	3.27

Connector, steel set screw
1/2"	EA.	6.33
3/4"	EA.	7.11
1"	EA.	8.58

Insulated throat
1/2"	EA.	6.75
3/4"	EA.	7.80
1"	EA.	9.60

Connector, die cast set screw
1/2"	EA.	5.18
3/4"	EA.	5.79
1"	EA.	7.11

Insulated throat
1/2"	EA.	6.17
3/4"	EA.	7.32
1"	EA.	9.54

Coupling, steel set screw
1/2"	EA.	5.20
3/4"	EA.	6.37
1"	EA.	8.53

Diecast set screw
1/2"	EA.	3.71
3/4"	EA.	4.20

	Unit	Total

16110.22 EMT CONDUIT (Cont.)

Coupling
  Diecast set screw
    1" .... EA. | 5.06

1 hole malleable straps
    1/2" .... EA. | 3.27
    3/4" .... EA. | 3.42
    1" .... EA. | 3.75

EMT to rigid compression coupling
    1/2" .... EA. | 11.60
    3/4" .... EA. | 13.47
    1" .... EA. | 20.45

Set screw couplings
    1/2" .... EA. | 8.40
    3/4" .... EA. | 8.98
    1" .... EA. | 13.37

Set screw offset connectors
    1/2" .... EA. | 9.81
    3/4" .... EA. | 10.68
    1" .... EA. | 16.72

Compression offset connectors
    1/2" .... EA. | 11.47
    3/4" .... EA. | 12.58
    1" .... EA. | 18.21

Type "LB" set screw condulets
    1/2" .... EA. | 28.50
    3/4" .... EA. | 36.00
    1" .... EA. | 50.00

Type "T" set screw condulets
    1/2" .... EA. | 36.50
    3/4" .... EA. | 47.75
    1" .... EA. | 59.25

Type "C" set screw condulets
    1/2" .... EA. | 30.75
    3/4" .... EA. | 37.25
    1" .... EA. | 51.25

Type "LL" set screw condulets
    1/2" .... EA. | 30.75
    3/4" .... EA. | 36.75
    1" .... EA. | 51.00

Type "LR" set screw condulets
    1/2" .... EA. | 30.75
    3/4" .... EA. | 36.75
    1" .... EA. | 51.00

Type "LB" compression condulets
    1/2" .... EA. | 49.75
    3/4" .... EA. | 78.00
    1" .... EA. | 89.75

Type "T" compression condulets
    1/2" .... EA. | 66.75
    3/4" .... EA. | 82.00
    1" .... EA. | 122.00

Condulet covers
    1/2" .... EA. | 10.68
    3/4" .... EA. | 11.06
    1" .... EA. | 11.83

Clamp type entrance caps
    1/2" .... EA. | 27.59
    3/4" .... EA. | 32.50
    1" .... EA. | 42.00

Slip fitter type entrance caps
    1/2" .... EA. | 25.07
    3/4" .... EA. | 29.64
    1" .... EA. | 38.81

		Unit	Total
16110.23 FLEXIBLE CONDUIT			
Flexible conduit, steel			
3/8"		L.F.	2.95
1/2		L.F.	3.05
3/4"		L.F.	4.08
1"		L.F.	5.14
Flexible conduit, liquid tight			
3/8"		L.F.	4.29
1/2"		L.F.	4.56
3/4"		L.F.	6.13
1"		L.F.	7.77
Connector, straight			
3/8"		EA.	9.36
1/2"		EA.	9.61
3/4"		EA.	11.28
1"		EA.	15.86
Straight insulated throat connectors			
3/8"		EA.	13.24
1/2"		EA.	13.24
3/4"		EA.	16.79
1"		EA.	20.23
90 deg connectors			
3/8"		EA.	16.75
1/2"		EA.	16.75
3/4"		EA.	21.90
1"		EA.	31.75
90 degree insulated throat connectors			
3/8"		EA.	17.93
1/2"		EA.	17.93
3/4"		EA.	23.50
1"		EA.	34.25
Flexible aluminum conduit			
3/8"		L.F.	2.64
1/2"		L.F.	2.72
3/4"		L.F.	3.62
1"		L.F.	4.26
Connector, straight			
3/8"		EA.	8.62
1/2"		EA.	9.14
3/4"		EA.	9.80
1"		EA.	16.47
Straight insulated throat connectors			
3/8"		EA.	7.77
1/2"		EA.	9.10
3/4"		EA.	9.27
1"		EA.	14.10
90 deg connectors			
3/8"		EA.	12.67
1/2"		EA.	14.15
3/4"		EA.	16.24
1"		EA.	22.20
90 deg insulated throat connectors			
3/8"		EA.	13.19
1/2"		EA.	14.55
3/4"		EA.	17.26
1"		EA.	23.25

	Unit	Total

16110.24 GALVANIZED CONDUIT

Galvanized rigid steel conduit

1/2"	L.F.	6.19
3/4"	L.F.	7.28
1"	L.F.	9.57
1-1/4"	L.F.	13.09
1-1/2"	L.F.	15.02
2"	L.F.	18.26

90 degree ell

1/2"	EA.	26.16
3/4"	EA.	30.52
1"	EA.	40.50
1-1/4"	EA.	49.75
1-1/2"	EA.	57.75
2"	EA.	70.00

Couplings, with set screws

1/2"	EA.	7.59
3/4"	EA.	9.52
1"	EA.	14.14
1-1/4"	EA.	21.51
1-1/2"	EA.	27.19
2"	EA.	51.75

Split couplings

1/2"	EA.	17.12
3/4"	EA.	22.63
1"	EA.	26.14
1-1/4"	EA.	34.25
1-1/2"	EA.	43.50
2"	EA.	77.75

Erickson couplings

1/2"	EA.	36.25
3/4"	EA.	41.13
1"	EA.	54.60
1-1/4"	EA.	82.25
1-1/2"	EA.	95.50
2"	EA.	141.25

Seal fittings

1/2"	EA.	61.00
3/4"	EA.	72.00
1"	EA.	90.25
1-1/4"	EA.	104.00
1-1/2"	EA.	128.75
2"	EA.	160.50

Entrance fitting, (weather head), threaded

1/2"	EA.	38.98
3/4"	EA.	44.50
1"	EA.	52.00
1-1/4"	EA.	66.50
1-1/2"	EA.	82.25
2"	EA.	101.50

Locknuts

1/2"	EA.	3.81
3/4"	EA.	3.85
1"	EA.	3.98
1-1/4"	EA.	4.11
1-1/2"	EA.	5.08
2"	EA.	5.44

Plastic conduit bushings

1/2"	EA.	9.33
3/4"	EA.	11.10
1"	EA.	14.60
1-1/4"	EA.	17.36
1-1/2"	EA.	19.76
2"	EA.	25.67

	Unit	Total
16110.24 GALVANIZED CONDUIT (Cont.)		
Conduit bushings, steel		
1/2"	EA.	9.46
3/4"	EA.	11.16
1"	EA.	14.75
1-1/4"	EA.	17.68
1-1/2"	EA.	20.30
2"	EA.	26.41
Pipe cap		
1/2"	EA.	4.14
3/4"	EA.	4.18
1"	EA.	4.52
1-1/4"	EA.	7.33
1-1/2"	EA.	8.19
2"	EA.	8.48
Threaded couplings		
1/2"	EA.	5.54
3/4"	EA.	6.64
1"	EA.	9.29
1-1/4"	EA.	10.79
1-1/2"	EA.	12.58
2"	EA.	14.99
Threadless couplings		
1/2"	EA.	14.63
3/4"	EA.	16.62
1"	EA.	20.46
1-1/4"	EA.	25.25
1-1/2"	EA.	32.00
2"	EA.	42.50
Threadless connectors		
1/2"	EA.	10.77
3/4"	EA.	14.55
1"	EA.	19.36
1-1/4"	EA.	28.75
1-1/2"	EA.	41.25
2"	EA.	66.25
Setscrew connectors		
1/2"	EA.	8.37
3/4"	EA.	10.00
1"	EA.	12.79
1-1/4"	EA.	18.76
1-1/2"	EA.	24.75
2"	EA.	42.00
Clamp type entrance caps		
1/2"	EA.	30.83
3/4"	EA.	37.75
1"	EA.	46.25
1-1/4"	EA.	52.75
1-1/2"	EA.	74.50
2"	EA.	88.50
"LB" condulets		
1/2"	EA.	31.93
3/4"	EA.	39.50
1"	EA.	49.75
1-1/4"	EA.	66.50
1-1/2"	EA.	84.25
2"	EA.	118.00
"T" condulets		
1/2"	EA.	40.00
3/4"	EA.	46.75
1"	EA.	58.25
1-1/4"	EA.	73.50
1-1/2"	EA.	87.75
2"	EA.	119.00

	Unit	Total

16110.24 GALVANIZED CONDUIT (Cont.)

"X" condulets

1/2"	EA.	50.25
3/4"	EA.	55.50
1"	EA.	73.50
1-1/4"	EA.	86.50
1-1/2"	EA.	102.25
2"	EA.	173.75

Blank steel condulet covers

1/2"	EA.	10.02
3/4"	EA.	10.68
1"	EA.	11.92
1-1/4"	EA.	14.63
1-1/2"	EA.	14.92
2"	EA.	18.94

Solid condulet gaskets

1/2"	EA.	5.91
3/4"	EA.	6.10
1"	EA.	6.48
1-1/4"	EA.	9.35
1-1/2"	EA.	9.54
2"	EA.	9.98

One-hole malleable straps

1/2"	EA.	3.28
3/4"	EA.	3.43
1"	EA.	3.66
1-1/4"	EA.	5.15
1-1/2"	EA.	5.38
2"	EA.	7.05

One-hole steel straps

1/2"	EA.	3.00
3/4"	EA.	3.04
1"	EA.	3.14
1-1/4"	EA.	3.97
1-1/2"	EA.	4.09
2"	EA.	4.23

Grounding locknuts

1/2"	EA.	7.90
3/4"	EA.	8.45
1"	EA.	9.62
1-1/4"	EA.	10.54
1-1/2"	EA.	10.72
2"	EA.	12.79

Insulated grounding metal bushings

1/2"	EA.	15.24
3/4"	EA.	18.44
1"	EA.	21.37
1-1/4"	EA.	27.24
1-1/2"	EA.	33.97
2"	EA.	41.25

16110.25 PLASTIC CONDUIT

PVC conduit, schedule 40

1/2"	L.F.	2.89
3/4"	L.F.	3.06
1"	L.F.	4.16
1-1/4"	L.F.	4.64
1-1/2"	L.F.	5.70
2"	L.F.	6.28

Couplings

1/2"	EA.	4.06
3/4"	EA.	4.15
1"	EA.	4.43
1-1/4"	EA.	5.36
1-1/2"	EA.	5.76
2"	EA.	6.22

	Unit	Total

16110.25 PLASTIC CONDUIT (Cont.)

PVC conduit, schedule 40
 Couplings
 90 degree elbows

1/2"	EA.	8.92
3/4"	EA.	10.76
1"	EA.	11.81
1-1/4"	EA.	14.50
1-1/2"	EA.	19.17
2"	EA.	23.82

 Terminal adapters

1/2"	EA.	7.89
3/4"	EA.	8.27
1"	EA.	8.52
1-1/4"	EA.	13.10
1-1/2"	EA.	13.54
2"	EA.	14.30

 LB conduit body

1/2"	EA.	19.19
3/4"	EA.	20.76
1	EA.	21.47
1-1/4"	EA.	34.00
1-1/2"	EA.	36.25
2"	EA.	47.25

 PVC cement

1 pint	EA.	15.00
1 quart	EA.	22.00

16110.27 PLASTIC COATED CONDUIT

Rigid steel conduit, plastic coated

1/2"	L.F.	9.75
3/4"	L.F.	11.40
1"	L.F.	15.00
1-1/4"	L.F.	19.01
1-1/2"	L.F.	23.19
2"	L.F.	29.00

 90 degree elbows

1/2"	EA.	46.25
3/4"	EA.	52.75
1"	EA.	61.00
1-1/4"	EA.	71.50
1-1/2"	EA.	88.00
2"	EA.	118.50

 Couplings

1/2"	EA.	11.17
3/4"	EA.	13.00
1"	EA.	15.98
1-1/4"	EA.	18.99
1-1/2"	EA.	24.44
2"	EA.	30.00

 1 hole conduit straps

3/4"	EA.	15.38
1"	EA.	15.63
1-1/4"	EA.	21.80
1-1/2"	EA.	23.05
2"	EA.	31.30

	Unit	Total

16110.28 STEEL CONDUIT

Intermediate metal conduit (IMC)

1/2"	L.F.	4.32
3/4"	L.F.	5.52
1"	L.F.	7.59
1-1/4"	L.F.	9.38
1-1/2"	L.F.	12.15
2"	L.F.	14.73

90 degree ell

1/2"	EA.	34.50
3/4"	EA.	39.25
1"	EA.	54.00
1-1/4"	EA.	68.50
1-1/2"	EA.	81.00
2"	EA.	105.75

Couplings

1/2"	EA.	7.63
3/4"	EA.	9.21
1"	EA.	13.08
1-1/4"	EA.	15.55
1-1/2"	EA.	18.76
2"	EA.	22.99

16110.35 SURFACE MOUNTED RACEWAY

Single Raceway

3/4" x 17/32" Conduit	L.F.	4.57
Mounting Strap	EA.	4.32
Connector	EA.	4.47
Elbow		
45 degree	EA.	11.25
90 degree	EA.	6.06
internal	EA.	6.69
external	EA.	6.46
Switch	EA.	48.75
Utility Box	EA.	42.25
Receptacle	EA.	52.50
3/4" x 21/32" Conduit	L.F.	4.80
Mounting Strap	EA.	4.57
Connector	EA.	4.60
Elbow		
45 degree	EA.	13.05
90 degree	EA.	6.23
internal	EA.	7.15
external	EA.	7.15
Switch	EA.	48.75
Utility Box	EA.	42.25
Receptacle	EA.	52.50

16120.41 ALUMINUM CONDUCTORS

Type XHHW, stranded aluminum, 600v

#8	L.F.	.64
#6	L.F.	.74
#4	L.F.	.95
#2	L.F.	1.16
1/0	L.F.	1.62
2/0	L.F.	1.93
3/0	L.F.	2.33
4/0	L.F.	2.55

Type S.E.U. cable

#8/3	L.F.	3.15
#6/3	L.F.	3.37
#4/3	L.F.	4.24
#2/3	L.F.	5.05
#1/3	L.F.	5.99
1/0-3	L.F.	6.53
2/0-3	L.F.	7.22

	Unit	Total

16120.41 ALUMINUM CONDUCTORS (Cont.)

Type S.E.U. cable

3/0-3	L.F.	9.30
4/0-3	L.F.	9.74

Type S.E.R. cable with ground

#8/3	L.F.	3.65
#6/3	L.F.	4.35

16120.43 COPPER CONDUCTORS

Copper conductors, type THW, solid

#14	L.F.	.42
#12	L.F.	.56
#10	L.F.	.74

THHN-THWN, solid

#14	L.F.	.42
#12	L.F.	.56
#10	L.F.	.74

Stranded

#14	L.F.	.42
#12	L.F.	.56
#10	L.F.	.74
#8	L.F.	1.10
#6	L.F.	1.47
#4	L.F.	2.02
#2	L.F.	2.66
#1	L.F.	3.28
1/0	L.F.	3.95
2/0	L.F.	4.90
3/0	L.F.	6.15
4/0	L.F.	7.45

Bare stranded wire

#8	L.F.	1.03
#6	L.F.	1.48
#4	L.F.	1.90
#2	L.F.	2.66
#1	L.F.	3.35

Type "BX" solid armored cable

#14/2	L.F.	2.68
#14/3	L.F.	3.40
#14/4	L.F.	4.13
#12/2	L.F.	2.93
#12/3	L.F.	3.64
#12/4	L.F.	4.48
#10/2	L.F.	3.86
#10/3	L.F.	4.86
#10/4	L.F.	6.53

Steel type, metal clad cable, solid, with ground

#14/2	L.F.	2.02
#14/3	L.F.	2.54
#14/4	L.F.	3.12
#12/2	L.F.	2.18
#12/3	L.F.	3.02
#12/4	L.F.	3.81
#10/2	L.F.	3.16
#10/3	L.F.	4.13
#10/4	L.F.	5.67

	Unit	Total

16120.47 SHEATHED CABLE

Non-metallic sheathed cable

Type NM cable with ground

#14/2	L.F.	1.37
#12/2	L.F.	1.60
#10/2	L.F.	1.98
#8/2	L.F.	2.58
#6/2	L.F.	3.60
#14/3	L.F.	2.27
#12/3	L.F.	2.56
#10/3	L.F.	2.96
#8/3	L.F.	3.66
#6/3	L.F.	4.72
#4/3	L.F.	7.87
#2/3	L.F.	10.88

Type U.F. cable with ground

#14/2	L.F.	1.49
#12/2	L.F.	1.88
#14/3	L.F.	1.91
#12/3	L.F.	2.29

Type S.F.U. cable, 3 conductor

#8	L.F.	3.46
#6	L.F.	4.71

Type SER cable, 4 conductor

#6	L.F.	6.18
#4	L.F.	7.80

Flexible cord, type STO cord

#18/2	L.F.	.89
#18/3	L.F.	1.06
#18/4	L.F.	1.42
#16/2	L.F.	.98
#16/3	L.F.	.91
#16/4	L.F.	1.18
#14/2	L.F.	1.44
#14/3	L.F.	1.44
#14/4	L.F.	1.74
#12/2	L.F.	1.82
#12/3	L.F.	1.52
#12/4	L.F.	2.08
#10/2	L.F.	2.22
#10/3	L.F.	2.21
#10/4	L.F.	3.18

16130.40 BOXES

Round cast box, type SEH

1/2"	EA.	45.25
3/4"	EA.	50.50

SEHC

1/2"	EA.	49.25
3/4"	EA.	54.50

SEHL

1/2"	EA.	49.75
3/4"	EA.	56.25

SEHT

1/2"	EA.	56.75
3/4"	EA.	62.50

SEHX

1/2"	EA.	64.75
3/4"	EA.	73.25
Blank cover	EA.	15.34
1/2", hub cover	EA.	15.12
Cover with gasket	EA.	18.06

Rectangle, type FS boxes

1/2"	EA.	35.50
3/4"	EA.	40.00
1"	EA.	48.00

16130.40 BOXES (Cont.)

	Unit	Total
Rectangle		
FSA		
1/2"	EA.	43.75
3/4"	EA.	46.25
FSC		
1/2"	EA.	36.75
3/4"	EA.	43.00
1"	EA.	52.00
FSL		
1/2"	EA.	43.50
3/4"	EA.	47.25
FSR		
1/2"	EA.	44.25
3/4"	EA.	48.50
FSS		
1/2"	EA.	36.75
3/4"	EA.	41.50
FSLA		
1/2"	EA.	33.08
3/4"	EA.	37.87
FSCA		
1/2"	EA.	48.25
3/4"	EA.	51.25
FSCC		
1/2"	EA.	43.00
3/4"	EA.	57.25
FSCT		
1/2"	EA.	43.00
3/4"	EA.	53.75
1"	EA.	55.75
FST		
1/2"	EA.	56.75
3/4"	EA.	62.00
FSX		
1/2"	EA.	68.25
3/4"	EA.	74.50
FSCD boxes		
1/2"	EA.	64.25
3/4"	EA.	73.25
Rectangle, type FS, 2 gang boxes		
1/2"	EA.	47.25
3/4"	EA.	51.50
1"	EA.	60.00
FSC, 2 gang boxes		
1/2"	EA.	48.50
3/4"	EA.	54.75
1"	EA.	67.50
FSS, 2 gang boxes		
3/4"	EA.	53.25
FS, tandem boxes		
1/2"	EA.	53.25
3/4"	EA.	57.25
FSC, tandem boxes		
1/2"	EA.	61.75
3/4"	EA.	67.25
FS, three gang boxes		
3/4"	EA.	68.00
1"	EA.	75.50
FSS, three gang boxes, 3/4"	EA.	82.25
Weatherproof cast aluminum boxes, 1 gang, 3 outlets		
1/2"	EA.	35.54
3/4"	EA.	43.35
2 gang, 3 outlets		
1/2"	EA.	48.75

	Unit	Total

16130.40 BOXES (Cont.)

Weatherproof cast aluminum boxes, 2 gang, 3 outlets

3/4"	EA.	52.00
1 gang, 4 outlets		
1/2"	EA.	56.25
3/4"	EA.	65.25
2 gang, 4 outlets		
1/2"	EA.	56.75
3/4"	EA.	66.00
1 gang, 5 outlets		
1/2"	EA.	62.20
3/4"	EA.	69.25
2 gang, 5 outlets		
1/2"	EA.	69.75
3/4"	EA.	78.75
2 gang, 6 outlets		
1/2"	EA.	81.00
3/4"	EA.	86.00
2 gang, 7 outlets		
1/2"	EA.	93.00
3/4"	EA.	105.00
Weatherproof and type FS box covers, blank, 1 gang	EA.	13.48
Tumbler switch, 1 gang	EA.	16.62
1 gang, single recept	EA.	14.35
Duplex recept	EA.	15.42
Despard	EA.	15.44
Red pilot light	EA.	33.75
SW and		
Single recept	EA.	24.75
Duplex recept	EA.	22.97
2 gang		
Blank	EA.	16.35
Tumbler switch	EA.	17.32
Single recept	EA.	17.32
Duplex recept	EA.	17.32
3 gang		
Blank	EA.	21.60
Tumbler switch	EA.	23.30
4 gang		
Tumbler switch	EA.	29.50
Box covers		
Surface	EA.	30.00
Sealing	EA.	31.50
Dome	EA.	38.00
1/2" nipple	EA.	44.50
3/4" nipple	EA.	45.50

16130.60 PULL AND JUNCTION BOXES

4"		
Octagon box	EA.	11.97
Box extension	EA.	10.47
Plaster ring	EA.	7.69
Cover blank	EA.	5.80
Square box	EA.	13.58
Box extension	EA.	9.47
Plaster ring	EA.	7.13
Cover blank	EA.	5.75
Switch and device boxes		
2 gang	EA.	24.30
3 gang	EA.	36.30
4 gang	EA.	49.00
Device covers		
2 gang	EA.	17.05
3 gang	EA.	17.55
4 gang	EA.	22.05

		Unit	Total

16130.60 PULL AND JUNCTION BOXES (Cont.)

	Unit	Total
Handy box	EA.	12.23
Extension	EA.	8.00
Switch cover	EA.	6.26
Switch box with knockout	EA.	16.40
Weatherproof cover, spring type	EA.	16.81
Cover plate, dryer receptacle 1 gang plastic	EA.	8.94
For 4" receptacle, 2 gang	EA.	10.25
Duplex receptacle cover plate, plastic	EA.	5.04
4", vertical bracket box, 1-1/2" with		
RMX clamps	EA.	18.10
BX clamps	EA.	18.66
4", octagon device cover		
1 switch	EA.	8.76
1 duplex recept	EA.	8.76
4", octagon swivel hanger box, 1/2" hub	EA.	16.30
3/4" hub	EA.	17.80
4" octagon adjustable bar hangers		
18-1/2"	EA.	9.17
26-1/2"	EA.	9.68
With clip		
18-1/2"	EA.	7.73
26-1/2"	EA.	8.23
4", square face bracket boxes, 1-1/2"		
RMX	EA.	19.57
BX	EA.	20.36
4" square to round plaster rings	EA.	7.32
2 gang device plaster rings	EA.	7.42
Surface covers		
1 gang switch	EA.	7.02
2 gang switch	EA.	7.08
1 single recept	EA.	8.40
1 20a twist lock recept	EA.	9.43
1 30a twist lock recept	EA.	10.87
1 duplex recept	EA.	6.84
2 duplex recept	EA.	6.84
Switch and duplex recept	EA.	8.54
4" plastic round boxes, ground straps		
Box only	EA.	12.43
Box w/clamps	EA.	16.75
Box w/16" bar	EA.	21.28
Box w/24" bar	EA.	23.01
4" plastic round box covers		
Blank cover	EA.	5.56
Plaster ring	EA.	6.36
4" plastic square boxes		
Box only	EA.	11.99
Box w/clamps	EA.	16.35
Box w/hanger	EA.	20.53
Box w/nails and clamp	EA.	21.51
4" plastic square box covers		
Blank cover	EA.	5.52
1 gang ring	EA.	5.79
2 gang ring	EA.	6.39
Round ring	EA.	5.96

	Unit	Total

16130.80 RECEPTACLES

Contractor grade duplex receptacles, 15a 120v

Duplex	EA.	16.11
125 volt, 20a, duplex, standard grade	EA.	26.50
Ground fault interrupter type	EA.	60.25
250 volt, 20a, 2 pole, single, ground type	EA.	34.50

120/208v, 4 pole, single receptacle, twist lock

20a	EA.	49.00
50a	EA.	70.50

125/250v, 3 pole, flush receptacle

30a	EA.	45.50
50a	EA.	51.25
60a	EA.	102.00
Dryer receptacle, 250v, 30a/50a, 3 wire	EA.	39.50
Clock receptacle, 2 pole, grounding type	EA.	26.50

125v, 20a single recept. grounding type

Standard grade	EA.	27.50

125/250v, 3 pole, 3 wire surface recepts

30a	EA.	41.75
50a	EA.	44.00
60a	EA.	74.75

Cord set, 3 wire, 6' cord

30a	EA.	39.75
50a	EA.	47.00

125/250v, 3 pole, 3 wire cap

30a	EA.	47.00
50a	EA.	61.75
60a	EA.	74.25

16199.10 UTILITY POLES & FITTINGS

Wood pole, creosoted

25'	EA.	620.00
30'	EA.	760.00

Treated, wood preservative, 6"x6"

8'	EA.	131.75
10'	EA.	198.00
12'	EA.	214.50
14'	EA.	286.75
16'	EA.	340.00
18'	EA.	400.00
20'	EA.	470.00

Aluminum, brushed, no base

8'	EA.	740.00
10'	EA.	870.00
15'	EA.	960.00
20'	EA.	1,150
25'	EA.	1,530

Steel, no base

10'	EA.	870.00
15'	EA.	980.00
20'	EA.	1,280
25'	EA.	1,480

Concrete, no base

13'	EA.	1,290
16'	EA.	1,780
18'	EA.	2,140
25'	EA.	2,580

	Unit	Total

16350.10 CIRCUIT BREAKERS

Load center circuit breakers, 240v
1 pole, 10-60a	EA.	34.75
2 pole		
10-60a	EA.	67.50
70-100a	EA.	168.50
110-150a	EA.	302.75
Load center, G.F.I. breakers, 240v		
1 pole, 15-30a	EA.	161.50
Tandem breakers, 240v		
1 pole, 15-30a	EA.	60.25
2 pole, 15-30a	EA.	96.00

16365.10 FUSES

Fuse, one-time, 250v
30a	EA.	6.15
60a	EA.	7.89
100a	EA.	21.38

16395.10 GROUNDING

Ground rods, copper clad, 1/2" x
6'	EA.	64.75
8'	EA.	75.00
5/8" x		
6'	EA.	74.25
8'	EA.	100.50
Ground rod clamp		
5/8"	EA.	15.56
Ground rod couplings		
1/2"	EA.	19.26
5/8"	EA.	24.26
Ground rod, driving stud		
1/2"	EA.	16.98
5/8"	EA.	18.76
Ground rod clamps, #8-2 to		
1" pipe	EA.	25.00
2" pipe	EA.	31.50

16430.20 METERING

Outdoor wp meter sockets, 1 gang, 240v, 1 phase
Includes sealing ring, 100a	EA.	148.50
150a	EA.	181.00
200a	EA.	214.75
Die cast hubs, 1-1/4"	EA.	29.18
1-1/2"	EA.	30.06
2"	EA.	31.48

16470.10 PANELBOARDS

Indoor load center, 1 phase 240v main lug only
30a - 2 spaces	EA.	179.25
100a - 8 spaces	EA.	273.50
150a - 16 spaces	EA.	460.00
200a - 24 spaces	EA.	750.00
200a - 42 spaces	EA.	810.00
Main circuit breaker		
100a - 8 spaces	EA.	480.00
100a - 16 spaces	EA.	520.00
150a - 16 spaces	EA.	750.00
150a - 24 spaces	EA.	850.00
200a - 24 spaces	EA.	830.00
200a - 42 spaces	EA.	1,090
120/208v, flush, 3 ph., 4 wire, main only		
100a		
12 circuits	EA.	1,300
20 circuits	EA.	1,760
30 circuits	EA.	2,410

	Unit	Total

16470.10 PANELBOARDS (Cont.)

120/208v, flush, 3 ph., 4 wire
Main only
225a

30 circuits	EA.	2,510
42 circuits	EA.	3,140

16490.10 SWITCHES

Photo electric switches
1000 watt

105-135v	EA.	86.25

Dimmer switch and switch plate

600w	EA.	53.00

Time clocks with skip, 40a, 120v

SPST	EA.	147.75

Contractor grade wall switch 15a, 120v

Single pole	EA.	13.13
Three way	EA.	17.47
Four way	EA.	29.25

Specification grade toggle switches, 20a, 120-277v

Single pole	EA.	18.08
Double pole	EA.	30.08
3 way	EA.	27.55
4 way	EA.	49.75
Combination switch and pilot light, single pole	EA.	34.00
3 way	EA.	40.50
Combination switch and receptacle, single pole	EA.	39.25
3 way	EA.	43.25

Switch plates, plastic ivory

1 gang	EA.	6.18
2 gang	EA.	8.14
3 gang	EA.	10.05
4 gang	EA.	14.02
5 gang	EA.	15.18
6 gang	EA.	17.59

Stainless steel

1 gang	EA.	8.98
2 gang	EA.	11.66
3 gang	EA.	15.69
4 gang	EA.	22.00
5 gang	EA.	25.00
6 gang	EA.	30.25

Brass

1 gang	EA.	11.72
2 gang	EA.	20.01
3 gang	EA.	28.44
4 gang	EA.	33.00
5 gang	EA.	39.50
6 gang	EA.	47.00

16510.05 INTERIOR LIGHTING

Recessed fluorescent fixtures, 2'x2'

2 lamp	EA.	122.00
4 lamp	EA.	146.25

Surface mounted incandescent fixtures

40w	EA.	158.50
75w	EA.	158.50
100w	EA.	168.50
150w	EA.	208.50

Pendant

40w	EA.	144.00
75w	EA.	153.00
100w	EA.	168.00
150w	EA.	178.00

Contractor grade recessed down lights

100 watt housing only	EA.	143.50

	Unit	Total

16510.05 INTERIOR LIGHTING (Cont.)

Recessed fluorescent fixtures
  Contractor grade recessed down lights

150 watt housing only	EA.	172.50
100 watt trim	EA.	94.50
150 watt trim	EA.	126.75

  Recessed incandescent fixtures

40w	EA.	260.00
75w	EA.	270.00
100w	EA.	280.00
150w	EA.	290.00

  Light track single circuit

2'	EA.	78.75
4'	EA.	86.25
8'	EA.	141.00
12'	EA.	206.75

  Fittings and accessories

Dead end	EA.	27.25
Starter kit	EA.	40.75
Conduit feed	EA.	32.25
Straight connector	EA.	29.75
Center feed	EA.	41.25
L-connector	EA.	32.25
T-connector	EA.	39.75
X-connector	EA.	49.75
Cord and plug	EA.	42.51
Rigid corner	EA.	57.00
Flex connector	EA.	46.75
2 way connector	EA.	114.50
Spacer clip	EA.	5.20
Grid box	EA.	19.27
T-bar clip	EA.	5.98
Utility hook	EA.	17.30

  Fixtures, square

R-20	EA.	53.50
R-30	EA.	77.25
40w flood	EA.	120.50
40w spot	EA.	120.50
100w flood	EA.	130.50
100w spot	EA.	107.75
Mini spot	EA.	51.50
Mini flood	EA.	105.00
Quartz, 500w	EA.	250.50
R-20 sphere	EA.	82.75
R-30 sphere	EA.	48.50
R-20 cylinder	EA.	61.50
R-30 cylinder	EA.	69.50
R-40 cylinder	EA.	70.50
R-30 wall wash	EA.	105.00
R-40 wall wash	EA.	130.50

16510.10 LIGHTING INDUSTRIAL

Surface mounted fluorescent, wrap around lens

1 lamp	EA.	143.75
2 lamps	EA.	204.50

Wall mounted fluorescent

2-20w lamps	EA.	124.75
2-30w lamps	EA.	136.25
2-40w lamps	EA.	148.50

Strip fluorescent
  4'

1 lamp	EA.	91.75
2 lamps	EA.	101.25

  8'

1 lamp	EA.	116.00
2 lamps	EA.	159.00

	Unit	Total

16510.10 LIGHTING INDUSTRIAL (Cont.)

Surface mounted fluorescent
  Compact fluorescent

	Unit	Total
2-7w	EA.	222.50
2-13w	EA.	276.75

16670.10 LIGHTNING PROTECTION

Lightning protection
  Copper point, nickel plated, 12'

	Unit	Total
1/2" dia.	EA.	116.50
5/8" dia.	EA.	122.00

16750.20 SIGNALING SYSTEMS

Contractor grade doorbell chime kit

	Unit	Total
Chime	EA.	109.25
Doorbutton	EA.	28.37

16850.10 ELECTRIC HEATING

Baseboard heater

	Unit	Total
2', 375w	EA.	114.25
3', 500w	EA.	122.00
4', 750w	EA.	138.00
5', 935w	EA.	174.75
6', 1125w	EA.	212.50
7', 1310w	EA.	230.00
8', 1500w	EA.	270.00
9', 1680w	EA.	290.00
10', 1875w	EA.	350.00

Unit heater, wall mounted

	Unit	Total
750w	EA.	290.00
1500w	EA.	340.00

Thermostat

	Unit	Total
Integral	EA.	73.75
Line voltage	EA.	74.75
Electric heater connection	EA.	19.90

Fittings

	Unit	Total
Inside corner	EA.	53.25
Outside corner	EA.	55.50
Receptacle section	EA.	56.50
Blank section	EA.	63.00

Radiant ceiling heater panels

	Unit	Total
500w	EA.	362.50
750w	EA.	392.50
Unit heater thermostat	EA.	88.50
Mounting bracket	EA.	103.75
Relay	EA.	109.75

16910.40 CONTROL CABLE

Control cable, 600v, #14 THWN, PVC jacket

	Unit	Total
2 wire	L.F.	.93
4 wire	L.F.	1.32

Section Three

Metro Area Multipliers

The costs presented in this Costbook attempt to represent national averages. Costs, however, vary among regions and states and even between adjacent localities.

In order to more closely approximate the probable costs for specific locations throughout the U.S., this table of Metro Area Multipliers is provided. These adjustment factors can used to modify costs obtained from this book to help account for regional variations of construction costs and to provide a more accurate estimate for specific areas. The factors are formulated by comparing costs in a specific area to the costs presented in this Costbook. An example of how to use these factors is shown below. Whenever local current costs are known, whether material prices or labor rates, they should be used when more accuracy is required.

| Cost Obtained from Costbook Pages | X | Metro Area Multiplier Divided by 100 | = | Adjusted Cost |

For example, a project estimated to cost $1,000,000 using the Costbook can be adjusted to more closely approximate the cost in Los Angeles where the Multiplier is 119:

$$1,000,000 \ X \ \frac{119}{100} = \mathbf{1,190,000}$$

State	City	Multiplier
AK	ANCHORAGE	132
AL	ANNISTON	81
	AUBURN	82
	BIRMINGHAM	82
	DECATUR	84
	DOTHAN	83
	FLORENCE	84
	GADSDEN	82
	HUNTSVILLE	84
	MOBILE	86
	MONTGOMERY	81
	OPELIKA	82
	TUSCALOOSA	81
AR	FAYETTEVILLE	79
	FORT SMITH	79
	JONESBORO	78
	LITTLE ROCK	82
	NORTH LITTLE ROCK	82
	PINE BLUFF	80
	ROGERS	79
	SPRINGDALE	79
	TEXARKANA	79
AZ	FLAGSTAFF	94
	MESA	94
	PHOENIX	95
	TUCSON	93
	YUMA	94
CA	BAKERSFIELD	116
	CHICO	118
	FAIRFIELD	120
	FRESNO	118
	LODI	117
	LONG BEACH	119
	LOS ANGELES	119
	MERCED	118
	MODESTO	114
	NAPA	120
	OAKLAND	124
	ORANGE COUNTY	118
	PARADISE	114
	PORTERVILLE	116
	REDDING	114
	RIVERSIDE	116
	SACRAMENTO	118
	SALINAS	120
	SAN BERNARDINO	116
	SAN DIEGO	117
	SAN FRANCISCO	129
	SAN JOSE	126
	SAN LUIS OBISPO	113
	SANTA BARBARA	116
	SANTA CRUZ	120
	SANTA ROSA	121
	STOCKTON	117
	TULARE	118

State	City	Multiplier
CA	VALLEJO	120
	VENTURA	116
	VISALIA	118
	WATSONVILLE	118
	YOLO	118
	YUBA CITY	118
CO	BOULDER	103
	COLORADO SPRINGS	100
	DENVER	101
	FORT COLLINS	110
	GRAND JUNCTION	99
	GREELEY	108
	LONGMONT	103
	LOVELAND	110
	PUEBLO	105
CT	BRIDGEPORT	113
	DANBURY	113
	HARTFORD	112
	MERIDEN	113
	NEW HAVEN	113
	NEW LONDON	110
	NORWALK	117
	NORWICH	110
	STAMFORD	117
	WATERBURY	112
DC	WASHINGTON	105
DE	DOVER	105
	NEWARK	106
	WILMINGTON	106
FL	BOCA RATON	80
	BRADENTON	80
	CAPE CORAL	78
	CLEARWATER	81
	DAYTONA BEACH	75
	FORT LAUDERDALE	83
	FORT MYERS	78
	FORT PIERCE	81
	FORT WALTON BEACH	76
	GAINESVILLE	80
	JACKSONVILLE	78
	LAKELAND	78
	MELBOURNE	75
	MIAMI	81
	NAPLES	79
	OCALA	79
	ORLANDO	77
	PALM BAY	75
	PANAMA CITY	77
	PENSACOLA	76
	PORT ST. LUCIE	81
	PUNTA GORDA	78
	SARASOTA	80
	ST. PETERSBURG	80
	TALLAHASSEE	75
	TAMPA	80

State	City	Multiplier
FL	TITUSVILLE	75
	WEST PALM BEACH	80
	WINTER HAVEN	78
GA	ALBANY	86
	ATHENS	89
	ATLANTA	92
	AUGUSTA	86
	COLUMBUS	79
	MACON	83
	SAVANNAH	87
HI	HONOLULU	138
IA	CEDAR FALLS	91
	CEDAR RAPIDS	102
	DAVENPORT	106
	DES MOINES	104
	DUBUQUE	95
	IOWA CITY	97
	SIOUX CITY	91
	WATERLOO	91
ID	BOISE CITY	102
	POCATELLO	102
IL	BLOOMINGTON	113
	CHAMPAIGN	109
	CHICAGO	125
	DECATUR	107
	KANKAKEE	113
	NORMAL	113
	PEKIN	111
	PEORIA	111
	ROCKFORD	113
	SPRINGFIELD	108
	URBANA	109
IN	BLOOMINGTON	102
	ELKHART	96
	EVANSVILLE	99
	FORT WAYNE	100
	GARY	107
	GOSHEN	96
	INDIANAPOLIS	103
	KOKOMO	101
	LAFAYETTE	101
	MUNCIE	101
	SOUTH BEND	102
	TERRE HAUTE	100
KS	KANSAS CITY	120
	LAWRENCE	109
	TOPEKA	96
	WICHITA	87
KY	LEXINGTON	91
	LOUISVILLE	102
	OWENSBORO	101
LA	ALEXANDRIA	89
	BATON ROUGE	93
	BOSSIER CITY	90
	HOUMA	93

State	City	Multiplier
LA	LAFAYETTE	91
	LAKE CHARLES	93
	MONROE	89
	NEW ORLEANS	95
	SHREVEPORT	90
MA	BARNSTABLE	124
	BOSTON	128
	BROCKTON	118
	FITCHBURG	120
	LAWRENCE	121
	LEOMINSTER	120
	LOWELL	124
	NEW BEDFORD	118
	PITTSFIELD	118
	SPRINGFIELD	119
	WORCESTER	120
	YARMOUTH	124
MD	BALTIMORE	95
	CUMBERLAND	98
	HAGERSTOWN	90
ME	AUBURN	87
	BANGOR	87
	LEWISTON	87
	PORTLAND	88
MI	ANN ARBOR	119
	BATTLE CREEK	111
	BAY CITY	116
	BENTON HARBOR	111
	DETROIT	120
	EAST LANSING	117
	FLINT	116
	GRAND RAPIDS	112
	HOLLAND	112
	JACKSON	107
	KALAMAZOO	111
	LANSING	117
	MIDLAND	115
	MUSKEGON	112
	SAGINAW	116
MN	DULUTH	107
	MINNEAPOLIS	112
	ROCHESTER	107
	ST. CLOUD	105
	ST. PAUL	112
MO	COLUMBIA	114
	JOPLIN	103
	KANSAS CITY	118
	SPRINGFIELD	96
	ST. JOSEPH	117
	ST. LOUIS	115
MS	BILOXI	79
	GULFPORT	79
	HATTIESBURG	79
	JACKSON	79
	PASCAGOULA	79

State	City	Multiplier
MT	BILLINGS	96
	GREAT FALLS	90
	MISSOULA	91
NC	ASHEVILLE	73
	CHAPEL HILL	79
	CHARLOTTE	82
	DURHAM	81
	FAYETTEVILLE	75
	GOLDSBORO	80
	GREENSBORO	81
	GREENVILLE	79
	HICKORY	72
	HIGH POINT	81
	JACKSONVILLE	72
	LENOIR	72
	MORGANTON	72
	RALEIGH	80
	ROCKY MOUNT	72
	WILMINGTON	72
	WINSTON SALEM	77
ND	BISMARCK	84
	FARGO	98
	GRAND FORKS	81
NE	LINCOLN	84
	OMAHA	91
NH	MANCHESTER	106
	NASHUA	106
	PORTSMOUTH	111
NJ	ATLANTIC CITY	126
	BERGEN	129
	BRIDGETON	125
	CAPE MAY	125
	HUNTERDON	128
	JERSEY CITY	130
	MIDDLESEX	129
	MILLVILLE	125
	MONMOUTH	129
	NEWARK	129
	OCEAN	130
	PASSAIC	130
	SOMERSET	128
	TRENTON	128
	VINELAND	125
NM	ALBUQUERQUE	91
	LAS CRUCES	91
	SANTA FE	91
NV	LAS VEGAS	109
	RENO	97
NY	ALBANY	119
	BINGHAMTON	116
	BUFFALO	118
	DUTCHESS COUNTY	119
	ELMIRA	118
	GLENS FALLS	120
	JAMESTOWN	112

State	City	Multiplier
NY	NASSAU	137
	NEW YORK	148
	NEWBURGH	119
	NIAGARA FALLS	121
	ROCHESTER	118
	ROME	109
	SCHENECTADY	119
	SUFFOLK	137
	SYRACUSE	118
	TROY	119
	UTICA	109
OH	AKRON	112
	CANTON	107
	CINCINNATI	105
	CLEVELAND	114
	COLUMBUS	115
	DAYTON	115
	ELYRIA	114
	HAMILTON	105
	LIMA	115
	LORAIN	114
	MANSFIELD	115
	MASSILLON	107
	MIDDLETOWN	115
	SPRINGFIELD	109
	STEUBENVILLE	115
	TOLEDO	109
	WARREN	111
	YOUNGSTOWN	111
OK	ENID	86
	LAWTON	86
	OKLAHOMA CITY	85
	TULSA	80
OR	ASHLAND	109
	CORVALLIS	112
	EUGENE	112
	MEDFORD	109
	PORTLAND	114
	SALEM	112
	SPRINGFIELD	112
PA	ALLENTOWN	118
	ALTOONA	110
	BETHLEHEM	118
	CARLISLE	113
	EASTON	118
	ERIE	112
	HARRISBURG	113
	HAZLETON	118
	JOHNSTOWN	104
	LANCASTER	93
	LEBANON	115
	PHILADELPHIA	134
	PITTSBURGH	116
	READING	119
	SCRANTON	116

State	City	Multiplier
PA	SHARON	112
	STATE COLLEGE	98
	WILKES BARRE	116
	WILLIAMSPORT	97
	YORK	113
PR	MAYAGUEZ	73
	PONCE	74
	SAN JUAN	75
RI	PROVIDENCE	122
SC	AIKEN	89
	ANDERSON	71
	CHARLESTON	76
	COLUMBIA	76
	FLORENCE	73
	GREENVILLE	76
	MYRTLE BEACH	73
	NORTH CHARLESTON	81
	SPARTANBURG	73
	SUMTER	76
SD	RAPID CITY	81
	SIOUX FALLS	85
TN	CHATTANOOGA	84
	CLARKSVILLE	83
	JACKSON	83
	JOHNSON CITY	83
	KNOXVILLE	80
	MEMPHIS	84
	NASHVILLE	83
TX	ABILENE	88
	AMARILLO	92
	ARLINGTON	87
	AUSTIN	89
	BEAUMONT	88
	BRAZORIA	88
	BROWNSVILLE	73
	BRYAN	86
	COLLEGE STATION	86
	CORPUS CHRISTI	84
	DALLAS	89
	DENISON	87
	EDINBURG	73
	EL PASO	81
	FORT WORTH	87
	GALVESTON	93
	HARLINGEN	73
	HOUSTON	88
	KILLEEN	77
	LAREDO	78
	LONGVIEW	78
	LUBBOCK	91
	MARSHALL	87
	MCALLEN	73
	MIDLAND	87
	MISSION	73
	ODESSA	87
	PORT ARTHUR	88
	SAN ANGELO	87
	SAN ANTONIO	90

State	City	Multiplier
TX	SAN BENITO	73
	SAN MARCOS	89
	SHERMAN	87
	TEMPLE	77
	TEXARKANA	79
	TEXAS CITY	93
	TYLER	84
	VICTORIA	74
	WACO	77
	WICHITA FALLS	87
UT	OGDEN	95
	OREM	93
	PROVO	93
	SALT LAKE CITY	92
VA	CHARLOTTESVILLE	86
	LYNCHBURG	83
	NEWPORT NEWS	88
	NORFOLK	91
	PETERSBURG	78
	RICHMOND	90
	ROANOKE	76
	VIRGINIA BEACH	91
VT	BURLINGTON	97
WA	BELLEVUE	119
	BELLINGHAM	111
	BREMERTON	113
	EVERETT	117
	KENNEWICK	101
	OLYMPIA	113
	PASCO	100
	RICHLAND	101
	SEATTLE	119
	SPOKANE	98
	TACOMA	116
	YAKIMA	104
WI	APPLETON	113
	BELOIT	117
	EAU CLAIRE	113
	GREEN BAY	112
	JANESVILLE	117
	KENOSHA	118
	LA CROSSE	114
	MADISON	116
	MILWAUKEE	118
	NEENAH	113
	OSHKOSH	113
	RACINE	118
	SHEBOYGAN	112
	WAUKESHA	118
	WAUSAU	113
WV	CHARLESTON	113
	HUNTINGTON	113
	PARKERSBURG	113
	WHEELING	113
WY	CASPER	85
	CHEYENNE	85

- A -

A-BAND HANGER 122
ABOVE GROUND TANK....................120
ABRASIVE SURFACE TILE................102-103
ABS PIPE 48, 143
ACCESS STAIR 117
ACCESSORY REINFORCING 58
ACID-PROOF COUNTER 118
ACOUSTICAL BLOCK 65
   CEILING 112
   PANEL 104
   TILE 105
ACRYLIC CARPET 106
AD PLYWOOD 81
ADAPTER CUBICLE..............................154
   TERMINAL 161
ADDITION INDUSTRIAL FACILITY 13
ADHESIVE-BED TILE 102
ADJUSTABLE BAR HANGER 167
   SHELF 81
ADMINISTRATION BUILDING 23
ADMIXTURE 59
AIR COMPRESSOR 39
   CONDENSER 151
   CONDITIONING...............................151
   ENTRAINING AGENT 59
   TOOL 39
AIRPORT RESTAURANT 26
ALL THREAD ROD 154
ALUMINUM CONDUIT 157
   DOOR 98
   DOWNSPOUT 90
   FLASHING 89
   GUTTER 90
   LOUVER 70
   POLE 168
   RAILING 69
   ROOF 89
   SHINGLE 86
   SIDING PANEL 87
   THRESHOLD 97
AMBIENT DAMPER 151
AMBULATORY SURGICAL CENTER............20
ANCHOR 68
   BOLT 68
   BRICK 63
   DOVETAIL 63
   RAFTER 71
   SLOT 63
   WOOD 71
ANGLE STEEL.....................................66
   VALVE 146
ANTI-SIPHON BREAKER 147
APRON 79
ARCHITECTURAL FEE 37
ASPHALT DAMPPROOFING....................84
   EXPANSION JOINT 57
ASPHALTIC PAINT 84
ATHLETIC COMPLEX 23
ATTIC INSULATION 85
AWNING WINDOW................................96

- B -

BACK MOUNTED TILE 102
   SPLASH 81
BACKFILL 46
   HAND 44
BACKHOE..40
BACKHOE/LOADER 40
BACK-UP BLOCK 65
   BRICK 64
BALANCING VALVE 146
BALL VALVE 146
BALUSTER 80
BANK RUN GRAVEL 43
BAR HANGER 167
   REINFORCING 62
BARE STRANDED WIRE........................163

BARRICADE 38
BARRIER VAPOR............................58, 84
BASE CABINET 81, 118
   COLONIAL 79
   COLUMN 71
   FLASHING 89
   GROUTING 61
   MANHOLE 49
   TERRAZZO 104
BASEBOARD HEATER 172
   RADIATION 151
BATCH DISPOSAL 148
BATH FAUCET 148
BATHROOM LOCK................................97
BATTEN SIDING...................................88
BEAD MOLDING 80
   PARTING 80
   PLASTER...............................100, 102
   SASH 80
BEAM 68
   BOLSTER 58
   BOND 62, 66
   CHAIR 58
   FURRING 68, 99
   GRADE 60
   HANGER 71
   PLASTER.......................................101
   REINFORCING 57
   SHEETROCK 101
BEAUTY STORE 7
BENTONITE MEMBRANE 84
BEVELED SIDING 88
BIBB HOSE 145
BI-FOLD DOOR 94
BINDER COURSE 50
BI-PASSING DOOR 94
BIRCH DOOR 92
   PANELING 82
   VENEER 82
BITUMINOUS MEMBRANE 84
   SIDEWALK 50
BLACK IRON FITTING 144
   STEEL 144
BLOCK CONCRETE 61, 65
   DAMPPROOFING 84
   DEMOLITION 41
   GLASS 66
   GRANITE 64
   GROUT 62
   REMOVAL 41
   SPLASH 61
   VENT 115
BLOWN-IN INSULATION 85
BLUESTONE 64
BOARD RAFTER 75
   RIDGE 75
   SIDING 88
   SUB-FLOORING 77
BOLSTER SLAB 58
BOLT CARRIAGE 71
   WOOD 71
BOLTED STEEL 68
BOND BEAM 62, 66
BONDERIZED FLAGPOLE 115
BOOKKEEPER 38
BOTTOM BEAM....................................55
   PLATE 76
BOUNDARIES 38
BOX DEVICE 166
   JUNCTION 166
   PLASTIC 167
   WEATHERPROOF 166
BRACKET BOX 167
BRASS FITTING 134-135, 138
BREAKER CIRCUIT 154
   VACUUM 147
BRICK ANCHOR...................................63
   CHIMNEY 64
   MANHOLE 49
   PAVER 64

BRIDGING 71
BRONZE RAILING.................................69
BROOM FINISH....................................59
BRUSH CUTTING.................................43
BUCKET TRAP 147
BUDGET CONSTRAINTS..........................1
BUFF BRICK 64
BUILDING METAL 120
   PAPER 84
   TYPE 1
BUILT-IN OVEN 117
BUILT-UP ROOF 88
BULKHEAD FORMWORK 56
BULLDOZER 40
BURLAP CONCRETE 59
   RUB 59
BUS DUCT 154
BUSHING BRASS 135
   CONDUIT 158
   FLUSH COPPER 129
BUTT HINGE 97
BX CABLE 163
   CLAMP 167

- C -

C CONDULET 156
CABINET BASE 81
   KITCHEN 118
CABLE BX 163
   SER 163
   SEU 162
   THHN-THWN 163
CANT STRIP 76, 88
CAP BLACK IRON 144
   BRASS 135
   CONDUIT 159
   COPPER 129, 133
   ENTRANCE 156
   PILE 55, 60
   PILE REINFORCING 57
   PVC 140-142
   STEEL 145
CARPENTRY ROUGH.............................72
CARPET CLEAN 107
   TILE 107
CARRIAGE BOLT 71
CARRIER CHANNEL 105
CARVED DOOR 94
CASED BORING 41
CASEMENT WINDOW 96
CASING 79
   BEAD 102
   RANCH 79
   TRIM 80
CAST ALUMINUM BOX 165
   BOX 164
   IRON BOILER 150
   IRON FITTING 144
   IRON STRAINER 147
CAVITY WALL 62, 64
   WALL ANCHOR 63
CDX 77
CEDAR CLOSET 82
   DECKING..78
   SHINGLE 87
   SIDING 87-88
CEILING BLOCKING 72
   DIFFUSER 152
   FURRING.............................73-74, 99
   GRILLE 153
   HEATER 117
   INSULATION 84
   JOIST 72
   LATH 100
   REMOVAL 41
CEILINGS 113
CEMENT KEENES 101
   PLASTER......................................101
CENTER BULB 58

CHAIN LINK..42
    LINK FENCES..............................108
CHAIR RAIL..79
    REINFORCING..............................58
CHAMFER STRIP....................................56
CHANNEL FURRING..........................68, 99
    STRAP...154
CHECK VALVE.....................................145
CHERRY VENEER...................................82
CHESTNUT VENEER................................82
CHIMNEY BRICK....................................64
    FLUE...67
    MASONRY......................................67
CHURCH..28-29
CIRCUIT BREAKER...............................154
CITY SERVICES BUILDING........................27
CLAMP BEAM.....................................154
    GROUND ROD..............................169
    ROD BEAM..................................154
    TYPE CAP....................................159
CLASSROOM BUILDING...........................23
CLAY BRICK FLOOR..............................106
    PIPE..49-50
CLEANING MASONRY..............................67
CLEARING TREE.....................................43
CLEFT NATURAL....................................64
CLOCK RECEPTACLE.............................168
CLOSET CEDAR.....................................82
    DOOR...94
    FLANGE.......................................133
    POLE...79
CLOTH FACED FIBERGLASS.....................104
CMU...65
    GROUT..62
COLLEGE BUILDING................................22
COLONIAL BASE....................................79
    MOLDING.......................................80
COLOR GROUP TILE..............................102
COLUMN..68
    BASE..71
    COVER...98
    FURRING..68
    PIER..56
    PLASTER.......................................101
    SHEETROCK..................................101
    TIMBER...78
COMBINATION SWITCH...........................170
COMMON BRICK....................................64
COMMUNITY COLLEGE BUILDING..............22
COMPACT BASE.....................................45
    BORROW.......................................43
    FLUORESCENT..............................172
COMPACTOR RESIDENTIAL......................117
COMPRESSION COUPLING.......................156
    FITTING.................................137, 155
COMPRESSOR.......................................39
CONCEALED Z BAR...............................105
CONCRETE BLOCK................................107
    BLOCK REMOVAL............................41
    CUTTING.......................................42
    FILLED PILE...................................47
    MANHOLE......................................49
    PILING..47
    PLACEMENT...................................59
    POLE...168
    PUMP..59
    RECEPTOR....................................115
    REINFORCEMENT.............................56
    SLEEPER.......................................76
    TESTING.......................................38
    WATERPROOFING...........................84
CONDUCTIVE FLOOR.............................106
CONDUCTOR ALUMINUM.........................162
    COPPER.......................................163
    STRANDED...................................163
CONDUIT ALUMINUM......................155, 157
    BODY..161
    BUSHING......................................158
    CAP...159
    EMT..155

CONDUIT FLEXIBLE...............................157
    GALVANIZED.................................158
    LOCKNUT.....................................158
    PENETRATION...............................154
    PLASTIC COATE............................161
    PVC..160
    STEEL...157
CONDULET..156
    COVER..................................156, 160
    GASKET.......................................160
    LB...159
CONFERENCE CENTER...............................5
CONNECTOR COMPRESSION......................155
    DIE CAST.....................................155
    SET SCREW..................................155
CONTINUOUS DISPOSAL.........................148
    FOOTING......................................60
    HIGH CHAIR...................................58
CONTROL JOINT....................................63
COPING PRECAST...................................61
COPPER DOWNSPOUT...............................90
    FLASHING......................................89
    HANGER.......................................122
    PIPE FITTING................................133
    WIRE HOOK..................................123
CORD ELECTRIC...................................164
    SET..168
CORED PLUG.......................................136
CORING CONCRETE................................42
CORK WALL COVERING..........................114
CORNER BEAD...............................100, 102
    CABINET......................................118
    GUARD..114
    POST..51
CORNICE MOLDING.................................81
CORRUGATED DOWNSPOUT........................90
    METAL PIPE...................................50
    PANEL..87
    ROOF..89
COUNTER FLASHING................................89
    LAVATORY....................................149
COUNTERSUNK PLUG.............................136
COUNTERTOP..81
    RANGE..117
COUNTY HOSPITAL.............................17-18
    HOSPITAL PARKING DECK.................18
COUPLING BLACK IRON..........................144
    BRASS..135
    COMPRESSION..............................155
    COPPER.......................................133
    EMT..156
    ERICKSON....................................158
    NO-HUB.......................................123
    PLASTIC.......................................48
    PVC......................................140-142
    SET SCREW..................................155
    SPLIT...158
    STEEL...145
    THREADED...................................159
    THREADLESS................................159
    WITH STOP..................................126
COURSE BINDER....................................50
COURTHOUSE.......................................10
COVE BASE..106
    BASE TILE....................................103
    MOLDING......................................79
COVER CONDULET........................156, 160
CPVC FITTING.....................................142
    PIPE.....................................139, 142
CRACK PATCH.....................................101
CRANE..40
CRAWL SPACE INSULATION......................85
CRAWLER CRANE...................................40
CREOSOTE...82
CREOSOTED POLE................................168
CREW TRAILER......................................38
CROSS NO-HUB...................................124
CROWN MOLDING..................................80
CRUSHER RUN......................................46
CSI DIVISIONS..1

CURB TERRAZZO..............................103-104
CURING PAPER......................................59
CURTAIN WALL......................................98
CURVED CURB FORM...............................55
    STAIR TERRAZZO...........................104
CUSTOM DOOR......................................94
CUT AND FILL.......................................46
    TREE..43
CUT-OUT COUNTERTOP.............................81
CYLINDER PILING..................................47

- D -

DANDY CLEANOUT.................................132
DARBY...59
DECKING WOOD....................................78
DECKS, WOOD, STAINED.........................109
DEMOLITION..4
DESANCO FITTING COPPER......................132
DESCRIPTION..1
DEVICE COVER.....................................166
DIECAST SET SCREW.............................155
DIMMER SWITCH...................................170
DISAPPEARING STAIR.............................117
DISCOUNT SHOE STORE.............................9
DISH SOAP..103
DISHWASHER RESIDENTIAL......................117
DISPENSER TISSUE...............................116
DISPOSAL RESIDENTIAL..........................117
DIVIDER STRIP TERRAZZO.......................103
DOMESTIC WELL....................................47
DOOR ALUMINUM...................................98
    CLOSER..97
    FLUSH..94
    FRAME..92
    FRAME GROUT................................62
    HEADER..76
    HOLDER..97
    REMOVAL......................................41
    SHOWER......................................115
    SLIDING GLASS..............................94
    SOLID CORE...................................92
DOORS...107
    AND WINDOWS..............................107
DOORS, WOOD................................109, 113
DOUBLE HUNG WINDOW..........................95
    WALLED TANK...............................120
    WYE NO-HUB................................125
DOUGLAS FIR.......................................78
DOVETAIL ANCHOR SLOT.........................63
DOWEL REINFORCING..............................56
DOWNSPOUT...90
    ALUMINUM....................................90
DOZER EXCAVATION...............................43
DRAIN FIELD..50
    TILE..50
DRAINAGE PIPE.....................................48
    UNDERSLAB...................................50
DRAPERY TRACK...................................118
DRAWER BASE.....................................118
DRILLED WELL......................................47
DRILLING ROCK.....................................41
DRIVING STUD.....................................169
DROP EAR ELL.....................................129
DROPCLOTHS.......................................107
DRUM TRAP..133
DRY STONE WALL..................................67
DRYER RECEPTACLE..............................168
DRYWALL...101
    REMOVAL......................................41
DUCT BUS..154
    INSULATION.................................123
DUCTWORK METAL................................152
DUMBELL JOINT.....................................58
DUMP TRUCK..40
DUMPSTER...41
DWV COPPER.......................................126
    FITTING COPPER...........................130

Index

- E -

EDGE FORM 55
ELASTIC SHEET ROOF 89
ELASTOMERIC FLASHING.....64
ELBOW ABS.....49
  CAST IRON.....48
  PLASTIC.....48
  PVC.....141
ELECTRIC BOILER 151
  FURNACE.....151
EMERGENCY CENTER 27
ENAMEL PAINT.....114
END CLEANOUT.....132
ENGINEERING FEE 37
ENTRANCE CAP 156, 159
  FITTING 158
ENTRY LOCK 97
EQUIPMENT MOBILIZATION.....38
  PAD.....60
  PAD REINFORCING.....56
ERICKSON COUPLING.....158
ESTABROOK TY 133
EXPANDED LATH 100
EXPANSION JOINT 57, 100
EXPOSED AGGREGATE 64
EXTENSION BOX 166
EXTERIOR DOOR 94
  TILE 103

- F -

FABRIC CHAIN LINK 51
FACTORY FINISH FLOOR 105
FAMILY HOMELESS RESIDENTIAL 31
FAN EXHAUST.....152
FASCIA BOARD 75
  PLASTER.....101
FASTENER INSULATION 85
FAUCET.....148
FEE PROFESSIONAL 37
FELT CONTROL JOINT.....58
FEMALE ADAPTER COPPER 127, 132
  ADAPTER PVC.....140-142
  CONNECTOR 137
  DROP EAR ELL.....129
  FLANGED ELL.....129
  FLUSH BUSHING 129
FENCE.....51
  REUSE.....42
FENCES, WOOD OR MASONRY 108
FIBER CANT.....76
  FORM CONCRETE.....55
  PANEL.....104
FIBERBOARD SHEATHING 78
FIBERGLASS INSULATION.....84-85
  PANEL.....104
  TANK.....120
FIBROUS DAMPPROOFING 84
FILL BORROW 43
  CAP.....120
FILLED BLOCK.....61, 65
FILLER JOINT.....63
  PAINT.....114
FILTER BARRIER.....46
FINISH PLASTER.....100
  SHOTCRETE.....59
FINISHING SHEETROCK 102
FINK TRUSS.....79
FIR DECKING.....78
  FLOOR.....105
  SIDING.....87
FIRE RESISTANT SHEETROCK.....102
  RETARDANT.....82
  RETARDENT ROOF.....87
  STATION.....11-12
FITTING CPVC.....142
  NO-HUB.....123, 125
  PVC.....141
  REDUCER COPPER 132

FIXED WINDOW.....95
FIXTURE PLUMBING 147
  SQUARE.....171
FLANGE PVC.....140-142
FLARE FITTING BRASS.....137
FLASHING.....89-90
  MASONRY.....64
FLAT APRON.....79
  CONDUIT CABLE.....154
  RIB.....100
  WASHER.....154
FLEXIBLE CONDUIT.....157
  CORD.....164
FLOAT.....59
  TRAP.....147
FLOOR CLEANOUT.....145
  DRAIN.....147
  FINISH.....59
  FINISHING.....105
  GYM.....105
  INDUSTRIAL WOOD 105
  JOIST.....73
  MASONRY.....106
  SAFE.....120
  SHEATHING.....77
  TERRAZZO.....103
  TILE.....102-103
FLUE LINER.....67
FLUID APPLIED FLOOR 106
FLUORESCENT FIXTURE 170-171
FLUSH BUSHING COPPER 129
  DOOR.....92, 94
FLUTED STEEL CASING 47
FOAM POLYETHYLENE 58
FOAMGLASS CANT 88
FOIL BACKED INSULATION 85
FOLDING STAIR 117
FOOTING EXCAVATION 45
FOREMAN 37
FORMICA 81
FOUNDATION BACKFILL 44, 46
  BLOCK.....65
  VENT.....62
FRAME COVER.....49
  DOOR.....94
FRAMING ANCHOR 71
  CEILING.....72
  DOOR.....76
  ROOF.....74
  SOFFIT.....76
  TIMBER.....78
  WALL.....76
  WINDOW.....76
FRESH MARKET.....6
FRICTION PILING.....47
FRONT-END LOADER 44
FS BOX.....164
FSA BOX.....165
FSC BOX.....165
FSCA BOX.....165
FSCD BOX.....165
FSL BOX.....165
FSR BOX.....165
FURRING CEILING.....99
  CHANNEL.....68
  STEEL.....99
FUSIBLE SWITCH 154

- G -

GABLE LOUVER 115
  TRUSS.....79
GABLE-END RAFTER 74
GALVANIZED ACCESSORY 58
  DUCTWORK.....152
  MESH.....57
  RAILING.....69
  SHINGLE.....86
  WALL TIE.....62
GARAGE.....3

GAS FURNACE 151
GASKET CONDULET 160
GATE POST.....51
  SWING.....51
  VALVE.....145
GENERATOR.....39
GFI BREAKER.....169
GIRDER.....68
GLASS BEAD.....80
  CLOTH TILE.....105
  DOOR.....94
  FRAMING.....98
GLAZED BRICK.....64
  FLOOR.....106
  WALL TILE.....102
GLOBE VALVE.....146
GRAB BAR.....115
GRADALL.....45
GRADING.....46
GRANITE BLOCK.....64
  VENEER.....67
GRAPHIC REPRESENTATION 1
GRASS CLOTH 114
GRAVEL MULCH.....54
  ROOF.....89
GRAY SPONGE.....58
GRILLE VENTILATION.....152
GROUND FAULT.....169
  ROD.....169
  SLAB.....56
  STRAP.....167
GROUNDING LOCKNUT 160
GROUT BEAM.....62
  BLOCK.....61-62, 65
  MASONRY.....62
  WALL.....62
GRS CONDUIT.....158
GRUBBING.....43
GUNITE.....59
GUTTER.....90
  COPPER.....90
  REMOVAL.....42
  STEEL.....90
GUTTERS AND DOWNSPOUT.....109
GYM FLOOR.....105
GYPSUM PLASTER 100
  SHEATHING.....78

- H -

HALF ROUND GUTTER 90
  ROUND MOLDING.....80
HAND BUGGY.....59
  EXCAVATION.....45
  LOADING.....43
  SEEDING.....52
  SPLIT SHAKE.....87
  SPREADING.....52
HANDICAPPED PLUMBING.....148
HANDLING RUBBISH.....41
HANDY BOX.....167
HANGER CHANNEL.....154
  JOIST.....71
  ROD.....154
HARDBOARD DOOR.....93
  UNDERLAYMENT.....77
HAULING RUBBISH.....41
HAVEN FOR HOPE.....30-31
HEADER.....76
  CEILING.....72
HEATER.....39
  ELECTRIC.....117, 172
  UNIT.....151
  WATER.....150
HEAVY DUTY DOOR.....92
  DUTY TERRAZZO.....103
HERRINGBONE FLOOR 106
HEX BUSHING.....135
  NUT.....154
  TRAP COPPER 132

HIGH CHAIR REINFORCING 58
HIP RAFTER 75
HOLE CLIP 122
   CONDUIT 154
   PLASTER 101
HOLLOW BLOCK 65
   COLUMN 83
   CORE DOOR 93
   METAL DOOR 92
   METAL FRAME 92
HOMELESS CAMPUS 30-31
HOOD RANGE 117
HORIZONTAL DAMPER 152
   REINFORCING 57, 62
   SIDING 87
   WINDOW 95
HOSPITAL EXPANSION 17
HOT WATER DISPENSER 148
   WATER STORAGE TAN 150
H-SECTION PILE 47
HVAC SYSTEM 20
HYDRAULIC EXCAVATOR 43, 45

- I -

ICE MAKER 117
IMC CONDUIT 162
IMMEDIATE CARE 16
INCANDESCENT FIXTURE 170
INCREASING FEMALE ADA 127
   MALE ADAPT 127
INDEPENDENT LIVING COTTAGES 15
   LIVING FACILITY 32
INDUSTRIAL FACILITY 13-14
   WOOD FLOOR 105
INSULATED BLOCK 65
   GLASS DOOR 94
   SIDING 87
   THROAT 155, 157
INSULATION BLOWN-IN 85
   FASTENERS 85
   MASONRY 86
   SPRAYED 86
INTERMEDIATE CONDUIT 162
IRREGULAR STONE 64
IRRIGATION LAWN 50
ISOLATOR VIBRATION 123

- J -

JACK RAFTER 75
JALOUSIE WINDOW 95
JOB BUILT FORM 55
   TRAILER 38
JOINT CLIP 100
   EXPANSION 57
   FILLER 63
   REINFORCING 62
JOIST BRIDGING 71
   FLOOR 73
   HANGER 71
   SISTER 72-73
JUDICIAL CENTER 10
JUMBO BRICK 64
JUTE PADDING 106

- K -

K COPPER 126
   TUBE 126
KEENES CEMENT 101
KEYWAY FORM 56
KILN DRIED 82
KING POST TRUSS 79
KITCHEN CABINET 81, 118
   FAUCET 148
   SINK 149
KNOTTY PINE 82

- L -

L TUBE 126
LADDER REINFORCING 62
LAMINATED PLASTIC 81
   RAILING 69
LANDING TERRAZZO 104
LANDSCAPE TIMBER 54
LATCHSET 97
LATEX PAINT 114
LATH EXPANDED 100
   STUCCO 100
LATTICE MOLDING 80
LAUAN DOOR 92
   VENEER 82
LAVATORY FAUCET 148
LB CONDULET 156, 159
LEACHING PIT 50
LEAD COATED COPPER 90
LECTURE HALL 22
LEED® 3, 21-23, 25
LEVEL GAUGE 147
   INDICATOR 120
LIGHT GAGE FRAMING 68
   STEEL 68
   TRACK 171
LIGHTING 171
LIGHTWEIGHT BLOCK 65
LIMESTONE AGGREGATE 64
LIMING 52
LINCOLN CENTER 5
LINE POST 51
LINER FLUE 67
LINTEL STEEL 66
LIQUID LEVEL GAUGE 147
LL CONDULET 156
LOAD BEARING STUD 99
   CENTER BREAKER 169
   CENTER INDOOR 169
LOADER 40
LOCKNUT BRASS 136
   CONDUIT 158
   GROUNDING 160
LOCKWASHER 155
LONG FORGED NUT 138
   SWEEP ABS 143
   TURN TEE 131
LOT LINES 38
LOUVER DOOR 94
LR CONDULET 156

- M -

M TUBE 126
MAHOGANY VENEER 82
MALE ADAPTER COPPER 127, 132
   ADAPTER PVC 140-142
   CONNECTOR 137
MALL 4
MALLEABLE IRON 144
   STRAP 156, 160
MANHOFF ADAPTER COPPER 131
MANHOLE 49
MAPLE FLOOR 105
MARBLE CHIP 54
MARKET 6
MASKING PAPER AND TAP 107
MASONRY CHIMNEY 64, 67
   CLEANING 67
   DEMOLITION 41
   FENCE 42
   FURRING 73
   GLASS 66
   INSULATION 86
   PLASTER 67
   REINFORCING 57
   SLATE 67
   WATERPROOFING 84
MAT FORMWORK 55
   REINFORCING 57

MECHANICAL FEE 37
   JOINT PIPE 47
   SEEDING 52
MEDICAL CENTER PARKING DECK 18
   OFFICE BUILDING 16
MEDICINE CABINET 115
MEMBRANE CURING 59
   WATERPROOFING 84
MEN'S HOMELESS RESIDENTIAL 30
MESH SLAB 57
   TIE 63
   WIRE 60
METAL BASE 100
   BUILDING 120
   CLAD CABLE 163
   FENCE 51
   LINTEL 66
   POLE 168
   RAILING 69
   STUD 68
   WINDOW REMOVAL 41
METALLIC COLOR TILE 103
METRO AREA MULTIPLIERS 171
MIDDLETON HALL 24
MILL FRAMED STRUCTURE 78
MILLED WINDOW 96
MINERAL FIBER PANEL 104
   FIBER TILE 105
   WOOL 85
   WOOL INSULATION 85
MIRROR 115
   PLATE 98
MIXING VALVE 146
MONOLITHIC TERRAZZO 103
MOP SINK 150
MORTISE LOCKSET 97
MOSAIC TILE 103
MOSS PEAT 54
MOUNTING BRACKET HEAT 172
MOVING SHRUB 54
   TREE 54
MULCH 54

- N -

NAILER CEILING 72
NARROW STILE DOOR 98
NATURAL CLEFT SLATE 64
   LIGHT 3, 14, 20, 33
NEOPRENE FLASHING 89-90
   MEMBRANE 84
   ROOF 89
NIPPLE BLACK IRON 144
   STEEL 145
NM CABLE 164
NO-HUB ADAPTER COPPER 132
   PIPE 123, 125
NON-DRILLING ANCHOR 68
NON-METALLIC GROUT 61
NON-SLIP TERRAZZO 104
NORMAN BRICK 64
NORTH HALL 21
NUT HEX 154
NYLON CARPET 106

- O -

OAK DOOR 94
   FLOOR 105
   VENEER 82
OFFICE TRAILER 38
OFFSET CONNECTOR 156
OGEE MOLDING 80
OIL FIRED BOILER 151
   FURNACE 151
   TANK 120
ONE-HOLE STRAP 160
ORGANIC BED TILE 102
OUT PATIENT SERVICES 16
OVERHEAD 37
OVERSIZED BRICK 64

Index

- P -

PACKAGED HEATER 151
PAD EQUIPMENT.................................55
   REINFORCING 56
PADDING CARPET 106
PAINT ASPHALTIC 84
PALM TREE...54
PANEL ACOUSTICAL..............................104
   SIDING 87
PANIC DEVICE 97
PAPER BACKED INSULATION 85
   BACKED LATHE 100
   BUILDING 84
   CURING 59
PARALLEL DAMPER 152
PARGING 67
PARKING DECK 18
   DECK COUNTY HOSPITAL 18
   GARAGE 3, 23
   STRUCTURE 18
PARQUET FLOOR...................................105
PARTING BEAD 80
PARTITION REMOVAL 41
PATCH HOLE 101
PATIO BLOCK 64
PAVEMENT CUTTING 42
   REMOVAL 42
PAVER GRANITE 64
   STONE 64
PAVING CONCRETE.................................50
PEA GRAVEL 46
PEAT MOSS 54
PECAN VENEER 82
PEDESTRIAN BARRICADE 38
PEGBOARD 82
PENNSYLVANIA SLATE 86
PERFORATED CLAY PIPE 50
   PVC PIPE 50
   STRAP 122
PERFORMANCE HALL 5
PERLITE INSULATION 86
   ROOF INSULATION 85
PHOTOGRAPHS 38
PICKUP TRUCK 40
PICTURE WINDOW 96
PILASTER..56
PINE DECKING 78
   DOOR 94
   RISER 82
   SIDING 88
PIPE CAP 159
   CLAY 49
   COLUMN...68
   COPPER 126
   CPVC 142
   FLASHING 89
   GALVANIZED 144
   NO-HUB 123, 125
   PILE POINT 47
   PVC 141
   RAILING 69
PLACEMENT SLAB 59
PLANT BED PREPARATION.........................52
PLASTER MASONRY 67
   PATCH 101
   RING 167
PLASTERBOARD 101
PLASTIC CONDUIT BUSHING 158
   FILTER FABRIC 50
   SHEET 84
   SQUARE BOX 167
PLATE...76
   GLASS 97
   MIRROR 98
   SHEAR 71
   SWITCH 170
PLAZA 4
PLEXIGLASS 97
PLUG CAST IRON 145

PLUG CONDUIT 166
   NO-HUB 125
PLYWOOD 77
   FINISH 81
   SHEATHING 77
   SHELVING 81
   STRUCTURAL 78
   UNDERLAYMENT 77
PNEUMATIC TOOL 39
PODIATRY CLINIC 19
POLE CLOSET 79
   UTILITY 168
POLYETHYLENE VAPOR BARRIER.............84
POLYSTYRENE INSULATION 85-86
POLYURETHANE FLOOR 105
PORCELAIN SHINGLE 86
   SINK 149
POROUS CONCRETE PIPE 50
   FILL 58
PORTLAND CEMENT GROUT 61
POSTS TREATED 78
POURED INSULATION 85
   VERMICULITE 86
PRECAST LINTEL 66
   MANHOLE 49
   SEPTIC TANK 50
   TERRAZZO 103
PREFINISHED SHELVING 81
PREMOLDED JOINT 57
PRESSURE REDUCING VALVE 146
PRIMARY CARE 16
PRIMED DOOR 94
   SIDING 88
PRIMER PAINT 114
PROFESSIONAL FEE 37
PROFIT 37
PROJECTING WINDOW 95
P-TRAP 133
   ABS 143
   NO-HUB 124-125
PUBLIC WORKS DEPARTMENTS 27
PULL BOX 166
PUMP 39
PUMPED CONCRETE 59, 61
PUTTYING 107
PVC CEMENT 161
   CHAMFER STRIP 56
   COATED HANGER 122
   CONDUIT 160
   FITTING 141
   FOAM 58
   PIPE 48, 50, 141
   ROOF 89
   SEWER PIPE 49
   WATERSTOP 58

- Q -

QUARTER ROUND 80

- R -

RACEWAY 162
RAFTER...74
   ANCHOR 71
   HIP 75
RAIL CHAIR 79
RAILING...80
   METAL 69
RANCH CASING 79
   MOLDING 80
RANDOM WIDTH FLOOR 105
RANGE ELECTRIC 117
   HOOD 117
RECEPTOR SHOWER 115, 149
RECESSED LIGHT FIXTURE 105
RECTANGULAR BOX 165
   WALL TIE 62
RED BRICK 64
   LEAD PAINT 114
   NIPPLE 136

REDUCER COPPER 127
   NO-HUB 125
REDUCING COUPLING COP.........................126
   ELL STEEL 145
   FEMALE ADAPT 127
   INSERT PVC 140-142
   MALE ADAPTER 128
   TEE 144
REDWOOD SIDING...............................87-88
REFRIGERATION TUBING 126
REGIONAL MEDICAL CENTER 17-18
REGISTER WALL 153
REINFORCING ACCESSORY 58
   MASONRY 62, 66
RELIEF VALVE 146
REMOVE DRAINAGE PIPE 42
   FENCING 42
   GAS PIPING 42
   SEPTIC TANK 41
   SEWER PIPE 42
   TOPSOIL 52
   WATER PIPE 42
RESEED 52
RESET HYDRANT 42
RESIDENTIAL LOUVER 70
   TRANSITIONAL HOME 34
RESTAURANT AIRPORT 26
RETAIL CENTER 6
   STORE 8
RETARDANT FIRE 82
RETIREMENT COMMUNITY 33
   LIVING FACILITY 32
RIB LATH 100
RIBBED BLOCK 65
   SIDING 88
   WATERSTOP 58
RIDGE BOARD 75
   ROOF 89
RIGID STEEL CONDUIT............................158
   URETHANE INSULA 85
RING SPLIT 71
   TOOTHED 71
RISER TERRAZZO 104
   WOOD 82
ROCK DRILLING 41
ROCKWOOL INSULATION 85
ROD BEAM CLAMP 154
   COUPLING 154
   GROUND 169
   HANGER 154
   THREAD 154
   TRAVERSE 118
ROLL ROOF 86, 89
ROOF ASPHALT 88
   BUILT-UP 88
   DRAIN 147
   HIP 75
   SHINGLE 86
ROOFTOP AC 152
ROSEWOOD VENEER................................82
ROUGH-IN PLUMBING 148
ROUGH-SAWN SIDING 87
ROUND CAST BOX...........................164, 166
   COLUMN...55
   QUARTER 80
   TRAP COPPER 132
RUBBISH REMOVAL.................................41
RUBBLE STONE 67

- S -

SALAMANDER 39
SALES TAX 37
SALLY PORT SYSTEM 26
SALT PRESERVATIVE 82
SAMPLE SOIL 41
SAND BED PAVER...................................64
   BORROW 43
   FINISH STUCCO 101
SANDING 107

SANITARY CROSS NO-HUB......................123
   T ABS...143
   T COPPER....................................131
   T NO-HUB.....................................123
SASH BEAD...80
SCAFFOLDING...39
SCHEDULE-40 PIPE..................................48
SCHEDULE-80 PIPE..................................48
SCIENCE AND TECHNOLOGY BUILDING 25
   BUILDING......................................25
SCRATCH COAT......................................101
SCREED...59
SCREEN MOLDING 80
   VENT..115
SEAL FITTING......................................158
SEDIMENT FENCE.....................................46
SEEDING..52
SEH BOX...164
SEHC BOX..164
SEHL BOX..164
SEHT BOX..164
SEHX BOX..164
SELECT COMMON BRICK...............................64
SELF-DRILLING ANCHOR...............................68
SENIOR LIVING COMMUNITY............................15
SER CABLE......................................163-164
SERVICE SINK.......................................149
SERVICES BUILDING..................................27
SET RETARDER..59
   SCREW..155
   SCREW CONDULET 156
   SCREW COUPLING 155-156
SEU CABLE..162
SFU CABLE..164
SHAG CARPET..107
SHAKE ROOF..87
SHEAR PLATE...71
SHEATHING ROOF......................................77
   WALL...77
SHEET FLASHING......................................90
   FLOOR...106
   GLASS..97
   METAL ROOF.....................................89
   PLASTIC..84
SHEETROCK..101
   FINISHING.....................................102
SHELF...81
SHINGLE CEDAR.......................................87
   METAL..86
   WOOD...87
SHOE MOLDING..80
   STORE...9
SHOP AREA DESIGN....................................14
SHORT FORGED NUT...................................138
SHOTCRETE...59
SHOWER DOOR..115
   FAUCET..149
SHRUB...52
   MAINTENANCE....................................54
SHUTTERS AND LOUVRES...............................111
SIDE BEAM...55
SIDEWALK REMOVAL....................................42
SIDING..87
   STEEL..88
SILICONE DAMPPROOFING...............................84
SILL ANCHOR...71
   MARBLE...67
   SLATE..67
   WINDOWWALL.....................................98
SIMULATED PEG FLOOR................................105
SINK ELL...129
SISTER JOIST.....................................72-73
   RAFTER...75
SITE GRADING..46
SLAB BOLSTER..58
   CONCRETE....................................59-60
   MESH...57
   REINFORCING.................................56-57
SLATE...64
   PANEL..67

SLIDING GLASS DOOR..................................94
   WINDOW...96
SLIP COUPLING COPPER..........................127, 130
   FITTER..156
   JOINT ADAPTER.................................132
   JOINT COPPER.................................132
SLOT ANCHOR...63
SMOKESTACK MASONRY..................................67
SNAPPED PAVER.......................................64
SOAP DISH.....................................103, 116
SOCIAL SECURITY.....................................37
SOCKET METER.......................................169
SOFFIT TILE..103
SOFTENER WATER.....................................117
SOIL BORING...41
SOLAR SCREEN BLOCK..................................66
   VALVE...146
SOLID ARMORED CABLE................................163
   BLOCK..65
   CORE...93
   WALL...64
SOUND DEADENING BOARD..............................100
SPECIALTY CARE......................................16
SPIGOT ADAPTER COPPER..............................131
SPLASH BLOCK..61
SPLIT COUPLING.....................................158
   GROUND FACE....................................65
   RIB PROFILE....................................65
   RING...71
SPONGE NEOPRENE.....................................57
   RUBBER PADDING................................106
SPREAD FOOTING......................................60
   TOPSOIL.....................................46, 52
SPREADING TOPSOIL...................................52
SQUARE COLUMN.......................................55
   FACE BRACKET..................................167
   FIXTURE.......................................171
   FOOT COSTS......................................1
   HEAD COCK.....................................146
   HEAD PLUG................................135, 145
   NUT...154
   TUB...148
STAGING...39
STAINLESS COUNTER..................................118
   FLASHING.......................................89
   GRAB BAR......................................115
   RAILING..69
STAIR ACCESS.......................................117
   RAIL...69
   TERRAZZO......................................103
   TREAD...104
   TREAD CERAMIC.................................103
STALL SHOWER.......................................115
STANDING-SEAM ROOF..................................89
STEAM BOILER.......................................150
   CLEAN MASONRY..................................67
   TRAP..147
STEEL ANGLE...66
   EDGING...54
   GUTTER...90
   LINTEL...68
   PIPE..144
   POLE..168
   SHINGLE..86
   SIDING PANEL...................................87
   STRAP...160
   STRUCTURAL.....................................68
   STUD...99
   TANK..120
   WELDING..68
STEP MANHOLE..49
STEPPING STONE......................................54
STONE...46
   PAVER..64
STOOL MARBLE..67
   MOLDING..80
   SLATE..67
STOP MOLDING..80
STORM DOOR..95
   WINDOW...95

STRAIGHT CURB FORM..................................55
STRANDED WIRE......................................163
STRAP CHANNEL......................................154
   CONDUIT.......................................161
   MALLEABLE................................156, 160
   STEEL....................................155, 160
   TIE..71
STRAW BALE..46
STREET ELL COPPER.............................128, 130
STRINGER TERRAZZO..................................104
STRIP CANT..76
   CHAMFER..56
   FLOORING......................................105
   FLOURESCENT...................................171
   SHINGLE..86
STRUCTURAL BACKFILL.................................46
   EXCAVATION.....................................44
   FEE..37
   PLYWOOD..78
   TUBE...68
STUCCO...101
   LATH..100
STUD CLIP..100
   METAL......................................68, 99
   REMOVAL..41
STUMP...43
STYROFOAM INSERT....................................65
SUB-BASE..43
SUB-FLOORING..77
SUBMERSIBLE PUMP....................................39
SUN SCREEN..61
SUPERINTENDENT......................................37
SURFACE COVER......................................167
   MOUNTED CLOSE..................................97
SURGERY CENTER......................................19
SURGICAL CENTER.....................................20
SUSPENDED CEILING...................................84
   CEILING REM....................................41
SUSPENSION SYSTEM..................................105
SWING GATE..51
SWITCH BOX...167
   DIMMER..170
   FUSABLE.......................................154
   PLATE...170
SWIVEL HANGER BOX..................................167
   JOINT...133
   TRAP..133
SY-PINE DECKING.....................................78
   SIDING...87
   TIMBER...78

- T -

T CONDULET.....................................156, 159
T&G SIDING..88
TANDEM BOX...165
   BREAKER.......................................169
TAPERED FRICTION PILE...............................47
TAPPED T NO-HUB....................................124
TARPAULIN...39
TAX...37
T-BAR SYSTEM.......................................105
TEAK VENEER...82
TECHNOLOGY BUILDING.................................25
TEE ABS..143
   BLACK IRON....................................144
   BRASS....................................134, 137
   COPPER...................................129, 133
   PLASTIC..48
   PVC.......................................140-142
   STEEL...144
TEMPERED PEGBOARD...................................82
TEMPERING VALVE....................................146
TERMINAL ADAPTERS..................................161
TERMITE CONTROL................................46, 115
TERRAZZO RECEPTOR..................................115
TEST CAP COPPER....................................129
   PIT..41
   T NO-HUB......................................123
TEXTURE 1-11..87

THEATER 5
THERMOSTAT 172
THERMOSTATIC VALVE 146
THHN-THWN CONDUCTOR 163
THIN-SET TERRAZZO 103
THREAD ROD 154
THREADED BOLT 71
    COUPLING 159
    ROD COUPLING 154
    VALVE 145
THREADLESS COUPLING 159
THRESHOLD DOOR 97
    MARBLE 67
THROAT INSULATED 155
THROUGH-WALL FLASHING 64
THWN CONDUCTOR 163
TIE MESH 63
    STRAP 71
TILE ACOUSTICAL 105
    QUARRY 103
    RESILIENT 106
    TERRAZZO 103
TIMBER FRAMING 73, 78
    LANDSCAPING 54
TIME CLOCK 170
TIMEKEEPER 38
TINTED GLASS 97
TISSUE DISPENSER 116
TOGGLE SWITCH 170
TOILET 150
TOOTHBRUSH HOLDER 116
TOOTHED RING 71
TOP PLATE 76
TOPDRESS SOIL 52
TOWEL BAR 116
    BAR CERAMIC 103
TRACK LIGHTING 171
    MOUNTED LOADER 44
TRAILER 38
TRAP FLOAT 147
TRAVERSE ROD 118
TRAVERTINE FLOOR 106
TREAD WOOD 82
TREATED LUMBER 54
    POLE 168
    POST 78
TREE REMOVAL 43
    SMALL 52
TRELLIS PRECAST 61
TRENCHER 46
TRIM 107, 110, 113
    ALUMINUM 90
    CARPENTRY 79
    CASING 79-80
TROWEL FINISH 100
    FINISH STUCCO 101
TRUCK 40
    CRANE 40
TRUSS REINFORCING 62
    WOOD 79
TUB BATH 148
TUBE STRUCTURAL 68
TUMBLER HOLDER 116
    SWITCH 166
TUMBLESTONE AGGREGATE 64
TWIN ELL COPPER 130
TWIST LOCK RECEPTACLE 168

- U -

UF CABLE 164
UNCASED BORING 41
UNDER SLAB SPRAYING 115
UNDERGROUND TANK 120
UNDERLAYMENT 77
UNDERSLAB DRAINAGE 50
UNEMPLOYMENT TAX 37
UNFACED INSULATION 85
UNGLAZED FLOOR 106
    FLOOR TILE 102

UNGLAZED WALL TILE 102
UNION BLACK IRON 144
    BRASS 135
    COPPER 129, 133
    ELBOW BRASS 137
    PVC 140-142
    STEEL 145
UNIT COSTS 35
    HEATER 172
UNIVERSITY HALL 21, 24
UNRATED DOOR 92
URETHANE INSULATION 85-86
    PADDING 106

- V -

VACUUM CARPET 107
    SYSTEM 117
VALLEY FLASHING 89
VALVE VACUUM 117
VANITY BATH 118
VAPOR BARRIER 58, 84, 123
VARNISH PAINT 114
V-BEAM ROOF 89
VEGETATION CONTROL 54
VENEER 82
    BRICK 64
    GRANITE 67
VENETIAN BLIND 119
    TERRAZZO 104
VENT CAP 120
    FOUNDATION 62
    MASONRY 115
VERMICULITE INSULATION 86
    PLASTER 101
VERMONT SLATE 86
VERTICAL CHECK VALVE 146
    GRAIN FLOOR 105
    REINFORCING 57, 62, 66
VINYL COATED FENCE 51
    FENCE 51
    SHEET 106
    SHEET FLOOR 106
    SHEETROCK 102
    SIDING 87
    TILE 106
    WALL COVERING 114

- W -

WAFERBOARD SHEATHING 77
WAINSCOT TERRAZZO 104
WALK 60
WALL BASE 106
    BLOCKING 72
    BRICK 64
    CABINET 81, 118
    CAVITY 62
    CLEANOUT 145
    FABRIC 114
    FINISH 59
    FOOTING 55
    FORMWORK 56
    FURRING 68, 73
    GRILLE 153
    HEATER 117
    HUNG SINK 149
    HYDRANT 149
    INSULATION 85
    LATH 100
    MASONRY REINFORCING 57
    MOUNTED HEATER 172
    PENETRATION 122
    PLASTER 100
    RAILING 69
    RETAINING 56
    SHEETROCK 101
    STONE 67
    TIE 62
    TILE 102-103

WALLS 110, 113
    AND FLAT SURFACE 107
WALNUT DOOR 94
    VENEER 82
WARDROBE 118
WASHER FLAT 154
WASHING BRICK 67
    MACHINE BOX 150
WASHROOM FAUCET 148
WATCHMAN 38
WATER REDUCING ADMIXTURE 59
    SOFTENER 117
    VALVE 146
WATER-RESISTANT SHEET 102
WATERSTOP 58
WAX FLOOR 105
WEARING SURFACE 50
WEATHERHEAD 158
WEATHERPROOF BOX 165-166
    COVER 167
WELDED RAILING 69
WELDING 68
WET BED TILE 102
WHEEL BARROW 45
WHITE CEDAR SHINGLE 87
WINDOW 95-96
    FRAME 96
    HEADER 76
    REMOVAL 41
    SILL 64
    SILL MARBLE 67
    STILL CERAMIC 103
    STOOL MARBLE 67
WINDOWS 111
WINDOWWALL 98
WIRE HOOK HANGER 123
    MESH 57, 60
    MESH REMOVAL 42
    STRANDED 163
WOMAN'S HOMELESS RESIDENTIAL 31
    TRANSFORMATIONAL HOME 34
WOOD ANCHOR 71
    CANT 76, 88
    CHIP MULCH 54
    COLUMN 83
    CUTTING 43
    DECKING 78
    DOOR REMOVAL 41
    FENCE REMOVAL 42
    FIBER PANEL 104
    FRAME 94
    HANDRAIL 69
    INDUSTRIAL FLOOR 105
    PILE 47
    PLATE 76
    POLE 168
    RISER 82
    SHELVING 81
    SLEEPER 76
    SOFFIT 76
    STUD REMOVAL 41
    WALL 76
    WINDOW REMOVAL 41
WOODWORK ARCHITECTURAL 82
WOOL CARPET 106
    MINERAL 86
WYE ABS 143
    NO-HUB 123

- X -

X CONDULET 160

- Z -

ZONING CODES 1
Z-TIE WALL 63

ENR

Engineering News-Record